Imam Abū Ḥanīfah
Life and Work

IMAM ABŪ ḤANĪFAH

LIFE AND WORK

امام ابو حنيفة

SHIBLI NOMANI

Translated by M. Hadi Hussain

TOP

The Other Press

Kuala Lumpur

First published 1972
Institute of Islamic Culture

This new edition 2015
The Other Press Sdn. Bhd.
607 Mutiara Majestic
Jalan Othman
46000 Petaling Jaya
Selangor, Malaysia
www.ibtbooks.com

The Other Press is affiliated with Islamic Book Trust.

Perpustakaan Negara Malaysia Cataloguing-in-Publication Data

Shibli Nomani, 1857-1914
Imam Abu Hanifah : Life and Work / Shibli Nomani.
Translated by M. Hadi Hussain.
Includes index
ISBN 978-983-9541-99-1
1. Abu Hanifah, -767 or 768. 2. Muslim scholars--Iraq--Biography.
3. Hanafites--Biography. 4. Islamic law--Biography. I. Hussain, M. Hadi.
II. Title.
922.97

Printed by
Real Sharp (M) Sdn. Bhd.
No. 30, Jalan Tembaga SD 5/2G
Bandar Sri Damansara
52200 Kuala Lumpur

Contents

Author's Preface vii

1 Name, ancestry and birthplace 3

2 Maturity, education and teachers 12

3 Lectures, rulings and later life 40

4 Death 49

5 Children 53

6 Character and habits 55

7 Anecdotes about Abū Ḥanīfah's wit and wisdom 71

8 Abū Ḥanīfah's writings 99

9 Beliefs and *kalām* 106

10 Tradition and principles of tradition 119

11 Fiqh 171

Appendix: Abū Ḥanīfah's disciples 241

Index 267

Author's Preface

My series of eminent Muslims' biographies, launched with the publication of *al-Ma'mūn*, was originally conceived on a grand scale. I proposed to select my heroes, not only from ruling dynasties, but also from the world of learning. The task proved too gigantic for me and I had to reduce its size by confining myself to rulers and, further, by leaving out some of the dynasties. However, I did not altogether give up the idea of presenting some great men of learning, time permitting, for, as the Arabic saying goes, the sword and the pen are twins.

After the publication of *al-Ma'mūn* I started writing *al-Fārūq*. But after I had written a considerable part of it I had to come to a halt. Uncomprehending critics attributed all kinds of motives to me, although the reason was nothing more than this that a number of books, which it was necessary for me to consult and which were being published in Europe, had not yet become available. Rather than sit idle while waiting for those books I thought of writing on some other famous ruler, but was inhibited by the uneasy feeling of having an unfinished book on my hands, besides being haunted by my original idea of including men of learning among my heroes in keeping with the fact that in Islam the sword and the pen have always gone together.

Ultimately, the latter idea prevailed so that, turning away from ruling dynasties, I explored the world of learning for someone to write about. The sciences and arts to choose my hero from were *fiqh* (jurisprudence), Ḥadīth (tradition), *adab* (literature), *manṭiq* (logic), philosophy and mathematics. For certain reasons I decided to make my choice from *fiqh* and chose its founder and greatest master, Imam Abū Ḥanīfah. Abū Ḥanīfah's juristic pronouncements and formulations have held sway over the entire Muslim world for nearly twelve centuries. They were on the statute books of many Muslim empires and kingdoms and are still followed in the larger part of the Muslim world. His biographies have been written in Arabic, Persian, Turkish and several European languages, and it seemed to me deplorable that none had been written in Urdu, by and large the language of his followers.

No other Muslim has as many biographies written of him as Abū Ḥanīfah has, which shows how high he ranks among the celebrities of Islam. Research and writing on personalities were developed in Islam to a degree unparalleled anywhere else. The subject was divided into several branches, entitled *tarājim*, *ṭabaqāt*, *qurūn*, *wafayāt*, *a'yān* and *sinīn*, and innumerable books were written in each branch; but biography, properly so called, did not make much progress.

There are very few great men—scholars, poets, judges or philosophers—who have been fortunate enough to have had regular biographies written of them. Abū Ḥanīfah is not only one of the fortunate few, but the most fortunate of them, with al-Shāfi'ī as a close second; and many of his numerous biographers were themselves men fit to be the subject of full-blooded biographies.

I give below particulars[1] of such of Abū Ḥanīfah's biographers and biographies as I have been able to ascertain:

1. Aḥmad b. Muḥammad al-Ṭaḥāwī, *'Uqūd al-Marjān.* Al-Ṭaḥāwī (d. 321 H) is a well-known doctor of Ḥadīth and *fiqh* and by one remove a disciple of al-Shāfi'ī. Of his writings the *Ma'ānī al-Āthār* has been published.
2. Aḥmad b. Muḥammad al-Ṭaḥāwī, *Qalā'id 'Uqūd al-Durr wa al-'Iqyān.* This is a summary of *'Uqūd al-Marjān.*
3. Aḥmad b. Muḥammad al-Ṭaḥāwī, *al-Rawḍah al-'Āliyah al-Munīfah.*
4. Muḥammad b. Aḥmad b. Shu'ayb, *Manāqib al-Nu'mān.* Muḥammad b. Aḥmad (d. 357 H) was the Ḥadīth teacher of Ḥākim. The book is in twenty parts (*al-Jawāhir al-Muḍiyyah*).
5. Abū 'Abdullāh al-Ṣaymarī Ḥusayn b. 'Alī, *Manāqib al-Nu'mān.* Al-Ṣaymarī (d. 436 H) was a great *faqīh* and a disciple of al-Dāraquṭnī in Ḥadīth. The historian al-Khaṭīb quotes traditions from him. Qāḍī Abū al-Walīd al-Bājī has called him Imam al-Ḥanafiyyah. This is a voluminous book, the main source of information on Abū Ḥanīfah.
6. Abū al-'Abbās Aḥmad b. al-Ṣalt al-Ḥamānī, *Manāqib al-Nu'mān.* This is a book rich in details. The author of the *Kashf al-Ẓunūn* writes that al-Khaṭīb al-Baghdādī has tried to discredit Abū al-'Abbās, as is his wont in respect of Ḥanafīs. Died in 308 H.
7. Jārallāh al-Zamakhsharī, *Shaqā'iq al-Nu'mān fī Manāqib al Nu'mān.* Al-Zamakhsharī (d. 528 H) is a renowned writer: author of the famous *Tafsīr al-Kashshāf.*
8. Muwaffiq al-Dīn b. Aḥmad al-Mulkī al-Khawārizmī, *Manāqib al-Nu'mān.* The book consists of 40 chapters. The author (d. 568 H), a disciple of al-Zamakhsharī, was a great *fiqh* doctor and littérateur. Al-Suyūṭī mentions him in his *Bughyah al-Wu'āh.*

9. ʻAbdullāh b. Muḥammad al-Ḥarithī al-Kalābādhī, *Kashf al-Āthār.* Although he was a famous writer (d. 340 H) Ibn al-Jawzī quotes Abū Saʻīd as saying that he was unreliable in narrating traditions. Commenting on this, the author of *al-Jawāhir al-Muḍiyyah* says that ʻAbdullāh ranks higher than both Ibn al-Jawzī and Abū Saʻīd.
10. Ẓahīr al-Dīn al-Marghinānī, *Manāqib al-Nuʻmān.* A famous *faqīh.* The author of *al-Jawāhir al-Muḍiyyah* says that Qāḍī Khān was one of his disciples. Died in 506 H.
11. Muḥammad b. Muḥammad al-Kurdarī, *Manāqib al-Nuʻmān.* Consists of eleven chapters, which give accounts of Abū Ḥanīfah and his famous disciples, namely, Abū Yūsuf, Muḥammad, ʻAbdullāh b. al-Mubārak, Zufar, Dāwūd al-Ṭāʼī, Wakīʻ b. al-Jarrāḥ, Ḥafṣ b. Ghayāth, Yaḥyā b. Zakariyyā, Ḥasan b. Ziyād. The book is very popular in Turkey and was translated into Turkish by Muḥammad b. ʻUmar under the orders of Sultan Murād II. The author died in 827 H.
12. Abū al-Qāsim b. Kās, *Manāqib al-Nuʻmān.* There are many citations from this book in the *ʻUqūd al-Jumān.*
13. Qāḍī b. ʻAbd al-Birr, *Kitāb al-Intiqāʼ fī Manāqib al-Thalāthah al-Fuqahāʼ.* Contains accounts of Abū Ḥanīfah, Mālik and al-Shāfiʻī. Ibn Khallikān mentions it in his note on Abū Yūsuf. The author (d. 463 H) is a great *muḥaddith* and imam. His *Istīʻāb* is a famous and authentic book on the Companions.
14. Abū al-Qāsim ʻAbdullāh b. Muḥammad b. Aḥmad, better known as Ibn Abī al-ʻAwām, *Manāqib al-Nuʻmān.*
15. Al-Dhahabī, *Manāqib Abī Ḥanīfah.* The author refers to this book in his *Tadhkirah al-Ḥuffāẓ.* He was a very great *muḥaddith,* unsurpassed by any successor. His well-known

books are *Mīzān al-I'tidāl*, *al-Kāshif*, *al-'Ibar*, *Duwal al-Islām* and *Tadhkirah al-Ḥuffāẓ*.

16. Abū al-Ḥasan b. Abī al-Qāsim al-Bayhaqī, *al-Mawāhib al-Sharīfah fī Manāqib Abī Ḥanīfah.* A translation of this book has been published under the title *Tuḥfah al-Sulṭān fī Manāqib al-Nu'mān.*
17. Muḥyī al-Dīn 'Abd al-Qādir al-Qurashī, *Bustān fī Manāqib al-Nu'mān*, Also author of *al-Jawāhir al-Muḍiyyah fī Ṭabaqāt al-Ḥanafiyyah.* A disciple of Taqī al-Dīn al-Subkī in Ḥadīth. Died in 775 H.
18. Jalāl al-Dīn al-Suyūṭī, *Tabyīḍ al-Ṣaḥīfah fī Manāqib Abī Ḥanīfah.* A famous writer.
19. Muḥammad b. Yūsuf b. 'Alī al-Dimashqī, *'Uqūd al-Jumān fī Manāqib al-Nu'mān*, More details later.
20. Ibn Ḥajar al-Makkī, *al-Khayrāt al-Ḥisān fī Manāqib al-Nu'mān.* Also author of *al-Ṣawā'iq al-Muḥriqah.*
21. *Qalā'id 'Uqūd al-Jumān.* The name of the author is not known. The preface suggests that he was some scholar of Yemen.
22. Shams al-Dīn Aḥmad b. Muḥammad al-Satwāsī, *Manāqib al-Nu'mān.* In Turkish verse.
23. Abū Sa'īd 'Atīq b. Dāwūd al-Yamānī, *Manāqib al-Imām al-A'ẓam*, *Risālah fī Faḍl Abī Ḥanīfah.* In Persian.
24. Ṣārim al-Dīn Ibrāhīm b. Muḥammad b. Daqqāq, *Naẓm al-Jumān.* In three volumes, dealing, respectively, with Abū Ḥanīfah, Abū Yūsuf and Muḥammad. The author died in 809 H.
25. Muḥammad Kāmī Afandī, *qāḍī* of Baghdad, *Manāqib al-Imām al-A'ẓam.* In Turkish. The author died in 1136 H.
26. Mustaqīm Zādah Sulaymān Sa'd al-Dīn Afandī, *Manāqib al-Imām al-A'ẓam.* A voluminous book, written in 1168 H. In Turkish.

Unfortunately, these books are not available in our country. However, I possess a copy each of the *'Uqūd al-Jumān* and *al-Khayrāt al-Ḥisān* and have also read the *Qalā'id al-'Iqyān.*[2] The *al-Khayrāt al-Ḥisān*, because of being a work of Ibn Ḥajar al-Makkī, is more famous than the other two; but it is not a regular work in its own right, being, as the author admits in his preface, only a summary of the *'Uqūd al-Jumān.* The *Qalā'id al-'Iqyān* also, as is clear from its preface, is mostly derived from Ṣaymarī's work. The *'Uqūd al-Jumān*, a detailed and exhaustive work, which is my main source, is a work by Abū al-Maḥāsin Muḥammad b. Yūsuf b. 'Alī al-Dimashqī al-Ṣāliḥī, a visiting scholar at al-Khānqāh al-Barqūqiyah. Abū al-Maḥāsin is a disciple of Jalāl al-Dīn al-Suyūṭī and a well-known *muḥaddith.* The book, as mentioned by the author at its conclusion, was completed in Rabī' al-Thānī 939.

In the preface the author states that of the many books containing accounts of Abū Ḥanīfah that he had read he found Muwaffiq b. Aḥmad al-Khawārizmī's the best and most comprehensive. In the book's concluding passages, he mentions that with the material he had found in the numerous books he had consulted, he could have written two thick volumes.

Although this is the only regular book on Abū Ḥanīfah that I have been able to lay my hands on, I have consulted many books of *rijāl* (biographical dictionaries) and history in which Abū Ḥanīfah finds mention. Worthy of particular mention among these are *al-Ta'rīkh al-Ṣaghīr* of al-Bukhārī, *al-Ma'ārif* of Ibn Qutaybah, *Mukhtaṣar Ta'rīkh* of al-Khaṭīb al-Baghdādī, *al-Ansāb* of al-Sam'ānī, *Tahdhīb al-Asmā' wa al-Lughāt* of al-Nawawī, *Tadhkirah al-Ḥuffāẓ* of al-Dhahabī, *Duwal al-Islām* of al-Dhahabī, *al-'Ibar fī Khabar Man 'Abar* of al-Dhahabī, *Tahdhīb al-Tahdhīb* of Ibn Ḥajar al-'Asqalānī and the *Khulāṣah Tahdhīb al-Kamāl* of Safī al-Dīn Khazrajī. These are basic works of *rijāl* today and are mostly relied on in the criticism of traditions.

The account of Abū Ḥanīfah's life, which forms the first part of my book, is derived for the most part from the above-mentioned books; but they proved useless for the second part, which deals with Abū Ḥanīfah's personal judgement and principles of deduction. For in early times it was not customary for biographies to include discussion of the subjects' works or ideas. However, there are numerous polemical writings from which one could get material for a detailed review oi Abū Ḥanīfah's juristic pronouncements and writings.

There is, to begin with, the treatise written by al-Qāsim b. Quṭlūbaghā (d. 879 H) to refute the objections raised by Ibn Abī Shaybah against Abū Ḥanīfah's legal formulations, by which he tried to prove that they were opposed to Ḥadīth. Next there is Shams al-A'immah al-Kurdarī's reply to al-Ghazālī's *al-Mankhūl.* Then there are two books written under the title *al-Nukat al-Ẓarīfah fī Tarjīḥ Madhhab Abī Ḥanīfah* by Akmal al-Dīn Muḥammad (d. 786 H) and Abū 'Abdullāh Muḥammad b. Yaḥyā al-Jurjānī (d. 397 H). The historian Sibṭ b. al-Jawzī has two works to his name—a two-volume book entitled *al-Intiṣār li Imām A'immah al-Amṣār* and a book of thirty chapters, which is devoted to proving the excellence of Abū Ḥanīfah's legal pronouncements and which the author of the *Kashf al-Ẓunūn* describes as unparalleled in its class. There is a similar book entitled *al-Intiṣār wa al-Tarjīḥ* by 'Umar b. Muḥammad b. Sayyid al-Mawṣilī.

The most elaborate of all works on the subject is *al-Ibānah* by Qāḍī Abū Ja'far Aḥmad b. 'Abdullāh al-Sarmārī al-Balkhī, consisting of six chapters. The first chapter is devoted to proving that Abū Ḥanīfah's *madhhdb* is eminently in accord with the principles of government, the second to proving that his formulations are supported by Ḥadīth and *āthār*, and the sixth, after listing the questions on which he has been adversely criticised, gives detailed replies to the criticisms. About this book the author of *al-Jawāhir al-Muḍiyyah* writes,"I have read this book; it is an excellent book. The author supports with illustrations every claim that he makes."

Undoubtedly, these books would have proved a great help to me; but I did not have the good fortune of the author of the *Kashf al-Ẓunūn* to have access to them, rare as they are. The only one that I could lay hands on after much effort was Shams al-A'immah al-Kurdarī's treatise. Such as it is, it was something to be thankful for. I took from it whatever I could; for the rest, I had to rely on my own research, for which I was fortunate enough to have an adequate collection) of Ḥadīth and *fiqh* books.

A few words would not be out of place about the variations in style and treatment noticeable in the different parts of the present book. The facts of Abū Ḥanīfah's life—birth, upbringing and development, way of living, mode of earning a livelihood etc.—are historical matters to be dealt with as a historian would deal with them. The reliability of various accounts of them is, however, a question to be decided in accordance with the principles of Ḥadīth. Again, appraising Abū Ḥanīfah's juristic formulations and pronouncements in the capacity of a *mujtahid* is a task to be performed by a *mujtahid*. A book dealing with all these aspects must of necessity be a combination of three methods of treatment—the first that of a historian, the second that of a *muḥaddith* and the third that of a *mujtahid*.

Thus, in dealing with purely historical matters I regarded as adequate such evidence as is commonly accepted by historians. Where, however, a question of Ḥadīth was involved I made as thorough an examination as was possible, applying all the rules prescribed by the *muḥaddithīn* for appraising reports and narrations. The passages in which I have done so may not be interesting for the common reader, but it was not possible for me to leave them out for that reason. As regards common historical facts, although I have not scrutinised them as minutely as the *muḥaddithīn* examine their material, I have not recorded a single fact for which there was no authority and have not cited a single authority from any book which I had not myself read, conscious as I was of the fact that second-hand reports can seldom be accurate. Despite all this care, it is possible that I have made mistakes. However, I have the satisfaction of knowing that I have done my best.

Notes

1. Except where otherwise indicated, these particulars have been derived from the *Kashf al-Ẓunūn.*
2. I had occasion to read most of the books listed above during my travels in Turkey and Egypt. But none of them contained any material which could contribute much to this modest effort of mine.

First Part
The Imam's Life and Personality

1

Name, ancestry and birthplace

Acclaimed as the Great Imam and best known by his *kunyah* of Abū Ḥanīfah, al-Nu'mān b. Thābit b. Zūṭā b. Māh was of 'Ajamī (non-Arab) origin, as the etymology of the last two names suggests and as is generally accepted. There are, however, different theories about his origin and how he came to Arabia.

The Baghdadi historian al-Khaṭīb attributes the following statement to the Imam's grandson Ismā'īl: "I am Ismā'īl b. Ḥammād b. al-Nu'mān b. Thābit b. al-Nu'mān b. al-Marzbān. We are of Fārisī (Persian) origin and have never been slaves. My grandfather, Abū Ḥanīfah, was born in 80 H. His father, Thābit, called on 'Alī to pay his respects. 'Alī was gracious enough to pray for him and his family, and I believe that his prayer bore fruit."[1]

Ismā'īl gave the name of the Imam's grandfather as Nu'mān and that of his great-grandfather as Marzbān, but the correct names, as commonly accepted, are Zūṭā and Māh, respectively. It is probable that Zūṭā, when he adopted Islam, changed his name to Nu'mān, which Ismā'īl, from a legitimate pride in his Muslim ancestry, mentioned instead of Zūṭā. It is similarly probable that the name of Zūṭā's father was neither Māh nor Marzbān, but something else. Ismā'īl is further quoted as having claimed that his was a respected and renowned family of Persia. Since the mayor of a city was called Marzbān in Persia, it seems a reasonable conjecture that neither "Marzbān" nor "Māh" was a name and that both of them were titles or official designations. In fact, al-Ḥāfiẓ Abū al-Maḥāsin took "*māh*" and "*marzbān*" to be synonyms. As he knew no Persian, he perhaps only hazarded a guess, but the guess was right, as I can say with certainty. "*Māh*" is really a variant of "*mah*," which means "big" when an adjective and "a chief" when a noun. Arabic pronunciation turned "*mah*" to "*māh*."

Some historians have said about Zūṭā that, having come as a captive from Kabul, he was sold as a slave to a woman of the Banū Taymallāh tribe, who set him free after he had served her for some time. This, according to them, explains why the Imam's family was known as *mawlās* of the Banū Taymallāh. Enemies of the Imam, enjoying the attempt to detract from his status, have given much prominence to this story.

It makes little difference whether the story is true or not: the Imam is in good company in either case. The Chosroes of Iran were not spared the stigma of being descendants of slaves. Our scholars would have it that Hagar was a slave girl, although the Torah says nothing of the kind. In the earlier period of Islam most of the acknowledged masters of Ḥadīth were men to whom the appellation of slave actually applied. To name a few, al-Ḥasan al-Baṣrī, Ibn Sīrīn, Ṭāwūs, 'Aṭā' b. Yasār, Nāfi', 'Ikrimah and Makḥūl, all leading authorities in their time, were either slaves or descendants of slaves. Thus, even if it were established that Zūṭā was a slave, that would not detract one whit from the Imam's greatness. However, historical evidence disproves it.

There are other differences of opinion about the Imam's ancestry. Abū Muṭī', for example, describes him as an Arab and gives his ancestry thus: al-Nu'mān b. Thābit b. Zūṭā b. Yaḥyā b. Zayd b. Asad b. Rashīd al-Anṣārī. al-Ḥāfiẓ Abū Isḥāq gives it thus: al-Nu'mān b. Thābit b. Kā'ūs b. Hurmuz b. Bahrām. There are various accounts about Zūṭā's place of residence too.

These differences are quite understandable. We can well guess that Zūṭā must have remained a stranger in Arabia for some years after his arrival there. People might not have cared to acquaint themselves with facts about him or might have been prevented by the barrier of language from doing so. At the same time, social necessities must have led Zūṭā to establish friendly relations with them. Friendly relations between strangers and the local people were given a special name in Arabia at that time, namely, *wilā'*, from which is derived the word *mawlā*, which also means "slave." This verbal confusion may have later on given rise to the idea that Zūṭā was a slave, and the idea must have taken root in the course of time, so that Ismā'īl found it necessary to contradict it explicitly.

Ismā'īl was a very reliable and highly respected man, Therefore discriminating historians have accepted his version of the facts rather than any other. Qāḍī Ṣaymarī, a writer of high rank, has clearly stated that Zūṭā was an ally of the Banū Taymallāh.[2] That part of the slavery story which says that Zūṭā was brought as a captive from Kabul is also obviously false. Zūṭā's ancestors had Persian names. It is also an established fact about Abu Ḥanīfah that he knew Persian as his family tongue, and Persian was not spoken in Kabul at that time.

We cannot definitely name Zūṭā's native city. Different historians have mentioned different cities, and it is not possible to say which is the correct one. All that is established beyond doubt is that he came from Persia and was of Persian origin. Persia was in those days under Islamic influence, and most of its great families were gradually getting converted to Islam. Zūṭā was probably one of the new converts and migrated to Arabia either from a desire to spend the rest of his days in Islam's homeland or in order to escape the displeasure of his family. 'Alī was the caliph then, and Kūfah was his capital. Zūṭā took up residence at Kūfah and used occasionally to attend the caliphate court in order to pay his respects to 'Alī. Once, on the occasion of Nawrūz, which is a Persian festival, he sent some *fālūdah* (a type of dessert) to the caliph as a present. "For us," remarked the caliph on receiving the present, "every day is Nawrūz." It was at Kūfah that Abū Ḥanīfah's father, Thābit, was born. Zūṭā took the newborn infant to 'Alī, who blessed the infant and his family with his prayers.

Nothing is known about Thābit except that he was a trader. His first son was born when he was forty years old, and he named him Nu'mān, to which fame added in the fullness of time the title *al-Imām al-A'ẓam* (the Great Imam).

At the time of Abū Ḥanīfah's birth, 'Abd al-Malik b. Marwān, the second caliph of the house of Marwān, was on the throne. There were still many people alive who had had the good fortune of seeing the Prophet (ṣ), and some of them lived on till Abū Ḥanīfah's early youth. Thus, Anas b. Mālik, the Prophet's personal attendant, died in 93 H, Sahl. b. Sa'd in 91 H and Abū al-Ṭufayl 'Āmir b. Wāthilah in 100 H.

There is, however, no evidence that Abū Ḥanīfah quoted even a single tradition from any of these. This has caused surprise, and historians have explained it in different ways. Some of them think that Abū Ḥanīfah had not yet acquired any education, having been brought up to be a trader like his ancestors, and that, by the time he started educating himself at the instance of Imam al-Sha'bī, it was too late for him to make up for the opportunity he had lost, as all the Companions had passed away.

But I think that something else is the reason. There is a difference of opinion among Ḥadīth scholars about the minimum age for learning the discipline of Ḥadīth. The strictest in this matter were the scholars of Kūfah: they never admitted anybody below the age of twenty to a *ḥadīth* school.[3] The reason they advanced for this was that, since the traditions had been narrated in words having particular meanings, it was necessary for the student to have attained maturity of understanding, failing which there would be risk of his misunderstanding and misconstruing them. This, it seems to me, was what prevented Abū Ḥanīfah from achieving the honour of hearing traditions from the lips of the surviving Companions.

Nor was this restriction without justification. Although the traditions related by those who heard them from the Companions at the early age of ten or twelve years have this merit that they were only once removed from the Prophet (ṣ), there is always this danger inherent in them that, because of immaturity, their narrators may not have grasped their full meaning and may have committed grave errors in interpreting them.

Whatever the reason, it is a fact that Abū Ḥanīfah heard no tradition from a Companion. He, however, had the good fortune of meeting one of the Companions, namely, Anas, and deriving illumination from eyes that had seen the Prophet's glory face to face. This is a historical fact, but since it confers on him the rank of being a *Tābiʿī* (Successor), that is, one who has seen a Companion, it has been a subject of much religious controversy. There is, however, no doubt that Abū Ḥanīfah claimed this honour and was proud of it. Naive as it may appear to non-Muslims, the value attached by Muslims to such experiences bespeaks the profound love and fervent admiration they have for the Prophet (ṣ) and, through him, for his Companions.

Some writers of our day have disallowed to Abū Ḥanīfah the position of a *Tābiʿī*. This is nothing new: doubts were expressed on the subject in earlier times too. But Ḥadīth authorities, who have the right more than any others to decide issues of this kind, have decided in favour of the Imam, Ḥāfiẓ Ibn Ḥajar al-ʿAsqalānī, on a *fatwā* being sought from him, expressed the following opinion:

> There were many Companions still alive in Imam Abū Ḥanīfah's day. In 80 H, when he was born in Kūfah, one of the Companions, ʿAbdullāh b. Abī Awfā, who died in 88 H or perhaps later, was living in that city. Ibn Saʿd has reported on good authority that Abū Ḥanīfah met Anas b Mālik. Besides these two Companions, there were others living in different cities. Some people have compiled traditions purporting to have been heard by the Imam from some of the Companions, but the authority for these traditions is not free from weaknesses. What is factually correct is only this that the Imam was a contemporary of some of the Companions and met a number of them, as reported by Ibn Saʿd. In view of this, Abū Ḥanīfah belongs to the category of Successors to the Companions—a fact which has not been established in respect of other Imams who were alive in his time, as, for example, al-Awzāʿī in Syria, Ḥammād at Baṣrah, al-Thawrī in Kūfah, Mālik at Madīnah and al-Layth in Egypt. However, Allah knows best.[4]

The statement of Ibn Saʿd which Ibn Ḥajar has quoted can be traced to Abū Ḥanīfah through a single intermediary, namely, Sayf b. Jābir. In other words, Ibn Saʿd heard it from Sayf b. Jābir and the latter from Abū Ḥanīfah himself.[5] To Ibn Saʿd's trustworthiness al-Nawawī testifies in his *Tahdhīb al-Asmā'* in the following words: "Although his teacher, al-Wāqidī, is not reliable, he himself is very much so."

As regards Sayf b. Jābir, he was the *qāḍī* of Baṣrah and a truthful narrator. In view of the character of both its narrators, the story must be taken to be as authentic as the most perfect of traditions. On the basis of it, therefore, all great *muḥaddithīn*, such as al-Khaṭīb al-Baghdādī, al-Sam'ānī, author of *Kitāb al-Ansāb*, al-Nawawī, writer of the commentary on Muslim's *Saḥīḥ*, al-Dhahabī, Ibn Ḥajar al-'Asqalānī, Zayn al-Dīn al-'Irāqī, al-Sakhāwī, and Abū al-Maḥāsin al-Dimashqī, who are pillars of Ḥadīth, have finally decided that Abū Ḥanīfah did meet Anas.[6]

Ibn Khallikān has also quoted the statement of al-Khaṭīb al-Baghdādī, but as he has further said that Abū Ḥanīfah did not meet or hear traditions from any Companion, people have been misled into believing that Ibn Khallikān denies to Abū Ḥanīfah the status of a Successor to the Companions. The fact is that Ibn Khallikān denies only that Abū Ḥanīfah interviewed and heard traditions from any Companions and not that he saw one or two of them. Even if Ibn Khallikān's statement were understood to mean what certain superficial readers have taken it to mean, nobody could claim that his testimony overrides the testimony of the great masters of Ḥadīth whom we have named above. It is one of the settled principles of the science of tradition that if the evidence for and against a narrative is of equal weight the evidence for it will be accepted. In the present instance the negative evidence is of much less weight than the positive.

Some Ḥanafīs have gone beyond claiming that Abū Ḥanīfah saw some Companions and have claimed that he actually heard traditions from them. It is surprising that even 'Aynī, commentator on *al-Hidāyah*, has supported this erroneous claim. The truth of the matter is that the claim has not been established. Abū al-Maḥāsin has assembled in his *'Uqūd al-Jumān* all the traditions about which it is thought by some people that Abū Ḥanīfah had heard them from the Companions and then, after examining them in the light of the principles of Ḥadīth, has proved that they are not authentic.

Debate on matters of Ḥadīth is a complicated exercise. We shall, therefore, do well to refrain from getting involved in it. What is obvious is that, if the Imam had cited even a single tradition as having been heard by him from a Companion, his close disciples would have been the first to give publicity to this fact. But not a word has been quoted in his behalf from Qāḍī Abū Yūsuf, Imam Muḥammad, al-Ḥāfiẓ 'Abd al-Razzāq b. Hammām, 'Abdullāh b. al-Mubārak, Abū Na'īm al-Faḍl b. Dakīn, Makkī b. Ibrāhīm or Abū 'Āṣim al-Nabīl, who were all famous as faithful disciples of the Imam and, in fact, the principal architects of his fame.

The Imam's *kunyah*, which is better known than his name, was not a true *kunyah*, for he had no son named Ḥanīfah. The *kunyah* was not nominal, but epithetical, being an abbreviation of "Abū al-Millah al-Ḥanīfah," derived from the words "*Wattaba'a millata Ibrāhīma ḥanīfan*" (Therefore conform to the *millah* of Ibrāhīm, who was *ḥanīf*, that is, right in his beliefs), which Allah has addressed to the Muslims in the Qur'an.

Notes

1. Ibn Jazlah, *Mukhtaṣar Kitāb Ta'rīkh Baghdād*, notes on Imam Abū Ḥanīfah.

2. See *Qalā'id 'Uqūd al-'Iqyān,* Chapter 1. Al-Nawawī writes in the introduction to his *Tahdhīb al-Asmā' wa al-Lughāt* that the word *mawlā* is mostly used in the sense of "ally."
3. Ibn al-Ṣalāḥ, *Muqaddamah,* Lucknow edn., p. 58.
4. This *fatwā* has been quoted among other passages by al-Ḥāfiẓ Abū al-Maḥāsin in his *'Uqūd al-Jumān,* and what I have given is a literal translation of it.
5. Al-Dhahabī, *Tadhkirah al-Ḥuffāẓ.*
6. See notes on Abū Ḥanīfah in Ibn Jazlah, *Muhktaṣar Kitāb Ta'rīkh Baghdād, Kitāb al-Ansāb. Tahdhīb al-Asmā' wa al-Lughāt*; al-Dhahabī, *Tadhkirah al-Ḥuffāẓ, al-'Ibar fī Akhbār man 'Ghabar* and *Tahdhīb al-Tahdhīb.*

2

Maturity, education and teachers

The Imam's childhood fell in a time of troubles. Al-Ḥajjāj b. Yūsuf was then the governor of Iraq under the caliph 'Abd al-Malik, and oppression was the order of the day. As it was the opposition of the religious-minded which prevented the house of Marwān from establishing its rule firmly in Arabia and Iraq, al-Ḥajjāj chose people who were leaders in religion and learning as special victims of his cruelties.

Of al-Ḥajjāj there is no truer assessment than that made by 'Umar b. 'Abd al-'Azīz. "If the followers of all the other prophets," said that great caliph, "were to put forward together the great evildoers of their times, and we were to put forward al-Ḥajjāj alone, we would win the contest." 'Abd al-Malik died in 86 H and was succeeded by his son, al-Walīd.

Under al-Walīd, Islam's conquests were considerably extended. Spain and Sind, two large territories, were annexed. Crossing the frontiers of Khawārizm and Samarqand, the caliph's armies hoisted Islam's flag over Kabul and Farghānah; and in the west the islands of Minorca and Majorca were conquered. Of Islam's spiritual blessings, however, there remained no vestige. The higher the government functionaries, the more despotic and cruel they were.

'Umar b. 'Abd al-'Azīz summed up the tone of the administration in a sentence: "With al-Walīd in the Levant, al-Ḥajjāj in Iraq, 'Uthmān in Ḥijāz and Qurrah in Egypt the world was full of oppression." Even in that time of universal disaster religious education did not stop and schools of Ḥadīth continued to function, but not to the extent that Islam's still fresh vigour and missionary zeal warranted.

Fortunately for Islam and the Muslims, al-Ḥajjāj died in 95 H and al-Walīd followed him a year later. Al-Walīd was succeeded by Sulaymān b. 'Abd al-Malik, who is regarded by a consensus of historians as in many ways the best of the Umayyad caliphs. The best thing that Sulaymān did for the Muslim world was to appoint 'Umar b. 'Abd al-'Azīz as his counsellor and leave a written will appointing him as his successor. Sulaymān died in 99 H and, in accordance with his will, 'Umar b. 'Abd al-'Azīz ascended the caliphal throne.

With his accession the entire complexion of Marwānid government changed: justice, good administration and prosperity were restored. He stopped the reviling of the caliph 'Alī in public addresses which had been going on spontaneously, took back the lands granted to Umayyad princes and dismissed oppressive officials. The greatest service he rendered, however, was to encourage religious education: he gave it such a fillip that practically every home became a religious school. He commissioned al-Zuhrī to compile the traditions and, when the compilation was ready, despatched copies of it to all Islamic countries.

As long as al-Ḥajjāj and al-Walīd were alive, Abū Ḥanīfah neither felt any incentive nor got an opportunity to acquire education. Content with being a businessman like his ancestors, he set up a silk weaving factory, which he managed well enough to prosper. But when, during Sulaymān's reign, religious education began to come into its own, he felt an urge to acquire it. A happy coincidence turned the urge into a resolve.

One day, while passing by the house of al-Sha'bī, a famous Imam of Kūfah, he was called in by the Imam, who mistook him for a student. "Where are you going, young man?"[1] asked the Imam. Abū Ḥanīfah named a merchant whom he was going to see. "I meant to ask," said al-Sha'bī, "whose classes you attend." "Nobody's," replied Abū Ḥanīfah regretfully. "I see signs of intelligence in you," said al-Sha'bī. "You ought to sit in the company of learned men." The advice struck a responsive chord, and young Abū Ḥanīfah launched on an educational career in right earnest.

In those days the educational curriculum consisted of literature, genealogy, history of Arabia, *fiqh*, Ḥadīth and *kalām*. *Kalām* was not then what it is today, as philosophy had not yet influenced the discussion of Islamic religious questions. Nevertheless, it provided the widest scope then available for penetration, imaginativeness and originality in discussions relating to religion. So long as Islam remained confined to Arabia, discussion of its problems reflected its pristine simplicity. It was only when it reached Persia, Egypt and Syria that religious debate became an elaborate exercise. Although philosophy had lost its original hold on these countries, corrupted philosophical ideas enjoyed a wide vogue, and people's minds were inclined to hairsplitting and sceptical questioning. The Arabs had a broad understanding of what has been said in the Qur'an about Allah's essence and attributes, the beginning and end of the world and similar questions; and that was enough for the purposes of their simple and unadulterated beliefs.

As against this, complex debates arose in Persia and the Levant, as they were bound to do with the development of civilisation and the evolution of thought. The purity of Allah's nature, anthropomorphism, the identity or separateness of

Allah's essence and attributes, contingency, eternity and many like questions cropped up, discussion of each of which became an independent discipline. Gradually even common questions of belief were subjected to hairsplitting, and divergence of views crystallised into different schools of thought, such as the Qadariyyah, the Murji'ah, the Mu'tazilah, the Jahmiyyah, the Khawārij and the Rāfiḍah. So widespread did the evil of schism become that even simple believers, who had until then shunned controversies of this kind, were compelled to get involved in them, if for no other reason than to refute what they considered to be wrong. This gave rise to the science of *kalām* which in due course acquired such a high status that important Imams, as, for example, al-Ash'arī and Abū Manṣūr al-Māturīdī, were proud of their contributions to it.

Although *kalām*, after being systematised, subsequently became an academic discipline, at that time all that was needed for its acquisition was a keen intelligence and a modicum of religious learning. With his nimble Persian mind and his gift of originality, Abū Ḥanīfah was cut out for it. As for religious learning, narration of tradition and discussion of theological questions were so common in Kūfah that any man of ordinary intelligence could work up a fair acquaintance with them by simply attending learned gatherings. Abū Ḥanīfah in this way acquired so much competence in *kalām* that even leading masters of it used to fight shy of engaging in debate with him.

In connection with his trade, he frequently had to visit Baṣrah, which was the main forum of all the contending schools and particularly the Khawārij. He fought many battles of wit with members of the Ibāḍiyyah, the Ṣughrjyyah and the Ḥashwiyyah, always coming out victorious. Although in the course of time he gave up taking part in these debates and devoted himself wholly to *fiqh* for the rest of his days, he never completely lost his gusto for *kalām*, and records of his debates with the Khawārij and others are masterpieces of this genre. We shall recount some of them in detail when we discuss his works.

Abū Ḥanīfah grew out of his penchant for *kalām* with the maturing of his understanding and experience. How this came about is narrated in an interesting manner in the *'Uqūd al-Jumān*. In early youth, the story says, he thought *kalām* to be the highest of disciplines because it appeared to him to be the foundation of all faith. But later it dawned on him that the great Companions had always avoided getting embroiled in controversies of the kind that are the speciality of *kalām*, although no one understood the truth of these matters better than they did. They devoted most of their labours to questions of *fiqh*—to the learning and teaching of them. He also critically examined the way of life of the people whom he found engaged in *kalām*, and was disillusioned to discover that they did not have anything like the moral and spiritual qualities which had distinguished the great ones of earlier times.

About this time a woman one day posed to him a question as to how a man could divorce his wife in accordance with the Sunnah. He did not know the answer. So he advised the woman to go to Ḥammād, whose school was nearby, and put the question to him. He also requested her to tell him the answer on her way back. The woman returned some time later and told him what answer Ḥammād had given her. This revealed to him how little he knew and drove him to join Ḥammād's school at once.

There is another story about Abū Ḥanīfah's early education, which al-Khaṭīb has traced back to the Imam himself. When the Imam turned to acquiring education he could not for some time make up his mind as to which of the various disciplines that suggested themselves to him he should choose. His first thought was of *kalām*, but there was a nagging doubt in his mind as to whether it would be worthwhile labouring at a discipline the fruits of which he could not openly display for fear of being called a heretic. As regards literature and *qirā'ah*, they were not of much use unless one wanted to become a schoolmaster. So far as poetry was concerned, it was at that time nothing more than a collection of satires and false panegyrics. As for Ḥadīth, learning it needed a long time and, besides, one had to associate so much with young people that one was always afraid of being criticised and even derided. Ultimately, he settled for *fiqh*, which appealed to him as a discipline dealing with both the religious and the secular requirements of people.

This story, however, is completely false and is refuted by all reliable accounts. The remarks attributed to the Imam about the various disciplines are so preposterous that even an illiterate man could not have made them. If we were to believe this story, we should have to conclude that Abū Ḥanīfah took no interest at all in Ḥadīth and *kalām*, whereas the fact is that in these disciplines he has an undeniably high standing. What is probable is that after having acquired all the disciplines, the Imam decided to specialise in *fiqh*, because it seemed to him to cater to the needs of the common people.

Different narrators seem to have put different kinds of gloss on this simple probability, as is clear from the fact that, although the story had already been recorded, the author of the *'Uqūd al-Jumān* has narrated it in a very different way. I have before me Ibn Jazlah's summary of the *Ta'rīkh Baghdād*, in which also the story is related; but there the remarks quoted above about the various disciplines are attributed to other persons and Abū Ḥanīfah is reported only to have agreed with them.

Ḥammād was a famous Imam of Kūfah and an acknowledged master of *fiqh* in his time. He had heard traditions from the Prophet's personal attendant, Anas, and had associated with some of the most prominent *Tābi'īn*. His was the most largely attended school in Kūfah and counted among its pupils men of the eminence of Mis'ar and Shu'bah. He was the last surviving representative of the school of *fiqh* originated by the Companion 'Abdullāh b. Mas'ūd. He was also fortunate enough to be rich, which enabled him to devote himself fully to his teaching. For these reasons Abū Ḥanīfah, when he decided to learn *fiqh*, chose him for his teacher.

The method of teaching in those days was that the teacher would lecture on a particular subject and the pupils try to memorise what he said, sometimes also taking notes. On the first day, Abū Ḥanīfah was made to sit in the row on the teacher's left, which was the row for beginners; but before many days had passed, Ḥammād marked him out as the pupil with the best memory and intelligence in the class and made him sit right in front of him ahead of every other pupil.[2]

Although Abū Ḥanīfah had about the same time started learning Ḥadīth also, about which we shall have something to say in detail later on, he regularly attended Ḥammād's lectures. We have it on his own authority that he did so for two years, after which he began to think of starting his own class, but was prevented from doing so by respect for his teacher. As luck would have it, Ḥammād went to Baṣrah to attend the funeral of a relative, appointing Abū Ḥanīfah to take the class during his absence.

While lecturing in this way, Abū Ḥanīfah was frequently asked questions on which Ḥammād had narrated no tradition to him. He exercised his own judgement in answering these questions, keeping notes of his answers with the idea of showing them to Ḥammād later on. When Ḥammād returned from Baṣrah two months later, he showed him the notes. They dealt with sixty questions. Ḥammād found twenty of the answers wrong. This decided Abū Ḥanīfah to remain Ḥammād's pupil.

Ḥammād died in 120 H. Although Abū Ḥanīfah attended the *fiqh* lectures of other teachers as well, there is no doubt that he received his training mainly from Ḥammād, for whom he had the profoundest respect.

As we have already mentioned, Abū Ḥanīfah, while he was attending Ḥammād's *fiqh* lectures, started learning Ḥadīth also, because he felt that it would not be possible for him to do the kind of original work he wanted to do in *fiqh* without full knowledge of Ḥadīth.

At that period the teaching of Ḥadīth was going on vigorously in all Islamic countries, and everywhere authorities and narrations were being recorded. The Companions, at least ten thousand in number, had spread far and wide and become the nucleus of a great system of authorities and narrations. Wherever one of them was heard of, people flocked to him from far and near, eager to hear first-hand accounts of the Prophet (ṣ) and get authentic answers to questions of law exercising their minds. In this way a large body of *Tābi'īn*, who were called disciples of the Companions, had come into existence with its ramifications in all the Islamic countries. The cities which had comparatively large numbers of Companions or *Tābi'īn* acquired the name *dār al-'ilm* (centres of learning). Outstanding among these were Makkah, Yemen, Baṣrah and Kūfah—all of them cities full of mementoes of Islamic history.

Kūfah, Imam Abū Ḥanīfah's place of birth and residence, was in the vanguard of this expansion of Islamic learning. As the small territory of Arabia was becoming inadequate to accommodate the multiplying Arab population, the caliph ʻUmar wrote to Saʻd b. Abī Waqqāṣ, who was then stationed at Madā'in after having overthrown the empire of Chosroes, asking him to found a city to which some of the surplus Arab population could migrate. Saʻd selected the site of Kūfah and laid the foundation-stone of the city in 17 H.

The city began with a few simple buildings. As soon as the first few buildings were completed, tribesmen from different parts of Arabia began to flock to it, so that in a short while it became an extension of Arabia. ʻUmar fixed stipends for twelve thousand settlers from the Yemen and eight thousand from Nazār. Within a short time Kūfah became such an important Arab settlement that ʻUmar used to call it by names like "the Standard of Allah," "the Treasure House of the Faith" and "the Head of Arabia." He used to address his letters to Kūfah thus: "To the Head of Islam" or "To the Head of Arabia."

The caliph ʻAlī for his part made the city his capital. One thousand and fifty Companions, including twenty-four who had fought in the Battle of Badr by the side of the Prophet (ṣ), came over to Kūfah, and most of them settled there permanently. The presence of these Companions engendered so much popular interest in Ḥadīth and *riwāyah* that practically every house in the city became a school for these disciplines.[3]

Baṣrah was also founded under the orders of ʻUmar and soon became a rival to Kūfah in learning and particularly in Ḥadīth. Like Makkah and Madīnah these cities were regarded as twin centres of learning. Most of the personalities whom al-Dhahabī has described as transmitters of Ḥadīth in the second and third periods of Islam and on whom he has written full notes in his work, such as Masrūq b. al-Ajdaʻ, ʻUbaydah b. ʻUmar, al-Aswad b. Yazīd, Abū ʻUmar al-Nakhaʻī, Zirr b.

Hubaysh, al-Rabīʿ b. Khuthaym, ʿAbd al-Raḥmān b. Abī Laylā, Abū ʿAbd al-Raḥmān al-Salamī, Shurayḥ b. al-Ḥārth, Shurayḥ b. Hānī, Abū Wā'il Shaqīq b. Salamah, Qays b. Ḥāzim, Muḥammad b. Sīrīn. al-Ḥasan al-Baṣrī, Shuʿbah b. al-Ḥajjāj and Qatādah b. Diʿāmah, were residents of these two cities. Sufyān b. ʿUyaynah, regarded as one of the imams of Ḥadīth, often used to say that there were three important centres of Ḥadīth learning: Makkah for ceremonials of hajj, Madīnah for *Qirā'ah*, and Kūfah for what was lawful and what was unlawful, that is to say, *fiqh*.[4]

For learning *fiqh* Abū Ḥanīfah had thought it enough to attend Ḥammād's lectures; but when it came to learning Ḥadīth, he found that this would not do, for here one could not manage with intelligence and originality alone, but along with skill in criticism had to have a stock of traditions also. The traditions were at that time all scattered and still uncompiled, with the result that even great masters remembered not more than two or three hundred of them each. This number was not enough even for answering fundamental questions. Besides, such a large variety of *ṭuruq* (ways of transmission) had come into existence that unless one knew a *ḥadīth* according to a number of *ṭuruq* one could not be sure of its meaning and implications. Association with Ḥammād and maturing years had combined to make Abū Ḥanīfah realise this. So he devoted himself heart and soul to collecting traditions.

There was practically no *muḥaddith* in Kūfah at whose feet Abū Ḥanīfah did not sit to learn traditions. Abū al-Maḥāsin al-Shāfiʿī, giving a list of Abū Ḥanīfah's Ḥadīth teachers, says that ninety-three of them belonged to Kūfah. Although, unusually enough, the *Tahdhīb al-Tahdhīb*, *Tahdhīb al-Asmā'*, *Tadhkirah al-Ḥuffāẓ* etc., do not list the Imam's teachers, indications are available in these books that he learnt traditions from a large number of men, of whom twenty-nine were residents of Kūfah, most of them being *Tābiʿīs.* Of his Kūfah teachers al-Shaʿbī, Salamah b. Kuhayl, Muḥārib b. Dithār, Abū Isḥāq al-Sabīʿī, ʿAwn b. ʿAbdullāh, Samāk b. Ḥarb, ʿAmr b. Murrah, Manṣūr b. al-Maʿmar, Aʿmash, Ibrāhīm b. Muḥammad, ʿAdī b. Thābit al-Anṣārī, ʿAṭā' b. al-Sā'ib, Mūsā b. Abī ʿĀ'ishah and ʿAlqamah b. Murthid were particularly great authorities on Ḥadīth, *sanad* and *riwāyah.* The line of transmission of Sufyān al-Thawrī, Aḥmad b. Ḥanbal and several others generally goes back to these personalities.

Al-Shaʿbī, it will be recalled, was the one who first of all aroused in Abū Ḥanīfah an interest in learning. He narrated traditions he had heard from a large number of Companions. It is said that he had met as many as five hundred of them, and was one of four men acknowledged to be accomplished scholars of Ḥadīth in Iraq, Arabia and al-Shām. According to al-Zuhrī there were only four real scholars: Ibn al-Musayyib in Madīnah, al-Ḥasan in Baṣrah, Makḥūl in Syria and al-Shaʿbī in Kūfah. ʿAbdullāh b. ʿUmar, after attending a lecture of al-Shaʿbī on *maghāzī* (military campaigns), remarked, "By Allah, this man knows the subject better than I do." Al-Shaʿbī held the office of *qāḍī* for a long time and was highly respected by the caliphs and high state officials. He died in 104 or 106 H.

Salamah b. Kuhayl was a famous *Muḥaddith* and *Tābiʿī.* He had heard traditions from Jundub b. ʿAbdullāh, Ibn Abī Awfā, Abū al-Ṭufayl and many other Companions. Ibn Saʿd describes him as the transmitter of a large number of traditions. Sufyān b. ʿUyaynah, al-Shāfiʿī's teacher, called him one of the pillars of Ḥadīth. Ibn Mahdī named four men as the most accurate narrators of traditions in Kūfah: Manṣūr, ʿAmr b. Murrah, Abū al-Ḥuṣayn and Salamah.

Abū Isḥāq al-Sabīʿī was one of the high-ranking *Tābiʿīs* and had heard traditions from ʿAbdullāh b. ʿUmar, Ibn al-Zubayr, al-Nuʿmān b. Bashīr, Zayd b. Arqam and a number of Companions whose names have been given by al-Nawawī in *Tahdhīb al-Asmā'*. Al-ʿUjaylī says that he had met thirty-eight Companions face-to-face and heard traditions from them. ʿAlī b. al-Madīnī, teacher of al-Bukhārī, estimates the number of his masters in Ḥadīth at a minimum of three hundred. Of these al-Ḥāfiẓ Ibn Ḥajar has given a detailed account in *Tahdhīb*.

Samāk b. Ḥarb was a leading *Tābiʿī* and *muḥaddith*. Imam Sufyān al-Thawrī acknowledges that he never made a mistake in Ḥadīth, and he himself claims to have met eighty Companions.

Muḥārib b. Dithār had heard traditions from ʿAbdullāh b. ʿUmar, Jābir and others. Sufyān al-Thawrī says that he never saw a more pious man. Al-Dhahabī regards his pronouncements as conclusive. Imam Aḥmad, Ibn Muʿīn, Abū Zarʿah, al-Dāraquṭnī, Abū Ḥātim Yaʿqūb, Ibn Sufyān and al-Nasā'ī regard him as reliable. He was a *qāḍī* in Kūfah and died in 116 H.

ʿAwn b. ʿAbdullāh b. ʿUtbah b. Masʿūd had heard traditions from Abū Hurayrah and ʿAbdullāh b. ʿUmar, and was a reliable narrator and a pious man.

Hishām b. ʿUrwah was a venerable and well-known *Tābiʿī* who had heard traditions from many Companions and was the teacher of several great imams of Ḥadīth, such as Sufyān al-Thawrī, Mālik and Sufyān b. ʿUyaynah. He came to Kūfah in the time of Abū Jaʿfar al-Manṣūr and people heard traditions from him while he was there. The caliph al-Manṣūr held him in high esteem and on one occasion gave him a grant of a hundred thousand dirhams. He himself led the prayers at

Hishām's funeral. Ibn Sa'd says that he was reliable and had a large stock of traditions. Abū Ḥātim describes him as an imam of Ḥadīth.

Sulaymān b. Mihrān, better known as al-A'mash, was a famous imam of Kūfah. Of the Companions, he had met Anas b. Mālik and had heard traditions from 'Abdullāh b. Abī Awfā. Sufyān al-Thawrī and Shu'bah were his pupils.

The second city where Abū Ḥanīfah received his education in Ḥadīth was Baṣrah, a rich treasure house of Ḥadīth because of the presence of al-Ḥasan al-Baṣrī, Shu'bah and Qatādah. It is surprising that, although al-Ḥasan al-Baṣrī lived up to 110 H, there is no evidence that Abū Ḥanīfah attended his lectures; but so far as Qatādah is concerned, many *muḥaddiths* have mentioned that Abū Ḥanīfah was a pupil of his. Similarly, it appears from several passages in the *'Uqūd al-Jumān* that he heard traditions related by Shu'bah and that the latter during his own lifetime permitted him to give *fatwās* and narrate traditions.

Qatādah was a great *muḥaddith* and a famous *Tābi'ī* who had heard traditions from Anas b. Mālik, 'Abdullāh b. Sarakhs, Abū al-Ṭufayl and other Companions. He was one of the two most famous pupils of Anas. What he is particularly famous for is that he used to relate traditions with meticulous faithfulness, so that there was not the slightest difference between words and meanings.

There is a surprising story about his retentive memory related by 'Amr b. 'Abdullāh. Sa'īd b. al-Musayyib from whom he used to learn *fiqh* and Ḥadīth daily, said to him one day, "You ask me a lot of questions every day. But do you remember the answers I give you?" "I remember every word of what you tell me," replied Qatādah, who then began to repeat what he had learnt from Sa'īd giving the day and date of each lesson. Astonished, Sa'īd remarked, "Allah has created men like you also!" It was because of his memory that he used to be called *Aḥfaẓ al-Nās* (the Strongest of Memory). Aḥmad b. Ḥanbal praises him greatly for his knowledge of *fiqh*, *ikhtilāf* (difference of opinion) and exegesis. "In these subjects," he says, "Qatādah may have had equals, but had no superior at all." Ibn Ḥajar gives a detailed account of him in the *Tahdhīb al-Tahdhīb*, which shows how high he ranked.

Shu'bah also was a leading *muḥaddith*, who knew by heart two thousand traditions. Sufyān al-Thawrī has acclaimed him as the *Amīr al-Mu'minīn* of Ḥadīth. He was the first in Iraq to devise rules of criticism and appraisal. Al-Shāfi'ī used to say that if there had been no Shu'bah, Ḥadīth would have had no vogue in Iraq. He died in 160 H. On hearing of his death Sufyān al-Thawrī said, "The art of Ḥadīth has died with him."

Shu'bah was deeply attached to Abū Ḥanīfah and often used to praise his intelligence and quick understanding in his absence. On one occasion he said, "Just as I know that the sun is bright, I know for certain that learning and Abū Ḥanīfah are doubles of each other." Somebody having asked Yaḥyā b. Ma'īn, who was one of al-Bukhārī's teachers, what he thought of Abū Ḥanīfah, he said, "It is enough for me to know that Shu'bah permitted him to teach Ḥadīth and narration. Shu'bah after all was Shu'bah."[5]

Among the other Baṣrah masters from whom Abū Ḥanīfah heard traditions 'Abd al-Karīm b. Umayyah and 'Āṣim b. Sulaymān al-Aḥwal were prominent.

Although Abū Ḥanīfah had collected a vast store of traditions in these schools, it was necessary for him to go to the two holy cities of Makkah and Madīnah, the fountainheads of religious learning, in order to complete his education. It is not known definitely when he performed his first journey to the holy cities; but it seems most probable that he did so at an early stage of his educational career.

The historian Ibn Khallikān[6] quotes Wakī' as narrating a story connected with this journey, which he claims to have heard from Abū Ḥanīfah himself. A barber who shaved his head during the pilgrimage rebuked Abū Ḥanīfah several times. When he asked what he had to pay for the shave, the barber said, "One does not discuss what one has to pay for hajj rites." So Abū Ḥanīfah quietly let him go on to trim his beard. The barber suddenly remarked, "One does not remain silent during hajj; keep saying your *takbīr*." When he got up to go after finishing with the barber, the barber commanded him to perform two *rak'ahs* of prayer before going. Surprised, Abū Ḥanīfah asked him where he had learnt all these points of law. "I owe them all to 'Aṭā' b. Abī Rabāḥ," replied the barber. This story suggests that Abū Ḥanīfah was still a beginner then.

Abū Ḥanīfah went to Makkah as a student at a time when that city was a busy centre of education. A number of acknowledged masters of Ḥadīth, who had had access to the Companions had established their own schools there. The biggest and most respected of these was 'Aṭā' b. Abī Rabāḥ's school.

'Aṭā' was a famous *Tābi'ī*, who had associated with most of the Companions and acquired from this association the status of an authority. He had heard traditions from 'Abdullāh b. 'Abbās, Ibn 'Umar, Ibn al-Zubayr, Usāmah b. Zayd, Jābir b. 'Abdullāh, Zayd b. Arqam, 'Abdullāh b. al-Sā'ib, 'Aqīl, Rāfi', Abū al-Dardā', Abū Hurayrah and many other Companions. He himself claims to have met two hundred men who had associated with the Prophet (ṣ). The leading Companions all acknowledged his learning. 'Abdullāh b. 'Umar, the son of the caliph 'Umar, often used to say, "Why do people come to me when 'Aṭā' b. Abī Rabāḥ is there for them to go to?" During hajj there used to be a government proclamation prohibiting anybody but 'Aṭā' from giving *fatwās*.[7] Many great imams of Ḥadīth, such as al-Awzā'ī, al-Zuhrī and 'Umar b. Dīnār, were alumni of his school.

When Abū Ḥanīfah presented himself to 'Aṭā' b. Abī Rabāḥ for enrolment, the latter questioned him about his beliefs. The Imam replied, "I do not speak ill of people of the earlier generations (*aslāf*), do not call sinners *kāfirs* and believe in *qaḍā'* and *qadar*." 'Aṭā' thereupon permitted him to attend his lectures.[8] His intelligence and intellect made an increasing impression on the teacher, so that there soon came a stage where, as soon as he came, 'Aṭā' would order room to be made for him to sit close to him.[9] As long as 'Aṭā' lived— he died in 115 H—Abū Ḥanīfah used to attend his lectures whenever he visited Makkah.

Of the other *muḥaddiths* of Makkah whose Ḥadīth classes Abū Ḥanīfah attended, one who deserves special mention is 'Ikrimah. He was a slave and pupil of 'Abdullāh b. 'Abbās, who educated him with great care and personal attention, making him so proficient that he, during his own lifetime, gave him the authority to exercise personal judgement and give rulings. 'Ikrimah had learnt traditions and points of *fiqh* from many other Companions, such as the caliph 'Alī, Abū Hurayrah, 'Abdullāh b. 'Umar, 'Uqbah b. 'Amr, Ṣafwān, Jābir and Abū Qatādah. Among those who were his pupils in Ḥadīth and exegesis were at least seventy famous *Tābi'īs*. Al-Sha'bī used to say that there had never been a man who knew the Qur'an better than 'Ikrimah. Sa'īd b. Jubayr, a top-ranking *Tābi'ī*, was once asked whether he knew of someone more learned than himself. He named 'Ikrimah.

About the same time, that is, before 102 H, Abū Ḥanīfah paid a visit to Madīnah, the treasure house of Ḥadīth and the Prophet's home during his last days. The Companions having all departed one after another, seven of the *Tābi'īs* living in Madīnah had become the central figures in *fiqh* and Ḥadīth, and all questions of law were generally referred to them. These people had received their education from leading Companions and were acknowledged throughout the Islamic world, in every corner of which their pupils were running schools. They were all contemporaries and constituted a consultative body to which all Sharī'ah questions were referred.[10] Madīnan *fiqh*, which was codified by Mālik, is based largely on their rulings.

When Abū Ḥanīfah arrived in Madīnah, only two of these eminent men, namely, Sulaymān and Sālim b. 'Abdullāh, were alive. Sulaymān, who had been a slave of Maymūnah, one of the Prophet's wives, ranked second among the seven. Sālim was a grandson of 'Umar and had been taught by his father. Abū Ḥanīfah attended on both these *Tābi'īs* and learnt traditions from them.

Although this completes the account of Abū Ḥanīfah's travels as a regular student, he did not cease to be a student until the end of his life. He used frequently to visit the holy cities and sojourn there for months together. Especially during hajj, he used to meet and learn all he could from the eminent men who came to Makkah from different parts of the Islamic world, not only to perform the pilgrimage but also to teach and learn. Among these were al-Awzā'ī and Makḥūl al-Shāmī, the latter of whom was acclaimed as an imam in Syria. Abū Ḥanīfah took a *sanad* in Ḥadīth from both of them. By that time the fame of his intellectual gifts and originality had spread far and wide, and it included the reputation, given to him by superficial observers, of being a *qayyās*, that is, one who made deductions by analogy.

About that time ʿAbdullāh b. al-Mubārak, a well-known pupil of Abū Ḥanīfah's, went to Beirut to complete his Ḥadīth education under al-Awzāʿī. At the very outset, al-Awzāʿī asked him, "Who is this man Abū Ḥanīfah who has appeared in Kūfah. I hear he makes all sorts of new points about religion." ʿAbdullāh went home without giving a reply, but returned two or three days later with some parts of a manuscript, which he presented to al-Awzāʿī. On the title page were written the words "Says al-Nuʿmān b. Thābit." Al-Awzāʿī started reading the manuscript and went on doing so for a long time, fully absorbed. Then he asked ʿAbdullāh, "Who is this worthy Nuʿmān?" ʿAbdullāh replied, "A shaykh of Iraq in whose company I have sat." "A great man," observed al-Awzāʿī. "This is the same Abū Ḥanīfah," ʿAbdullāh quietly put in, "whom you called an innovator."[11] Al-Awzāʿī expressed much regret over his mistake and made it a point to meet Abū Ḥanīfah when he went next for hajj. The two of them discussed the questions dealt with in Abū Ḥanīfah's manuscript. ʿAbdullāh b. al-Mubārak happened to be present. He reports that Abū Ḥanīfah spoke so beautifully on the questions that al-Awzāʿī was astonished. After Abū Ḥanīfah's departure, ʿAbdullāh stayed on. "This man's greatness," said al-Awzāʿī to him, "has made people jealous of him. My suspicions about him were completely wrong, and I am very sorry for them."

It is a historically established fact that Abū Ḥanīfah was a pupil of al-Awzāʿī in Ḥadīth. He probably attended his lectures during the period that we are speaking of.

Abū Ḥanīfah had a similar encounter with Imam al-Bāqir. He called on al-Bāqir on his second visit to Madīnah. After the introduction had been made by a companion of Abū

Ḥanīfah's, al-Bāqir addressed him thus: "So you are the man who contradicts the traditions of my grandfather on the basis of analogy."

"Allah forbid," replied Abū Ḥanīfah. "Who dare contradict Ḥadīth? After you resume your seat, sir, I shall explain my position."

Then the following conversation took place:

Abū Ḥanīfah: "Who is the weaker, man or woman?"

Al-Bāqir: "Woman."

Abū Ḥanīfah: "Which of them is entitled to the larger share in the inheritance?"

Al-Bāqir: "The man."

Abū Ḥanīfah: "Now, if I had been making deductions by analogy, I should have said that the woman should get the larger share, because on the face of it the weaker one is entitled to more consideration. But I have not said so. To take up another subject, which do you think is the higher duty, prayer or fasting?"

Al-Bāqir: "Prayer."

Abū Ḥanīfah: "That being the case, it should be permissible for a woman during menstruation to postpone her prayers and not her fasts. But the ruling I give is that she can postpone her fasting and not her prayers."

Al-Bāqir was so highly pleased with this dialogue that he got up and kissed Abū Ḥanīfah's forehead.[12]

Abū Ḥanīfah sat for a long time at Imam al-Bāqir's feet and acquired from him much valuable knowledge of *fiqh* and Ḥadīth not available anywhere else. Shī'ahs and Sunnīs are agreed that Abū Ḥanīfah derived much of his learning from al-Bāqir. He learnt a great deal from the Imam's son, Ja'far al-Ṣādiq also, a fact which is generally mentioned in the history books.

Ibn Taymiyyah, however, denies this on the ground that Abū Ḥanīfah and Ja'far al-Ṣādiq were contemporaries and equals, which ruled out the probability of the former being the latter's pupil. But I consider this sheer impudence and lack of comprehension on Ibn Taymiyyah's part. For all his greatness as an original thinker and master of *fiqh*, Abū Ḥanīfah could not compare in learning with Imam Ja'far al-Ṣādiq. The *Ahl al-Bayt* were the fountainhead of Ḥadīth and *fiqh* and, in fact, all religious learning. "The master of the house knows best what is in it," to quote a well-known Arabic saying.

At one time, as we have mentioned earlier, Abū Ḥanīfah had visited the holy cities as a student; but there soon came a time when news of his intended visits to Arabia travelled ahead of him, so that thousands of people assembled to meet him in every city or village that he passed through.

On one of his visits to Makkah, an interesting incident took place. Such a large audience, which included scholars of both Ḥadīth and *fiqh*, had gathered before his arrival that there was not an inch of space left unoccupied in the meeting-place and people were falling over each other in their eagerness to question and listen to him. Unable to keep order, the Imam said, "I wish somebody asked my host to come and manage this crowd."

One of the people present, Abū 'Āṣim al-Nabīl, offered to go and call the host, but added that he had a few questions still to ask. The Imam asked him to come forward and listened to his questions with special attention. In this process, calling the host was forgotten. After finishing with Abū 'Āṣim, the Imam became busy with another student, listening to and answering his questions. After a little while, he remembered that somebody had offered to go and bring the host. He inquired who it was who had made the offer. Abū 'Āṣim answered that it was he. "Then why haven't you gone?" asked the Imam. Abū 'Āṣim retorted with a polemicist's wit, "I never said I would go at once. I'll go when I am free." "In ordinary conversation," the Imam corrected him, "there is no room for equivocations of this kind. Your words were to be taken in the sense in which the common people would take them."[13] In an indirect manner this was a juristic ruling, which the Imam gave in passing.

The Imam's teachers used to treat him with so much respect that people used to be astonished. Muḥammad b. al-Faḍl relates how, on one occasion, when Abū Ḥanīfah, accompanied by him, called on Khuḍayb to inquire about a tradition, the latter stood up to receive him and with much respect made him sit next to him. "What is the *ḥadīth* about? An ostrich egg?" asked Abū Ḥanīfah. Khuḍayb replied, "Abū 'Ubaydah narrated from 'Abdullāh b. Mas'ūd that if an ostrich egg is broken by one who is clad in *iḥrām*, he will have to pay its price." 'Amr b. Dīnār,[14] a famous *muḥaddith* of Makkah, would not address anybody else whenever Abū Ḥanīfah was present in his class.

In spite of the high esteem enjoyed by him, Abū Ḥanīfah did not think it beneath his dignity to learn from anybody. Although Mālik was thirteen years his junior, he often attended his lectures and heard traditions from him.

Al-Dhahabī writes in the *Tadhkirah al-Ḥuffāẓ* that Abū Ḥanīfah used to sit before Mālik as one sits before one's teacher. Some uncomprehending people have attributed this to a consciousness of his own inferiority on the part of Abū Ḥanīfah, but I think that this was a sign of nobility of character and a token of recognition due from one great scholar to another. Mālik for his part reciprocated this respect. This is instanced by a story reported to have been told by 'Abdullāh b. al-Mubārak. One day, while he was sitting with Mālik, there came an old man, who was received with extreme respect by the Imam and made to sit beside him. After he had gone, the Imam said to 'Abdullāh, "Do you know who this man was? He was Abū Ḥanīfah of Iraq, who, if he wanted to, could prove this pillar to have been made of gold." After some time another man came. The Imam received him also respectfully, but not as respectfully as he had received Abū Ḥanīfah. After his departure the Imam told those present that this was Sufyān al-Thawrī.

The great masters of Ḥijāz and Iraq followed different principles of *riwāyah* (narration) and a variety of methods of teaching. Some of them thought writing to be more reliable, while others as, for example, Ibrāhīm and al-Sha'bī, thought memory to be sufficient authority. The majority considered it permissible to leave out a part of a tradition in narrating it, so long as the meaning was not affected. Others were totally opposed to this. One group held the view that a narration could not be made unless the narrator was physically present. Abū Ḥanīfah's teacher, Shu'bah, belonged to this group. Another group admitted narration from a writing while the narrator was present behind a veil. Al-Zuhrī's practice was to explain the meanings and implications of the words along with narrations. Some people were severely opposed to this, so much so that on one occasion a man told al-Zuhrī not to mix his own words with a *ḥadīth Nabawī* (i.e. a *ḥadīth* of the Prophet (ṣ)).

As regards the method of teaching, Mālik liked his pupils to read aloud, while he himself listened. Some people objected to this. Yaḥyā b. Salām, for example, left Mālik's school simply on this ground. There were a number of differences in other matters also, which have been recorded in detail in *Fatḥ al-Mughīth.*

One main reason why Abū Ḥanīfah attached himself to so many masters and attended so many schools was that he wanted to acquaint himself with the different principles and methods in vogue so that by a comparative study of them he could arrive at some system of his own. What reforms he made in the principles of *fiqh* I shall have occasion to describe later on.

It was a matter of good fortune for Abū Ḥanīfah that by the time he started his education the method of teaching Ḥadīth had been systematised. Until then the common practice had been oral narration: some imams of Ḥadīth went so far as to consider reduction to writing impermissible.

It was the caliph ʿUmar b. ʿAbd al-ʿAzīz who took the initiative in introducing writing. He wrote as follows in a letter to the citizens of Madīnah around 101 H: "All traditions of the Messenger of Allah should be recorded, lest they are lost. I fear the end of this science with the passing away of its masters." He sent similar orders to other important cities as well. In obedience to his orders al-Zuhrī prepared at Madīnah a collection, copies of which were published in all Islamic countries.[15] From that time the practice of compiling traditions became common and scholars of Ḥadīth everywhere made collections of them. Even Abū Ḥanīfah's teacher, al-Shaʿbī, despite his insistence on oral narrations, used to keep a compilation by his side.

The method of education also underwent much improvement. The teacher would sit in a high seat with a Ḥadīth compendium in his hands, and the students, seated around him, would take down whatever he spoke. If the audience was too large for the people on the other fringes to hear the teacher, a man would stand up from among the audience and repeat the teacher's words; but it was compulsory that he should not alter the sense and, as far as possible, not even the words themselves. The man chosen to do the relaying was, therefore, always one with a strong memory and adequate knowledge of Ḥadīth, besides having a good pronunciation and a loud voice. Thus, in Shu'bah's classes Ādam b. Abī Ayās, and in Mālik's classes Ibn 'Uliyyah, used to render this service.

Abū Ḥanīfah is particularly famous for having had innumerable teachers. Abū Ḥafṣ claims that the Imam heard traditions from at least four thousand men. This is nothing unusual in the history of Islamic learning. The labour expended by the Muslims on collecting traditions was, indeed, immense beyond the imagination of the followers of other religions. We could name quite a few men whose Ḥadīth teachers numbered no less than four thousand, while the number of those who had more than a thousand teachers is legion. Al-Sakhāwī has listed these men in the *Fatḥ al-Mughīth.*

So far, however, as Abū Ḥanīfah is concerned, the claim that his teachers are innumerable does not stand the test of the principles of Ḥadīth. Nevertheless, there is no doubt that he heard traditions from a very large number of people. Al-Dhahabī, in the *Tadhkirah al-Ḥuffāẓ*, ends the list of Abū Ḥanīfah's teachers with the words "and numerous others." Abū al-Muḥāfiẓ al-Shāfi'ī in the *'Uqūd al-Jumān* gives the names of three hundred and nineteen men along with their parentage, and then ends with the words "in another book entitled *Taḥṣīl al-Sabīl ilā Ma'rifah al-Thiqāt wa āl-Majāhīl* I have given detailed facts about these men, but since their list is derived mainly from Ḥanafī jurists, it is likely that the *muḥaddiths* may not fully agree with it."

It is a pity that I have not been able to consult books written by *muḥaddiths* on the Imam, books in which they have given full details of his teachers. I have before me a number of authentic biographical dictionaries in which the Imam's name is included, but these deal with thousands of persons without giving full details about any of them. The names I have been able to ascertain from a scrutiny of the *Mukhtaṣar Ta'rīkh Baghdād*, *Tahdhīb al-Kamāl*, *Tahdhīb al-Asmā' wa al-Lughāt*, *Tadhkirah al-Ḥuffāẓ*, *Tahdhīb al-Tahdhīb*, *al-Ansāb* of al-Sam'ānī, *al-Muwaṭṭa'* of Imam Muḥammad and *Kitāb al-Āthār*[16] of Imam Muḥammad are listed below:

'Aṭā' b. Abī Rabāḥ of Makkah, 'Āṣim b. Abī al-Nujūd of Kūfah, 'Alqamah b. Marthad of Kūfah, al-Ḥakam b. 'Utbah of Kūfah, Salamah b. Kuhayl of Kūfah, Imam al-Bāqir of Madīnah, 'Alī b. al-Aqmar of Kūfah, Ziyād b. 'Ilāqah of Kūfah, Sa'īd b. Masrūq of Kūfah, 'Adī b. Thābit al-Anṣārī of Kūfah, 'Atiyyah b. Sa'īd of Kūfah, Abū Sufyān al-Sa'dī, 'Abd al-Karīm b. Umayyah of Baṣrah, Yaḥyā b. Sa'īd of Madīnah, Hishām b. 'Urwah of Madīnah (from *Tahdhīb al-Tahdhīb* of al-Ḥāfiẓ Ibn Ḥajar al-'Asqalānī); Abū Isḥāq al-Sabī'ī of Kūfah, Nāfi' b. 'Umar of Madīnah, 'Abd al-Raḥmān b. Hurmuz al-A'raj of Madīnah, Qatādah of Baṣrah, 'Umar b. Dīnār of Makkah, Muḥārib b. Dithār of Kūfah, Hushaym b. Ḥabīb al-Ṣarrāf[17] of Kūfah, Qays b. Muslim of Kūfah, Muḥammad al-Munkadir of Madīnah, Yazīd al-Faqīr of Kūfah, Simāk b. Ḥarb of Kūfah, 'Abd al-'Azīz b. Rafī' of Makkah, Makḥūl of Syria, 'Amr b. Murrah of Kūfah, Abū al-Zubayr Muḥammad b. Muslim of Makkah, 'Abd al-Malik b. 'Umar of Kūfah, Manṣūr b. Zādhān, Manṣūr b. al-Mu'tamir, 'Aṭā' b. al-Sā'ib of Thaqīf, 'Aṭā' b. Abī Muslim of Khurāsān, 'Āṣim b. Sulaymān al-Aḥwal of Baṣrah, al-A'mash of Kūfah, 'Abdullāh b. 'Umar b. Ḥafṣ of Madīnah, Imam al-Awzā'ī (from various parts of *Ṭabaqāt al-Ḥuffāẓ* of al-Dhahabī); Ibrāhīm b. Muḥammad of Kūfah, Ismā'īl b. 'Abd al-Malik of Makkah, al-Ḥārith b. 'Abd al-Raḥmān of

Makkah, Khālid b. 'Alqamah al-Widā'ī, al-Rabī'ah of Rayy, Shaddād b. 'Abd al-Raḥmān of Baṣrah, Shaybān b. 'Abd al-Raḥmān of Baṣrah, Ṭāwūs b. Kaysān of Yemen, 'Abdullāh b. Dīnār of Madīnah, 'Ikrimah Mawlā b. 'Abbās of Makkah, 'Awn b 'Abdullāh of Kūfah, Qābūs b. Abī Ẓabyān of Kūfah, Muḥammad b. al-Sā'ib al-Kalbī of Kūfah, Muḥammad b. Muslim b. Shihāb al-Zuhrī, Abū Sa'īd Mawlā b. 'Abbās (from the *Tahdhīb al-Kamāl*), Mūsā b. Abī 'Ā'ishah of Kūfah, al-Ṣalt b. Bahrām, 'Uthmān b. 'Abdullāh b. Ḥawshab, Bilāl, Haytham b. Abī al-Haytham, Ḥasīn b. 'Abd al-Raḥmān, Ma'n, Maymūn b. Siyāh, Jawwāb al-Taymī, Sālim al-Afṭas, Yaḥyā b. 'Umar b. Salamah, 'Amr b. Jubayr, 'Ubaydullāh b. 'Umar, Muḥammad b. Mālik of Hamadān, Abū al-Sawwār, Khārijah b. 'Abdullāh, 'Abdullāh b. Abī Ziyād, al-Ḥakam b. Ziyad, Kathīr al-Aṣamm, Ḥamīd al-A'raj, Abū al-'Aṭūf, 'Abdullāh b. al-Ḥasan, Sulaymān al-Shaybānī, Sa'īd b. al-Marzubān, 'Uthmān b. 'Abdullāh and Abū Ḥujayyah (from *Kitāb al-Āthār* of Imam Muḥammad).

I have selected the above names quite cursorily. Had I pursued my investigations further, it is likely that I might have ended by compiling a list as long as the one given in *'Uqūd al-Jumān*. However, it is not the large number of Abū Ḥanīfah's teachers but his diligent research which is praiseworthy. He understood very well that the longer the line of transmission of a tradition, the greater the probability of modification in the course of transmission. That was why he mostly chose for his teachers *Tābi'īs* who were only at one remove from the Prophet (ṣ), or people who had associated for long with *Tābi'īs* and were regarded as models of learning, honesty and piety. He seldom, if ever, chose a teacher who did not belong to either of these categories. His method of learning also was different from that of the common run of students. He was fond of discussion and individual judgement from the very beginning, and even the opposition of his teachers could not keep him away from these.

One day, while Ḥammād and he were walking with al-A'mash to see him off, it became time for the *maghrib* prayer, but there was no water to be found anywhere for the *wuḍū'* (ablution). So Ḥammād ruled that *tayammum* (performing the *wuḍū'* with sand) would be in order. Abū Ḥanīfah, however, disagreed, saying that they ought to wait for water to become available till a few minutes before the expiry of the time prescribed for the *maghrib* prayer. It so happened that they did find water after walking a little more distance and said their prayers after performing the *wuḍū'* with it. It is reported that this was the first occasion on which Abū Ḥanīfah disagreed with a teacher of his. He was probably in the early stages of his education at the time.

Abū Ḥanīfah's teacher, al-Sha'bī, was of the firm opinion that expiation of sin was not possible. One day, while teacher and pupil were going together in a boat, the question cropped up. Abū Ḥanīfah said, "There certainly is expiation of sin, as Allah has prescribed atonement for *ẓihār* (pronouncement of the words 'you are like a mother to me' as a formula of divorce) and has also clearly said that *ẓihār* is a sin." Al-Sha'bī could not think of a reply and angrily said, "You are a great analogist."[18]

Somebody asked 'Aṭā' b. Abī Rabāḥ the meaning of the *āyah* "We gave them their families and along with them the likes of them." 'Aṭā's explanation was that Allah had brought back to life Ayyūb's children and given him more children along with them. Abū Ḥanīfah objected, "How can children not born from a man's loins be called his children?"[19]

One main source of Abū Ḥanīfah's great learning was his association with a number of men of high attainments. In the cities where Abū Ḥanīfah spent his life, namely, Kūfah, Baṣrah, Makkah and Madīnah, one breathed in an atmosphere laden with religious traditions. Fondness for the company of scholars and for participating in learned gatherings was inborn in him. Besides, he had become so famous that wherever he went thousands of people gathered round him for interviews, discussions and debates with him.

Notes

1. *'Uqūd al-Jumān.*
2. *'Uqūd al-Jumān*, Chapter 7.
3. All these facts are given in detail in al-Balādhurī's *Futūḥ al-Buldān* (chapter on the monuments of Kūfah), *Mu'jam al-Buldān*, and *Fatḥ al-Mughīth*, p. 382.
4. *Tadhkirah al-Ḥuffāẓ.*
5. *'Uqūd al-Jumān*, Chapter 10.
6. Ibn Khallikān, *Ta'rīkh*, note on 'Aṭā' b. Abī Rabāḥ.
7. For an account of him, see Ibn Khallikān and books of *rijāl.*
8. Ibn Jazalah, *Mukhtaṣar Kitāb Ta'rīkh Baghdad.*
9. *'Uqūd al-Jumānt* Chapter 10.
10. *Fatḥ al-Mughīth.*
11. *Mukhtaṣar Ta'rīkh al-Khaṭīb al-Baghdādī.*
12. *'Uqūd al-Jumān*, Chapter 16.
13. *Al-Jawāhir al-Muḍiyyah*, note on Abū 'Āṣim al-Nabīl.
14. *'Uqūd al-Jumān*, Chapter 10.
15. *Fatḥ al-Mughīth*, p. 239; the *Muqaddamah* of al-Qasṭalānī to his *Sharḥ* of al-Bukhārī, pp. 6-13.
16. Of these books I have not seen *Tahdhīb al-Kamāl.* The late Mawlawī 'Abd al-Ḥayy has given the names of Abū Ḥanīfah's teachers in *Ta'līq al-Mumajjad* on the authority of *Tahdhīb al-Kamāl.* My list is also based on that book.
17. According to *Dhamm al-Kalām wa Ahlih* of Abū Ismā'īl al-Anṣārī, he is Haytham b. Ḥabib al-Ṣarrāf [Ed.].
18. *'Uqūd al-Jumān*, Chapter 8.
19. *Mukhtaṣar Ta'rīkh al-Khaṭīb al-Baghdādī.*

3

Lectures, rulings and later life

Although Imam Abū Ḥanīfah had acquired the status of a *mujtahid* (a final authority) during Ḥammād's lifetime at a comparatively early age—he was around forty years old at the time of Ḥammād's death—his sincere regard for his teacher did not permit him to establish a school of his own while the teacher was still alive. It is difficult in our day to imagine the love and reverence that people had for their teachers in those days. We have it on the Imam's own authority that as long as Ḥammād lived, he never stretched his feet towards his house. Ḥammād died in 120 H. As after Ibrāhīm al-Nakha'ī's death, he was the sole surviving authority on *fiqh*, his death was a great loss to *fiqh* studies in Kūfah.

Ḥammād was survived by an able son, who was installed in his father's chair; but as his real interest lay in lexicography and literature, he soon made room for Mūsā b. Kathīr, a senior pupil of Ḥammād's in both age and experience. Mūsā was not an expert in *fiqh*, but had had the advantage of associating with a number of eminent authorities and was, therefore, looked up to. He gave lectures until he went for hajj, when Abū Ḥanīfah was approached to accept the chair.

In his youth Abū Ḥanīfah had often longed for the professorial chair, but now that it was at last offered to him he declined it, feeling unequal to its responsibilities. However, the people's insistence prevailed and he accepted the chair—not without misgivings, though. Abū al-Maḥāsin writes thus on this subject: "About that time, he saw himself digging up the Prophet's grave in a dream. He woke up frightened and thought that the dream was a hint from Heaven at his unsuitability for the position. However, Ibn Sīrīn, an expert in the interpretation of dreams, interpreted the dream for him as symbolising the revival of a dead branch of learning. Satisfied, Abū Ḥanīfah settled down to his teaching." The dream has been mentioned by all historians and *muḥaddiths*, and the probability is that Abū Ḥanīfah actually dreamed it. But that part of the story which relates to interpretation by Ibn Sīrīn is obviously false, for Ibn Sīrīn died long before 110 H. Whatever the truth, Abū Ḥanīfah got down to teaching in right earnest. In the beginning only Ḥammād's former pupils attended his classes, but in a few days he became so famous that most of the Kūfah schools closed down and became part of his school. Even his teachers, such as Mis'ar b. Kidām and al-A'mash, began to attend his lectures and induced others to do so.

There was no part of the Islamic world except Spain which was not represented in his classes. It is not possible to count all the places from where his students came, but we give here the names of a few regions and cities: Makkah, Madīnah, Damascus, Baṣrah, Wāsiṭ, Mūṣil, Algiers, Raqqah, Naṣībīn, Ramlah, Egypt, Yemen, Yamāmah, Bahrain, Baghdad, Ahwaz, Kirmān, Isfahan, Ḥulwān, Astrābād, Hamadān, Nihāwand, Rayy, Qūmas, Dāmghān, Ṭabaristān, Georgia, Nīshāpūr, Sarakhs, Nisā, Bukhārā, Samarqand, Kas, Ṣana'an, Tirmidh, Herat, Nihistār, Alzam, Khawārizm, Sistān, Madā'in, Masīsah and Emessa.[1] In short, his territory as a teacher was conterminous with the territory of the caliph.

Gradually he acquired so much political influence in Iraq that he began to be suspected of complicity in every revolution in that country. Shāh 'Abd al-'Azīz says in his *Tuḥfah* that the Imam took part in the revolt led by Zayd b. 'Alī against the Umayyads. The compilers of the *Nāmah-i-Dānishwarān* have also made this statement. I, however, do not believe it. I have not come across it in any of the books of history and biography that I have consulted. Had it been true, the fact would have been too important to find no mention in one or another of these books.

Zayd b. 'Alī's revolt took place in 121 H during the reign of the caliph Hishām b. 'Abd al-Malik. For all his tight control of the purse strings, there was peace in Hishām's dominions, the people were happy and no illicit revenues found their way into the public exchequer. There was, therefore, no reason for Abū Ḥanīfah to be hostile to the caliph. Zayd b. 'Alī revolted because he believed that as a *sayyid* he had a special claim to the caliphal throne.

The story of Abū Ḥanīfah's participation in his revolt seems to have had its origin in a misunderstanding arising out of his close relations with the *Ahl al-Bayt.* His family had a special devotion for the *Ahl al-Bayt.* He himself sat at the feet of Imam al-Bāqir for a long time. Again, the atmosphere of Kūfah was for a period surcharged with Shī'ism. These facts combined to create the legend of Abū Ḥanīfah's joining Zayd b. 'Alī's revolt, which is clearly contradicted by all the historical evidence.

Hishām died in 125 H. He was succeeded by al-Walīd b. Yazīd, Yazīd al-Nāqiṣ, Ibrāhīm b. al-Walīd and Marwān al-Ḥimār, one after another. The conspiracy to install the 'Abbāsids on the caliphal throne, which had been going on for a long time, gathered strength during Marwān's reign. Abū

Muslim of Khurāsān spread a network of intrigue over the whole country, which sapped the foundations of Marwān's rule.

As Iraq and in particular the city of Kūfah were the main centres of the disturbances, Marwān appointed Yazīd b. 'Umar Hubayrah as the governor of Iraq. Yazīd was sagacious, courageous, generous, well-born and influential. He had carefully studied the structure of Marwān's administrative machinery and had come to the conclusion that what was lacking in it was religious paraphernalia. He, therefore, decided to erect the edifice of his government on the pillars of religion and appointed outstanding authorities on *fiqh*, such as Ibn Abī Laylā b. Shubramah and Dāwūd b. Hind, to important political posts.

To Abū Ḥanīfah he offered the post of Keeper of the Seal and Chief Treasurer, but Abū Ḥanīfah declined it. Yazīd declared on oath that he would compel him to accept the post, and Abū Ḥanīfah's friends tried their best to persuade him to accept it. But Abū Ḥanīfah stuck to his guns. "If Yazīd were to ask me," he declared, "to count the doors of the mosques, I would not agree to do it for him, not to speak of my sealing the death warrant of a Muslim signed by him."[2] Yazīd was so enraged that he sent Abū Ḥanīfah to prison and ordered a hundred stripes to be administered to him daily; and this monstrous order was actually carried out.

Abū Ḥanīfah, however, did not relent. It was Yazīd who had to relent and stop the punishment. On one account Abū Ḥanīfah proceeded to Makkah as soon as he was released and stayed there till the end of 136 H. Ibn Qutaybah and some others say that this quarrel took place over the post of *qāḍī*. It is possible that that post was also offered to Abū Ḥanīfah and refused by him.

In 132 H, events took a new turn: the Umayyads were overthrown by the ʿAbbāsids. The first caliph of the latter dynasty was Abū al-ʿAbbās al-Saffāḥ, who died in 136 H after ruling for four years, being succeeded by his brother, al-Manṣūr. The ʿAbbāsids exterminated the Umayyad dynasty, even digging up the graves of the Umayyad caliphs; but they had not yet established themselves and made their rule effective, so that there were rebellions afoot everywhere. In quelling these, al-Saffāḥ and al-Manṣūr committed excesses which revived memories of al-Marwān's reign. The people had been looking up to the new rulers with hope, but were disappointed by their atrocities.

One day, it is reported, al-Manṣūr asked ʿAbd al-Raḥmān, who was a childhood friend of his, how in his opinion his rule compared with that of al-Marwān. ʿAbd al-Raḥmān replied that he saw no difference between the two. "What can I do?" said al-Manṣūr. "I can't get good people to fill government positions." "Increased demand increases the supply of a commodity," retorted ʿAbd al-Raḥmān.

To cap his barbarities, al-Manṣūr started exterminating the *sayyids*. True the *sayyids* had for long been plotting to seize the caliphal throne, to which from one point of view they had a right. However, no plot of theirs had been unearthed until al-Saffāḥ's death. Therefore, it was on mere suspicion that al-Manṣūr started destroying them. The more prominent among them were special targets of his cruelties. Muḥammad b. Ibrāhīm, popularly known as Dībāj (cloth of gold) because of his matchless good looks, was by his orders interred alive in a wall which was erected round him. Al-Manṣūr's cruelties form a long tale which needs a strong heart to tell. At last in 145 H, one of the persecuted *sayyids*, Muḥammad al-Nafs al-Zakiyyah, took up arms in Madīnah with a handful of followers.

Al-Nafs al-Zakiyyah was a courageous man well versed in the art of war, but luck was against him and he died fighting bravely in Ramaḍān of 145 H. After his death his brother Ibrāhīm assumed the leadership of the uprising and came into the battlefield with such a strong force that al-Manṣūr was frightened out of his wits. It is said that he did not change his clothes for two months on end and would sit with his pillow in his hand, repeating the words "I don't know whether this pillow belongs to me or to Ibrāhīm." He did not even exchange a word with two slave girls newly added to his harem. On being questioned about this, he replied, "These things are for times of leisure. What I am worried about at the moment is whether in a short while Ibrāhīm's head will be lying before me or mine before him."

Ibrāhīm, besides being a brave fighter, was a great scholar and highly respected religious leader. His claim to the caliphal throne received much public support, particularly in Kūfah, where about a hundred thousand men came forward to fight for him. Most religious leaders, especially scholars and jurists, pledged their loyalty to him. Abū Ḥanīfah had been watching the excesses of the 'Abbāsids from the very outset. As early as during the reign of al-Saffāḥ, he had reached the conclusion that these people were not fit to be caliphs.

Ibrāhīm b. Maymūn, a man of great piety and scholarship, who was a friend of Abū Ḥanīfah's, used often to ask him whether it was right for religious leaders to keep quiet while such monstrous things were being done. The Imam used to reply, "Inculcating what has been enjoined is undoubtedly a duty, but you must have the wherewithal for that." Ibrāhīm b. Maymūn, however, could not control his religious ardour for long and, going to Abū Muslim al-Khurāsānī, who was the evil genius behind all the iniquities that were going on, spoke to him frankly and fearlessly about them. Either to punish him for his audacity or from fear of his example being followed, Abū Muslim had him put to death. Abū Ḥanīfah wept bitterly on hearing of his friend's sad end.[3] All this happened in 131 H. When in 145 H Ibrāhīm raised the caliphal standard, Abū Ḥanīfah supported him along with other religious leaders. He wanted even to join the fighting, but was prevented from doing so by some difficulties, a fact which he always regretted.

The following occurs in a letter supposedly written by Abū Ḥanīfah to Ibrāhīm, which has been quoted in the *Nāmah-i-Dānishwarān:* "I am sending you four thousand dirhams, which is all I possess at the moment. If I did not have articles belonging to people lying in trust with me, I would certainly have come to meet you. When you are victorious over your enemies, treat them in the same way as your ancestor ('Alī) treated the people of Ṣiffīn. The wounded and truants should all be put to death. Do not follow what your father thought fit to do at the Battle of Jamal, since the enemy is in great strength." *The Nāmah-i-Dānishwarān* says about this letter that it has been quoted in many reliable books, but does not name even one of those books. I, therefore, do not regard it as authentic.

Irrespective of whether the letter just mentioned was authentic or not, there is no doubt that Abū Ḥanīfah openly supported Ibrāhīm and gave him every kind of help, short of taking part in the fighting. Ibrāhīm overreached himself, was defeated and died fighting bravely at Baṣrah.

Having successfully completed the campaign against Ibrāhīm, al-Manṣūr dealt with Ibrāhīm's supporters, among whom was Abū Ḥanīfah. al-Manṣūr's capital at the time was al-Hāshimiyyah, a few miles from Kūfah. Since the Kūfans did not acknowledge the right of anybody but a *sayyid* to the caliph's throne, he decided to shift his capital farther away from Kūfah and selected Baghdad as the new capital. Immediately after his arrival at Baghdad in 146 H, he issued a command to Abū Ḥanīfah to present himself at the capital at once.

The Imam had left Makkah after the fall of the Umayyads and was then living at Kūfah. Al-Manṣūr had made up his mind to have him put to death, but had to find some excuse for doing so. When Abū Ḥanīfah appeared at the caliphal court, the chamberlain, al-Rabīʿ, introduced him in the following words: "This man is the greatest living *ʿālim.*" In reply to a question by al-Manṣūr, Abū Ḥanīfah gave the names of his teachers, whose line went back to a number of great Companions. Al-Manṣūr thereupon offered him the post of *qāḍī.* Abū Ḥanīfah declined the post point-blank, saying that he was not fit for it. Enraged, al-Manṣūr shouted, "You are a liar." "If I am a liar," retorted the Imam, "then my statement that I am unfit for the post of *qāḍī* is true, because a liar cannot be appointed a *qāḍī.*"

This logical counterthrust had behind it a genuine conviction that he would be unable to bear the responsibilities of a *qāḍī's* office. He advanced very valid reasons for this conviction. For one thing, he was not settled in his mind. For another, he was not of Arab origin, which would make it intolerable for Arabs that he should sit in judgement on them. Again, he would be required to be obsequious to the courtiers, which he would find it impossible to do.

Al-Manṣūr accepted none of these reasons and declared on oath that he would make Abū Ḥanīfah accept the post. The Imam replied by similarly declaring on oath that he would never accept it. All the courtiers were thunderstruck at the Imam's boldness and fearlessness. Al-Rabīʿ said angrily, "Abū

Ḥanīfah, you dare to oppose the Khalīfah's vow with a vow of your own." "Yes, I do," replied the Imam, "because it is easier for the Commander of the Faithful than it is for me to atone for the sin of swearing."

Another version of the event is, however, given by al-Khaṭīb. According to that version, the Imam, when pressed very hard by al-Manṣūr, went and took his seat on the judicial bench. The very first case that came up before him was a suit for the repayment of a loan. The plaintiff had no witnesses, and the defendant totally denied the claim. In accordance with the prescribed procedure, the Imam asked the defendant if he was ready to declare on oath that he owed nothing to the plaintiff. The defendant expressed his readiness to do so. But hardly had he uttered the words "By Allah" when the Imam, seriously perturbed, asked him to stop and, producing the money out of his own pocket, gave it to the plaintiff, saying, "Here is your loan. Take it. Why do you want to make a Muslim swear?" Thereafter he got up and, going to al-Manṣūr's court, told him that he would not be able to carry on with the work. Al-Manṣūr immediately ordered his imprisonment, which ended only with his (Abū Ḥanīfah's) death. Al-Manṣūr, however, used to send for him occasionally and hold religious debates with him.

Notes

1. *'Uqūd al-Jumān*, Chapter 5.
2. Ibid., Chapter 21.
3. *Al-Jawāhir al-Muḍiyyah*, note on Ibrāhīm b. Maymūn.

4

Death

Despite sending Abū Ḥanīfah to prison (in 146 H); al-Manṣūr had no peace of mind in regard to him. Because of its being the capital, Baghdad had become a great seat of learning, to which seekers after knowledge flocked from all Islamic countries, and Abū Ḥanīfah, whose fame had spread far and wide, was its most prominent figure. His imprisonment, far from reducing his influence and popularity, enhanced them a great deal, especially with the scholarly community, which had an importance all its own in Baghdad.

Al-Manṣūr had to bow before these facts and refrain from doing anything overt which might show disrespect towards Abū Ḥanīfah. He, therefore, permitted Abū Ḥanīfah to carry on with his teaching in prison, and it was there that Muḥammad b. al-Ḥasan, one of the stalwarts of Ḥanafī *fiqh*, received his education from its originator. As Abū Ḥanīfah constituted no less a danger to the ʿAbbāsid government in prison than he had done outside, al-Manṣūr decided to do away with him and had him poisoned. When Abū Ḥanīfah felt the effects of the poison, he bent down in prayer and died (Rajab 150) in that posture.

News of his death spread like wildfire in the city and brought the citizens in their thousands to the prison. The city *qāḍī*, al-Ḥasan b. ʿAmmārah, bathed the body and, while doing so, kept repeating, "By Allah, you were the greatest *faqīh* and the most pious man of our time. You had all the qualities of greatness in you. You were, indeed, so great that nobody after you may hope to reach your level." By the time the bathing was finished so many people had assembled that the first funeral prayer was performed attended by fifty thousand persons. But people still kept coming. So the prayer had to be performed six times over and it was not till sunset that the burial took place.

The Imam, while dying, had expressed the wish to be buried in the graveyard at Khayzurān, because the ground of that graveyard had not, in his opinion, been seized by force. Accordingly, his tomb was built in the eastern part of the graveyard. We have it on the historian al-Khaṭīb's authority that for a full twenty days people went on performing funeral prayers for him. There could be no better proof of the Imam's great popularity.

All the prominent religious leaders in Islamic countries mourned his death and paid high compliments to him. In Makkah Ibn Jurayj said, "A very great scholar has passed away." Shuʿbah b. al-Ḥajjāj, who was one of Abū Ḥanīfah's teachers and an imam of Baṣrah, remarked, "Kūfah has been plunged into darkness." A few days after Abū Ḥanīfah's death ʿAbdullāh b. al-Mubārak, who happened to come to Baghdad, visited Abū Ḥanīfah's grave and said with tears in his eyes, "Abū Ḥanīfah, may Allah have mercy on you! When Ibrāhīm died he left a successor, and so did Ḥammād, but, alas, there is no one in the whole world to take your place."

The Imam's tomb was for years and still is a place of pilgrimage. Sultan Alp Arslān al-Saljūqī, a great, just and generous monarch, had a dome erected over the tomb and a *madrasah* built close to it in 459 H. This was probably the first *madrasah* in Baghdad: the Niẓāmiyyah *madrasah*, which is generally considered the pioneer among *madrasahs*, was built in the same year, but a little later. The building of the *madrasah* attached to the Imam's tomb remained unmatched for a long time in beauty and grandeur. The opening ceremony was attended by almost all the learned men and prominent citizens of Baghdad. A famous poet, Abū Ja'far Mas'ūd, who happened to be present, recited some verses which he composed on the spot. Here is a translation of them:

Don't you know how learning was dissipating until the man who lies in this tomb compiled it? In the same way, this land was lying barren and Abū Sa'd's efforts gave it new life.

The *madrasah*, which is known as Mashhad Abū Ḥanīfah, continued into our time and had among its teachers some great scholars, the names and brief particulars of most of whom are given in *al-Jawāhir al-Muḍiyyah fī Ṭabaqāt al-Ḥanafiyyah*. In 493 H, Ḥakīm b. Jazlah, who was a famous court philosopher of the caliph al-Muqtadir Billāh, donated his whole library to the *madrasah*.[1] There was also a travellers' rest house attached to the *madrasah*, where scholars coming to Baghdad from different parts of the country on brief visits used to stay as state guests. The well-known traveller Ibn Baṭṭūṭah, who visited Baghdad during the last days of the 'Abbāsid caliphate, writes in his travel journal, "At present there is in Baghdad no place except Mashhad Abū Ḥanīfah where travellers are given free food." Even today Imam Abū Ḥanīfah's tomb is one of the famous holy places of Baghdad. The present ruler of Iran, Sultan Nāṣir al-Dīn Qājār, mentions it in the account of his travels. He writes, "I recited al-Fātiḥah and made an offering at the tomb of Imam Abū Ḥanīfah." Great is the glory of learning.

Notes

1. Ibn Khallikān, *Wafayāt al-A'yān*, note on Yaḥyā b. 'Īsā b. Jazlah al-Ṭabīb.

5
Children

Details of the Imam's children are not known, but what is certain is that he was survived only by a son named Ḥammād, who was a great scholar and of whose early education the Imam had taken great care. When the boy completed his book *al-Ḥamd*, the Imam gave his tutor a reward of five hundred dirhams and when the boy grew up the Imam himself taught him. Ḥammād was a worthy son of his father, not only in learning, but also in unworldliness and piety.

The Imam had left in his house many articles belonging to different people who had deposited them with him as a trustee. Ḥammād took them to the city *qāḍī* and requested him to return them on his father's behalf to their owners. The *qāḍī* advised him to let them remain in his custody for some time more, as he thought that they were quite safe with him. Ḥammād, however, left the articles with the *qāḍī* and retired to some unknown place, making his appearance again only after the articles had been deposited with somebody else. He took service with nobody and did not have any connections even with the caliphal court. He died in Dhū al-Qa'dah 176, survived by four sons, 'Umar, Ismā'īl, Abū Ḥayyān and 'Uthmān.

Ismā'īl attained to much fame as a scholar and was appointed a *qāḍī* by Ma'mūn al-Rashīd, the duties of which post he discharged with such conscientiousness and fairness that when he left Baṣrah he was seen off by a big crowd, which prayed for him.[1]

The Imam's spiritual progeny is today spread over the whole Islamic world and numbers not less than sixty or seventy million. It includes some actual descendants of his, who are to be found in different countries. In India itself there are a number of families that trace their ancestry to him and which have kept alive from generation to generation the tradition of scholarship inherited from him.

Notes

1. Ibn Khallikān, *Wafayāt al-A'yān*, note on Hammād.

6
Character and habits

The writers of the *tadhkirahs* (biographical memoirs) in which Imam Abū Ḥanīfah figures have allowed their admiration for him to make them portray his character and personal habits with so much palpable exaggeration that after reading their accounts one finds it hard to visualise what he was really like. Here are a few of the incredible things they mention.

For forty years he said his morning prayers with the *wuḍū'* (ritual ablution) he had performed for his *'ishṣā'* prayer (the night prayer). For thirty years on end he fasted from day to day. He completed seven thousand readings of the Qur'an at the place where he died. There having been found in the canal at Kūfah a piece of meat about which it could not be ascertained whether or not it was part of a lawfully slaughtered animal, he abstained from eating fish for a long time for fear that the fish, which are long-lived, may have eaten of that piece of meat. For a similar reason he gave up eating goat meat. His personal expenditure was equivalent to ten annas a month only.

There are many other fantastic stories of the same kind current about him. The surprising thing is that our historians regard impossible things of this kind as real evidence of the Imam's spiritual attainments, although these have not been historically established and, in any case, are no proof of spiritual or moral excellence.

I must admit that the facts I have accepted about Imam's personality and way of life are also derived from these very biographical memoirs; but then every incident or fact mentioned in a book has to be considered on its own merits. In regard to ordinary incidents the ordinary kind of evidence is sufficient; but so far as extraordinary things of the kind that I am speaking of are concerned, they need some authority absolutely beyond doubt; in fact, they need to conform to something more than the conditions to be fulfilled by a *ḥadīth* before it can be accepted as *ṣaḥīḥ* (authentic), *marfū'* (connected with a saying or an act of the Prophet (ṣ)) and *muttaṣil* (uninterruptedly continuous)—and must also stand examination in accordance with the principles of scrutiny (*dirāyah*).

When one thinks of the Imam's sagacity and keen intellect, of which we have first-hand proof, one cannot believe his doing things which even a rabid anchorite would not do.

An accurate, though sketchy, portrait of the Imam's personality is to be found in the description that Qāḍī Abū Yūsuf gave of him to Hārūn al-Rashīd at the latter's request. "As far as I know," said the Qāḍī, "Abū Ḥanīfah was extremely pious, avoided forbidden things, remained silent and absorbed in his thoughts most of the time and answered a question only if he knew the answer. He was very generous and self-respecting, never asked a favour of anybody, shunned the company of the worldly minded and held worldly power and position in contempt. He avoided slander and only talked well of people. He was a man of profound learning and as generous with his knowledge as with his money." On hearing this account, Hārūn al-Rashīd observed, "You have described a great and good man."

To superficial observers, the qualities described by Qāḍī Abū Yūsuf may not appear to be of much significance, but connoisseurs of the spiritual character know that, easy as this way of life may look, it is very difficult to follow and as praiseworthy as it is difficult.

Along with beauty of character, Allah had endowed the Imam with good looks. He had a medium height, handsome features and a well-proportioned figure. His way of speaking was pleasing and his voice loud and clear. When he spoke on a problem, he did so with such eloquence and clarity that, no matter how complicated it was, it became simplified.

He was a man of good taste and liked to dress well. Sometimes he even put on ermine *jubbahs.* Abū Muṭīʿ al-Balkhī, one of his pupils, mentions that on one occasion he found him dressed in a shirt and mantle which could not have cost less than four hundred dirhams. One day he borrowed the mantle of Naṣr b. Muḥammad, who called on him when he was getting ready to go out. On coming back, he complained that he had felt ashamed of the mantle, because it was dirty. Naṣr had bought it for five dinars and was proud of it. He was, therefore, surprised at the Imam's complaint, but he understood the reason for it when, a few days later, he found the Imam wearing a mantle which could not have cost less than thirty dinars.

The caliph al-Manṣūr had invented a special straw cap covered with black cloth for his courtiers to wear. The cap was so very tall that it provoked the poet Abū Dalāmah into saying humorously, "We were expecting some enhancement from the caliph. So he has enhanced the length of caps."

Although the Imam kept away from the caliph's court as much as he could, he did not mind occasionally wearing the new courtiers' cap. In fact, it raised eyebrows in learned circles that he sometimes had seven or eight of the caps in his wardrobe, although for the *beau monde* this was nothing to marvel at.

In some other matters too the Imam's style of living was quite different from that of the common run of *'ulamā'*. Most of the contemporary *'ulamā'* were stipendiaries of the caliph or of rich courtiers, and did not consider this a thing to be apologetic about. Somebody having taunted Qāḍī Ibn 'Abd al-Barr with being a stipendiary of wealthy people, he replied by citing the example of a number of Companions, *Tābi'īs* and *Tābi' al-Tābi'īn* who had lived on the generosity of the rich.

However, I do not consider this, as perhaps some modern-minded people do, to be tantamount to idleness or parasitism. Teaching was not yet a salaried profession. The *'ulamā'* used to teach honorarily either at their own homes or in mosques—a system which has not yet been surpassed in extensiveness and usefulness. What these honorary teachers received from their rich patrons by way of regular stipends or occasional gifts could well be regarded as a salary. All the same, it cannot be denied that it was this practice which in the course of time grew into the system of professional and hereditary religious preceptors (*pīrs*), parasites living by exploiting people's credulity, which has rendered a large part of the Muslim population idle.

There is no doubt that Abū Ḥanīfah was strongly opposed to the practice, and he was right in the light of its subsequent development. One great advantage that accrued to him from his being attached to nobody was that he could express his true opinions without fear or favour. However independent-minded and frank a man may be, he cannot help being influenced by those from whom he accepts favours. Abū Ḥanīfah never accepted a favour from anybody throughout his life, and so he retained his independence. He sometimes used to mention this fact too.

Ibn Hubayrah, governor of Kūfah and a man of renown, once said to Abū Ḥanīfah, "I would consider it a favour if you could come and see me occasionally." "What is the point in my visiting you?" replied the Imam. "If you treated me kindly, I might fall into your trap. If, on the other hand, you received me rudely, I would consider it a disgrace. I do not need anything from your treasury, and whatever I have nobody can snatch away from me." A similar conversation is said to have taken place between him and ʿĪsā b. Mūsā.

A dispute having arisen between the caliph al-Manṣūr and his wife al-Ḥurrah over an accusation made by the latter that the former was not a just ruler, Abū Ḥanīfah was called in to arbitrate between them. The queen sat behind a curtain in order to hear the Imam's verdict with her own ears. Al-Manṣūr began by asking how many wives a Muslim was permitted to have at a time according to Sharīʿah. The Imam replied, "Four." "Do you hear?" shouted al-Manṣūr to the queen. "Yes, I heard it," replied the queen. At that point the Imam addressed himself to the caliph and added, "But this permission is for a man who is capable of doing justice. No other man can have more than one wife. Allah Himself says, 'If you doubt your ability to do justice (between your wives), have only one wife." Al-Manṣūr remained silent.

A little while after the Imam returned home, a servant came to him with a gift of fifty thousand dinars. "The queen," he said, "sends you her respectful salutations and says that she is grateful to you for your truthful verdict." The Imam returned the money with a message for the queen that he had expressed the opinion he had expressed not in the expectation of a reward but because it was his duty as an arbitrator to express it.

The Imam's business was on a large scale. He traded in goods worth millions, had his agents in a number of cities and had dealings with many big merchants. With such a vast establishment under him he personally took care to see that no illicitly gained money came into his coffers, even though this subjected him to occasional losses. Once he sent some lengths of silk to Ḥafṣ b. ʿAbd al-Raḥmān for sale with instruction to point out to prospective customers certain defects in some of the lengths. Ḥafṣ forgot the instruction and sold off the defective lengths without telling the customers anything about their defects. When the Imam learnt of this, he was very sorry and gave away in charity the entire price of the lengths, which amounted to thirty thousand dirhams.

One day a woman came to him with a length of silk which she wanted him to sell for her and quoted a hundred dirhams for it. When the Imam expressed surprise at that figure, she raised it to two hundred dirhams. But the Imam told her that it was worth not less than five hundred dirhams. "Are you making fun of me?" said the woman. The Imam took out five hundred dirhams, gave them to her and kept the cloth. This kind of scrupulous honesty, far from harming his business, made it flourish.

His object in carrying on business and making money was to be able to help others. He had fixed stipends for all his needy friends and acquaintances and had reserved a part of his profits for distribution among scholars and *muḥaddiths* annually.[1] Whenever he bought anything for his family, he would buy the same thing for the scholars and *muḥaddiths* of his acquaintance. If anybody came to call on him, he would tactfully find out about his economic condition and, if he was in want, help him. He used to provide those of his pupils who were poor with money for their household expenses, so that they could attend to their studies undistracted by domestic worries. Many people who were too poor to meet the expenses of their education were educated with his help and attained to high positions. One of these was Qāḍī Abū Yūsuf, of whom I will speak of more later.

One day a man who looked poor came to see Abū Ḥanīfah. When his visitors were taking leave of him, the Imam asked the man to stay on. After the others had gone, he pointed to his prayer mat and asked the man to lift it. On doing so the man found a purse containing a thousand under the mat. Understanding that the Imam was offering the money to him, the man explained that he was well-to-do and did not need it. "Then you should not dress in such a way," said the Imam, "that people mistake you for a poor man."

On one occasion, on his way to see a sick acquaintance, the Imam saw at a distance a man who owed him ten thousand dirhams. The man tried to avoid him, he accosted the man and, stopping him, asked why he tried to avoid him. The man replied that he was ashamed to face him because he had not been able to repay his loan. Impressed with the man's confession of shame, the Imam said, "Well, if you are unable to repay the loan, you need not do so."

On one of his pilgrimages he was accompanied part of the way by 'Abdullāh al-Sahmī. At one of the halting stations a bedouin caught hold of 'Abdullāh and, bringing him to the Imam, complained that 'Abdullāh was not repaying a loan he had given him. 'Abdullāh denied the claim. So the Imam asked the bedouin the amount of loan involved. The bedouin informed him that it was forty dirhams. "Things have come to such a pass," exclaimed the Imam, "that people fight over a paltry sum like forty dirhams." Saying this, he paid forty dirhams to the bedouin out of his own pocket.

Ibrāhīm b. ʿUtbah owed somebody four thousand dirhams and, being unable to repay the money, stopped meeting people out of shame. A friend of his started collecting subscriptions to help him discharge the loan and approached the Imam also. The Imam asked about the amount of the loan. When he was told that it was four thousand dirhams, he said, "Why bother so many people for such a small amount?" Saying this, he gave Ibrāhīm's friend the entire amount.

There are many other stories in the history books about the Imam's generosity, which for want of space I refrain from relating.

Despite his wealth and high position in society, the Imam was extremely gentle and polite. One day, while he was sitting in the Ḥanīf Mosque, surrounded by his pupils and admirers, a stranger posed a question, which he answered. The man remarked that al-Ḥasan al-Baṣrī had given a ruling contrary to his. "Then al-Hasan al-Baṣrī made a mistake," replied the Imam. One of those present, who was a disciple of al-Ḥasan al-Baṣrī, was so enraged at this remark that he shouted, "You son of a whore, you dare to say that al-Ḥasan al-Baṣrī can be wrong?" This caused an uproar in the assembly, and some people wanted to catch hold of the man and punish him. The Imam, however, intervened and prevented them from doing so. This struck the whole assembly dumb. However, when order had been restored, the Imam turned to the man who had abused him, and very calmly said, "Yes, al-Ḥasan did make a mistake. The correct tradition on the subject is the one narrated by ʿAbdullāh b. Masʿūd."

Yazīd b. Kumayt relates that one day, when he was present, a man began to speak rudely to the Imam. The Imam went on answering his questions gently and calmly; but the man became more and more impolite, so much so that he called the Imam a *zindīq*. On hearing that word, the Imam said, "May Allah forgive you! He knows that you have used a wrong word about me." The Imam often used to say that he had never cursed anybody, never taken revenge on anybody, never done harm to a Muslim or a *dhimmī*, never deceived anybody and never broken a promise.

For some time, relations were strained between Abū Ḥanīfah and Sufyān al-Thawrī. One day a man reported to Abū Ḥanīfah that Sufyān was speaking ill of him. "May Allah forgive both of us," said the Imam. "Sufyān is so great a scholar that if he had died even when Ibrāhīm al-Nakhaʿī was alive, the Muslims would have mourned him."

One day, while he was taking a class, a man who bore him some grudge started saying improper things about him. He paid no attention to the man and carried on with his teaching. He even told his pupils to pay no heed to him. When, after the class was over, he went out, the man followed him and continued abusing him. When both of them reached the Imam's house, the latter stopped and, turning to the man, said, "Brother, we are now at the doorstep of my house. If you have anything more to say, say it, because I shall presently go in and you may not get another opportunity."

On another occasion, while the Imam was lecturing, a young man, who was not a regular pupil of his, put a question to him and, on hearing the answer, said, "Abū Ḥanīfah, your answer is wrong." One of the Imam's pupils, Abū al-Khaṭṭāb al-Jurjānī, angered by this, shouted to the audience, "All of you are shameless people. Here is a mere youngster speaking rudely to the Imam, and nobody seems to be bothered." The Imam, turning to Abū al-Khaṭṭāb, said, "I am here to give people an opportunity of pointing out my mistakes freely, and I must listen to them patiently."

There was a merry cobbler living in the Imam's neighbourhood. After his day's work he used to come home with meat and wine and entertain his friends at night. They would all eat *kabābs*, which he himself roasted, and drink his wine with him. Happily drunk, he would now and again sing a couplet which said, "People have let me go to waste, me who would have been useful to them in battle and closing breaches." The Imam, who used to spend the greater part of the night in prayer, would hear his singing, but never objected to it out of neighbourly consideration and his habitual kindness.

One night the prefect of police, who happened to pass that way, arrested the cobbler and locked him up. In the following morning, the Imam mentioned to his friends that he had not heard his neighbour's singing during the previous night. They informed him of what had happened. The Imam at once ordered his mount, put on his court dress and proceeded to the governor's house.

The governor then was 'Īsā b. Mūsā, a cousin of the caliph al-Manṣūr and distinguished among the 'Abbāsids for sagacity and bravery. On being informed that Imam Abū Ḥanīfah was coming to see him, he sent a number of his courtiers to receive him, with orders that he should be escorted on horseback right up to the courtyard of the governor's house. As soon as the Imam's horse approached, he stood up and, after the Imam had dismounted, took him to a seat with all respect. Then he said, "Why have you taken the trouble of coming here? You could have sent for me." The Imam said, "What brings me here is that a cobbler who is my neighbour has been arrested by the prefect of police and I want him released." 'Īsā immediately sent orders for the cobbler's release. The cobbler was brought to the governor's house and set free, and he accompanied the Imam on his way home. "Well, my friend," said the Imam to him, "have I allowed you to go to waste?" This was with reference to the couplet the cobbler used to sing. The cobbler replied, "No, sir, you have proved a good neighbour."[2] From that day he changed his way of life. Giving up his drunken merry-making, he joined the Imam's classes and in due course attained to such scholarship that he came to be known as a *faqīh*.

The Imam lost his father before he had come of age, but his mother lived for a long time, and the Imam looked after her with great affection and regard. She was of a superstitious nature and, like most women, had much faith in religious preachers and storytellers, especially in 'Amr b. Dharr, a well-known preacher of Kūfah. Whenever she had a religious question to be answered, she would tell the Imam to go to 'Amr and get the answer from him. The Imam would faithfully carry out her behest, much to the embarrassment of 'Amr, who would exclaim, "How dare I open my mouth before you?" The Imam would reply, "Such is my mother's command."

It sometimes happened that 'Amr did not know the answer to a question. He would then request the Imam to tell him the answer so that he could repeat it in front of him—in which case, it would become his answer. Now and again the old lady would insist on questioning 'Amr personally and would go to him mounted on a mule, with Abū Ḥanīfah walking by her side. On arriving at 'Amr's house she would put her question to him personally and hear the answer with her own ears; only then would she be satisfied.

Once she posed a problem to the Imam and asked him for the answer, but when he gave it, she turned it down, saying, "No, you are no authority. I shall accept your answer only if Zurqah confirms it." (Zurqah was a preacher.) The Imam took her to Zurqah and explained the problem to him. "Why don't you answer it yourself?" said Zurqah. "You know far more than I do." The Imam then told him what answer he had given. Zurqah said that the answer was correct. That satisfied the old lady and she returned home. When Ibn Hubayrah, having sent for Imam Abū Ḥanīfah, asked him to accept the post of Keeper of the Seal and on the latter's refusal ordered him to be whipped daily until he relented, the Imam's mother was still living. Hearing of what was happening, she was greatly grieved. Whenever the Imam recalled this episode in later life, he would say, "It was not so much my pain as the thought of the grief it was causing my mother that I found hard to bear."

The Imam was very tender-hearted and was greatly disturbed by other people's pain and sorrow. One day, while he was teaching in a mosque, somebody came with the news that a certain man had fallen from the roof of his house. He cried out aloud, left the class, ran barefoot to the man's house and attended to him. Until the man had fully recovered, the Imam visited him every morning. But, distressed as he was by other people's sufferings, he bore his own with an equanimity which astonished people. Through all the persecution to which he was subjected by the caliph and his officers, he never wavered for a moment. Patience and steadfastness were inborn in him.

One day, while he was lecturing in the mosque, surrounded by students and devotees, a snake fell into his lap from the ceiling. Everybody except him ran out of the mosque. As for him, he kept sitting calmly as if nothing had happened.

A similar story is told of Imam Mālik and forms one of the famous incidents of his life.

Abū Ḥanīfah was a man of few words and never took part in idle talk. In his classroom he would sit quietly, letting his pupils freely debate among themselves, and would speak only when the discussion had become long-drawn-out without any conclusion being reached. He would then give his decision, which would satisfy all present.

He always avoided speaking ill of people behind their backs and would often thank Allah for saving his tongue from being contaminated with this evil. One day a man said to him, "Sir, people go about saying so many bad things about you, but one has never heard an ill word from your lips." The Imam observed, "This is Allah's grace. He grants it to whomever He likes." On somebody telling Sufyān al-Thawrī that he had never heard Abū Ḥanīfah slander anybody, Sufyān said, "Abū Ḥanīfah is not such a fool as to ruin all his good deeds."

He thought it wrong to swear and always abstained from it. In order to enforce this on himself, he had taken a vow that every time he committed the error he would pay a voluntary penalty of one dirham. Once he did commit it inadvertently. Thereupon he raised the penalty to one dinar.

His piety and devotion knew no bounds. Praying was a delight to him and he used to engage in it with great gusto and sincerity, and he was famous for this. Al-Dhahabī writes, "Accounts of his piety and devotion have reached a degree of *tawātur* (i.e. an unbroken chain of uncontradicted narrations)." While saying his prayers or reading the Qur'an, he would be so overcome with feeling that he would start weeping and go on doing so for hours.

Ibrāhīm al-Baṣrī relates that one morning while he was saying his prayers together with the Imam, the latter recited the *āyah* "Do not think that Allah is forgetful of the conduct of the iniquitous," and in reciting it wept so much that his whole body shook with sobs.

Zā'idah relates that, having an important question to consult the Imam about, he joined the *'ishā'* prayers with him and waited for him to finish his *nafls*. But the Imam, when in reciting from the Qur'an he reached the *āyah* "*Wa waqānā 'adhāb al-samūm*" (Save us from the torture of Hell's hot wind), went on repeating it until the morning. On another occasion he spent the whole night repeating the *āyah* "Judgement Day is the sinners' promised hour and it is a difficult and unpleasant hour," and weeping while he repeated it.

Yazīd b. Kumayt, a contemporary of the Imam and famous for his piety, relates that he joined the Imam in an *'ishā'* prayer, during which the Imam leading the prayers recited the *āyah* "*Idhā zulzilat.*" After the other people had departed, he found the Imam still sitting and heaving deep sighs. Yazīd did not want to disturb the Imam. So he also went away, leaving the Imam sitting. When he went to the mosque on the following morning, he found the Imam sitting, looking very sad, holding his beard in his hands and saying tearfully, "O You who will reward even the smallest virtue and punish even the smallest sin, save Your slave Nu'mān from Hellfire."

One day while walking in the street the Imam inadvertently stepped on a small boy's foot. The boy cried, "You don't seem to fear Allah." On hearing these words the Imam fainted. Mis'ar b. Kidām, who was with him, stopped him from falling and attended to him. As soon as he came to, Mis'ar said, "Why were you so perturbed by a small boy's casual remark?" The Imam replied, "Who knows this was not an admonition from the unknown!"

One day when the Imam arrived at his shop, his servant put out some lengths of cloth and by way of a good augury said, "May Allah grant us Paradise!" The Imam started weeping and wept so much that his whole mantle became wet. Then he told the servant to shut shop and went out, covering his face with his handkerchief. When he came to the shop on the following day, he said to the servant, "Who are we to wish for Paradise? It will be enough if Allah spares us His wrath." 'Umar al-Fārūq used to say similarly, "If on Judgement Day I am neither punished nor rewarded, I shall be quite happy."

One day, when he was explaining a point, one of the men present said, "You should always have the fear of Allah in your heart when you give a *fatwā*." The Imam was so deeply affected by this remark that he went pale. Turning to the man, he said, "May Allah reward you for your good deeds, brother! If I were not sure that Allah will punish me for deliberately withholding the benefit of my knowledge from others, I would never give a *fatwā*."

Faced with a question to which he did not know the answer, he used to get disturbed and ask himself whether he had committed some sin, of which this was the punishment. He would then perform his ablution, say his prayers and beg Allah's forgiveness. Somebody having reported this to al-Fuḍayl b. 'Iyāḍ, a famous Sufi, he wept and said, "Abū Ḥanīfah did not have many sins to repent for. That was why he thought thus. But those who are drowned in sin have innumerable calamities sent down on them and yet do not realise that these are warnings from Allah."

The Imam's daily routine was as follows. After the morning prayer he would take his class in the mosque and then reply to references for *fatwās*, which came from far and near. That was followed by a session for *fiqh* compilation, in which his leading disciples took part. Decisions reached unanimously were recorded. After saying his *ẓuhr* prayer, the Imam would go home and, if it was summer, have a siesta. The *'aṣr* prayer was followed by another session of teaching, after which the Imam would go round the city, meeting friends, visiting the sick, condoling the bereaved and helping the poor. After the *maghrib* prayer there was a third teaching session, which continued till the *'ishā'* prayer. Having said his *'ishā'* prayer, the Imam would start his private devotions, often continuing them throughout the night. During winter, he often slept in the mosque until the *'ishā'* prayer, after which he would spend the whole night in performing the *tahajjud* prayer, reciting chosen passages from the Qur'an and repeating devotional formulas. Sometimes he performed these in his shop.

Notes

1. Al-Nawawī relates these facts in the *Tahdhīb al-Asmā'*.
2. There are different versions of this story in different books. I have adopted the version of *Kitāb al-Aghānī*, Ibn Khallikān, *Wafayāt al-A'yān* and *'Uqūd al-Jumān*.

7
Anecdotes about Abū Ḥanīfah's wit and wisdom

It is in his writings and pronouncements on *fiqh* that Abū Ḥanīfah's inventiveness, originality, penetration and breadth of learning show at their best. In the compilation and codification of *fiqh* he occupies the same position as Aristotle does in logic and Euclid in geometry. But as this subject needs full treatment by itself, I have reserved the second part of the present work for it. In this chapter I content myself with relating certain facts and events which are incidental to a historical study of his work. These, I may however mention, by themselves furnish us with principles on which hundreds of points of law rest.

It is necessary at the outset to make it clear that many fictitious stories are current about the Imam's debates and utterances. What is surprising is that some eminent writers have included them in their books without properly investigating them, thus providing documentary corroboration of them. It is quite a common thing for all sorts of good and bad stories to come into existence about people who have attained eminence in the sciences and arts and to become so widely accepted as to appear authentic. The irony of it all is that admirers in their enthusiasm sometimes make claims which they think to be complimentary but which are, in fact, derogatory, while detractors sometimes make allegations intended as disparagements but in effect constituting praise. Abū Ḥanīfah did not escape this common fate of famous men. Some authors have narrated incidents intended to demonstrate his great intelligence and intellectual reach, but which, if believed, would rather go to show that he was merely crafty, prevaricative, good at repartee and glib-tongued.

These incidents, however, are not historically established and, apparently for that reason, careful scholars and especially traditionists have refrained from mentioning them. I propose to do the same and to confine myself to facts and incidents with a high degree of probability of being true.

There is no doubt that Abū Ḥanīfah took part in more polemic encounters and debating duels than any of the other imams of *fiqh*. His refinement of the legal sciences, which was beyond the comprehension of common minds, had brought into existence a group of people hostile to him, which included a number of pious simpletons. These people were always seeking to draw him into polemic trials of strength, and the Imam for his part could not but accept their challenge if he was to convince them. So he found himself involved in an unending round of debates. Apart from this, debate was one of the principal methods of teaching in those days, and the Imam himself had been educated by that method.

The author of *al-'Uyūn wa al-Ḥadā'iq* mentions in his biographical note on the Imam that he held debates with al-Sha'bī, Ṭāwūs and 'Aṭā'. These three were among the Imam's chief teachers, and he had much respect for them. What the biographer, therefore, apparently means is that the Imam was taught by the three through debates.[1]

Al-Awzā'ī, Imam of Syria and founder of a regular school of *fiqh*, during a meeting with Abū Ḥanīfah at Makkah, said to him, "It is surprising that the people of Iraq do not lift their hands during *rukū'* and at the time of raising the head after it, although I have heard it from al-Zuhrī, who heard it from Sālim b. 'Abdullāh, who heard it from 'Abdullāh b. 'Umar, that the Prophet (ṣ) used to lift his hands at these stages." Abū Ḥanīfah countered that with a tradition going back to 'Abdullāh b. Mas'ūd through Ḥammād, Ibrāhīm al-Nakha'ī and 'Alqamah, according to which the Prophet (ṣ) was not in the habit of lifting his hands at the stages in question. "Praise be to Allah," exclaimed al-Awzā'ī, "I cite a tradition transmitted by al-Zuhrī, Sālim and 'Abdullāh; but you cite against that a tradition transmitted by Ḥammād, al-Nakha'ī and 'Alqamah." "My transmitters," replied Abū Ḥanīfah, "were greater *faqīhs* than yours. As for 'Abdullāh b. Mas'ūd, you know his rank very well. A tradition transmitted by him must take precedence." Al-Rāzī relates this debate in his *Manāqib al-Shāfi'ī*, but, while not denying that it took place, comments that being a *faqīh* has nothing to do with reporting a matter of fact.[2]

The point of principle made by al-Rāzī will be discussed in the second part of this book. What is intended here by making a reference to him is to bring out the fact that the dialogue in question did take place and that even the Shāfi'īs do not deny it. Imam Muḥammad puts the point nicely in his *Kitāb al-Ḥujaj.* "Our tradition," he says, "ends with 'Abdullāh b. Mas'ūd, while that of the rival party goes only as far back as 'Abdullāh b. 'Umar. The basic question at issue here is which of the two is to be preferred. 'Abdullāh b. Mas'ūd attained maturity during the Prophet's life and, as has been mentioned in the traditions, was given a place in the first row of Companions. As against this, 'Abdullāh b. 'Umar was only a youth, who had a place assigned to him in the second or third row. Therefore, the opportunities of observing the ways of the Prophet (ṣ) at close quarters that ʿAbdullāh b. Masʿūd had were not available to ʿAbdullāh b. ʿUmar." This reasoning on the part of Muḥammad is based on one of the principles of Ḥadīth, and the reference made by Abū Ḥanīfah to the high rank enjoyed by ʿAbdullāh b. Masʿūd was a pointer to this principle.

One day a number of people came together to the Imam to discuss with him the question of recitation after the imam (the prayer leader). The Imam said, "How can I discuss the question with so many people at one and the same time? The only way for me to discuss it with you all is that you appoint one of yourselves as your spokesman." The people agreed to this. As soon as they did so, the Imam said, "There is no need for a discussion: the issue is decided. Just as one of you has been authorised to represent all of you, the leader at a prayer is authorised to recite passages from the Qur'an on behalf of the whole assembly."

It was not that the Imam settled a question of Sharīʿah by mere logical reasoning. What he did was to explain by a practical illustration the meaning of a tradition which he had traced back through an authentic chain of transmission to the Prophet (ṣ) himself, namely, the Prophet's saying "When a man prays behind an imam, the imam's recitation of Qur'anic *āyahs* is equivalent to recitation by himself."

The Imam had the special knack of explaining the most difficult problem in such a commonsense manner that his audience understood it easily and the discussion came to an end at once. On one occasion al-Ḍaḥḥāk, the well-known Khārijī leader who captured Kūfah during the reign of the Umayyads, came to the Imam and, pointing to his sword, said, "Repent." "Repent of what?" asked the Imam. "I am told you maintain that ʿAlī agreed to have his dispute with Muʿāwiyah decided by arbitration. As he was in the right, how could he agree to arbitration?" "If," said the Imam, "it is your wish to put me to death, I have nothing to say; but if you wish to find out the truth, then permit me to argue the question with you." "I too want a debate with you," said al-Ḍaḥḥāk. "If we cannot decide the issue between ourselves, what then?" asked the Imam. "We can appoint somebody as an umpire," replied al-Ḍaḥḥāk. Accordingly, one of al-Ḍaḥḥāk's followers was appointed umpire. As soon as that was done, the Imam said, "This is exactly what 'Alī did. Why blame him for it?" Outwitted, al-Ḍaḥḥāk retired quietly.

Another interesting encounter is reported between Abū Ḥanīfah and al-Ḍaḥḥāk. The latter, on his entry into Kūfah, ordered a general massacre. Hearing of this, the Imam hurried to him and asked, "What offence has the populace of Kūfah committed to deserve this?" "They are all apostates," replied al-Ḍaḥḥāk. "Have they changed their religion," asked the Imam, "or are they following the same religion as before?" "What did you say?" said al-Ḍaḥḥāk, "Repeat it." So the Imam explained his question. Al-Ḍaḥḥāk realised his error and ordered his soldiers to sheathe their swords.

Qatādah al-Baṣrī, a brief account of whom I have given while speaking of the Imam's teachers, on a visit to Kūfah issued a public notice inviting those interested to come and ask him questions on *fiqh*. As he was a famous *muḥaddith* and imam, a large number of people came and put questions to him one after another. Abū Ḥanīfah, who was also there, posed the following problem: "A man had gone abroad. After he had been away a year or two, news came of his death. His wife thereupon married another man, to whom she bore a child. After some time the man, who was still alive, came home. He denied, while the other man claimed, fatherhood of the child.

Did both the men or only the one who disowned the child impute adultery to the woman?" "Has such a situation actually arisen?" inquired Qatādah. "No," replied Abū Ḥanīfah, "but the *'ulamā'* should be ready to meet it, in case it arises." Qatādah claimed to be expert more in exegesis than in *fiqh*. So he said, "Leave these questions aside; ask me something about exegesis." "Then kindly tell me," said Abū Ḥanīfah, "what is the meaning of the *āyah* 'He who had knowledge of the Book said that he could produce her before him in the twinkling of an eye.'"

The allusion in this *āyah* is to the story of how, when Solomon ordered his courtiers to have the Queen of Sheba's throne brought to him, one of them (probably Solomon's vizier, Āṣaf b. Barkhiyā') offered to have it brought instantaneously. There was a legend among the Jews that Āṣaf knew the *ism al-a'ẓam*, by the prowess of which he transported the throne from Syria to the Yemen in a day. This legend had become popular among the Muslims too, and the *āyah* was commonly interpreted in accordance with it. Qatādah did the same.

Abū Ḥanīfah asked if Solomon himself knew the *ism al-a'ẓam*, to which Qatādah replied in the negative. "Do you then subscribe to the view," asked Abū Ḥanīfah, "that there can be in a prophet's time a man who knows more than the prophet himself?" Qatādah could give no reply to this and said, "Ask me something about beliefs." "Are you a *mu'min*?" asked Abū Ḥanīfah. Now, most *muḥaddiths* were afraid to call themselves *mu'mins* and carefully avoided doing so. There was a story in this connection about al-Ḥasan al-Baṣrī. Somebody having asked him if he was a *mu'min*, he had replied, "*Inshā' Allāh*" (if Allah wills). On the man's objecting that "*Inshā' Allāh*" was out of place in that context, al-Ḥasan had said, "I could call myself a *mu'min*, but I am afraid that Allah might say I was telling a lie." Qatādah gave the same reply to Abū Ḥanīfah's question.

The fact of the matter is that it is merely a kind of superstition to refrain from describing oneself as a *mu'min*. "*Īmān*" means belief, and if a person believes in Allah and His Messenger, he is definitely a *mu'min* and should consider himself one. If he has doubt about Allah and His Messenger, he is definitely a *kāfir* (unbeliever, and there is no point in his saying, "If Allah wills." Abū Ḥanīfah wanted to expose this error. So he asked Qatādah why he had given a conditional reply, "Ibrāhīm," replied Qatādah, "said that he had hoped Allah would forgive his sins on Judgement Day." "When Allah put to Ibrāhīm," asked Abū Ḥanīfah, "the question 'Are you a *mu'min?*' he replied, 'Yes,' meaning that he was a *mu'min*. Why have you not imitated Ibrāhīm in this?" Qatādah got up angrily and went into his house.[3]

Yaḥyā b. Sa'īd al-Anṣārī, *qāḍī* of Kūfah, was one of al-Manṣūr al-'Abbāsī's important courtiers, but was nevertheless unable to command in Kūfah anything like the influence enjoyed by Abū Ḥanīfah. He used to marvel at that and say to people, "These Kūfans are strange people: they blindly obey one man." One day Abū Ḥanīfah deputed Abū Yūsuf, Zufar and some other distinguished pupils of his to hold a debate with Qāḍī Yaḥyā. The discussion was opened by Abū Yūsuf. The question propounded was this: "If a slave belonged jointly to two men and one of the men wanted to set him free, would he have the right to do so?" Yaḥyā replied, "No, because there is a *ḥadīth* which says, 'An act which harms someone is not permissible.' Since the proposition in question entails loss on the second owner, the first owner cannot rightfully set the slave free." "What if the second owner sets him free?" asked

Abū Yūsuf. "He will be within his rights in doing so." "You are contradicting what you said earlier," rejoined Abū Yūsuf. "According to you, the slave does not become free if only one of the owners releases him, that is, he remains a slave. Now, if he still remains a slave, how can the second owner alone set him free? What was not permissible for the first owner cannot be permissible for the second."

Muḥammad b. ʻAbd al-Raḥmān, better known by his surname Abū Laylā, was an eminent jurist, who was *qāḍī* of Kūfah for thirty-three years. Relations between him and Abū Ḥanīfah were strained because the latter used to point out mistakes in the former's decisions, which the former disliked, but which the latter could not help, as he felt called on to express his opinion.

The *qāḍī* used to hear cases in a mosque. One day when he was going home after holding court, he found a woman quarrelling with a man in the street. In the course of the quarrel, the woman called the man the son of an adulteress. The *qāḍī* forthwith ordered her arrest, went back to his courtroom, had the woman produced before him and sentenced her to two rounds of whipping. When Abū Ḥanīfah was informed of this, he said, "The *qāḍī* has committed a number of errors in these proceedings. First, he held court irregularly, since he had already adjourned it after his day's work. Second, he had the sentence executed in the mosque notwithstanding the fact that the Prophet (ṣ) had prohibited the execution of sentences in mosques. Third, he had the woman whipped standing, which is not permissible in the case of women. Fourthly, he awarded double punishment for one offence, whereas he should have awarded a single sentence; and even if he had passed a sentence of double punishment, the two punishments could not be carried out simultaneously.

After, the first punishment there should have been allowed an interval for the culprit's wounds to heal. Fifth, as the man abused had not come forward with a complaint, the *qāḍī'* had no right to institute proceedings."

On hearing of this, Qāḍī Ibn Abī Laylā was infuriated and complained to the governor of Kūfah that Abū Ḥanīfah was making his life miserable. The governor issued orders restraining Abū Ḥanīfah from giving any more *fatwās.* Abū Ḥanīfah, although he was never deterred by the fear of displeasing an official or wealthy man from speaking out the truth, obeyed this order without demur, because the giving of *fatwās* was only a *farḍ kifāyah* (a collective duty) and there were in Kūfah many other *'ulamā'* to give them.

During the period when he was under restraint, his daughter asked him for a *fatwā.* She was fasting and had during her fast swallowed some blood from her gums. She wanted him to tell her if her fast had been broken or not. The Imam replied to her, "Darling, ask your brother Ḥammād, as I have been forbidden to give any *fatwās.*" The historian Ibn Khallikān, after reporting this, adds, "What better example could there be of obedience to orders and honesty?"[4] A few days later the governor, confronted with certain juristic questions which nobody else was able to solve, had to refer them to Abū Ḥanīfah, which automatically removed the ban imposed on the Imam.

In the records of the Imam's debates, one occasionally comes across indications of a certain assertiveness and combative ardour which appears to be at odds with his customary humility and self-effacement; but then no human being can be completely devoid of emotion. In accounts of the debates of al-Shāfi'ī, Mālik, al-Bukhārī and Muslim, I have found much more dogmatism and pugnacity. In fact, if the shortcomings of great men had not been brought out in the stories of their lives and the portraits of their personalities, we would have suspected that the writers of their memoirs had not presented them truthfully, but had allowed their admiration for them to colour their accounts. Very correctly has it been said by a sage that in narrating the life stories of great and eminent men, those traits of theirs should also be shown in which human nature is reflected, for this will engender in the reader's mind a desire to imitate them. If they are presented as perfect angels, people might begin to worship them, but would never think of following their example, considering them supermen incapable of being imitated.

One day Imam Sufyān al-Thawrī, Qāḍī Ibn Abī Laylā, Sharīk and Abū Ḥanīfah were all present at a learned gathering—too rare an opportunity for those eager to learn to let slip by. One of those present mooted the following question: A number of men were sitting together when a snake appeared and began to crawl up the body of one of them. He hurriedly shook it off, so that it landed on another man. The second man shook it off his body onto a third man. This went on until the last man on whom the snake landed was bitten by it and died in consequence. Now, which of these men is liable to pay *diyah* (mulct) for the man's death? This was a complex problem of *fiqh*, on which the learned men present expressed different opinions.

According to some, *diyah* was payable by all, and according to others, by the first man. There was a lot of discussion, but no agreed decision could be reached. Through all this, Abū Ḥanīfah sat silent and smiling. Ultimately everybody turned to him and asked him to express his opinion. The following is the ruling the Imam gave: When the first man threw the snake onto the second man, and the latter escaped being bitten, the former was absolved from responsibility. The same was true of all the succeeding men except the last one who shook off the snake. Now, as regards this last man there were two possible positions: if the snake bit the next man as soon as it landed on him, then the last man to throw the snake was liable to pay *diyah.* If, on the other hand, there was an interval between the two events, then the man bitten was guilty of contributory negligence in not throwing off the snake promptly enough to save himself. This view was accepted by all present, who complimented the Imam on his ingenuity.

Soundness in judgement, adroitness, sagacity, intelligence and penetration are qualities which friend and foe alike regard as characteristic of Abū Ḥanīfah. Muḥammad al-Anṣārī used to say that there was wisdom in everything that the Imam did or said—in his way of talking, in his manner of walking, even in his gestures. It was a favourite saying of 'Alī b. 'Āṣim that if the wisdom of half the world were put in one scale of a balance and Abū Ḥanīfah's wisdom in the other, the latter would outweigh the former. Khārijah b. Muṣ'ab was fond of saying that although he had met more or less a thousand learned men, he had found only three or four wise men among them, one of whom was Abū Ḥanīfah,

The qualities that are specially attributed to *'ulamā'* in our memoirs and biographies are keenness of intellect, a retentive memory, unworldliness, humility, contentment and piety; not a word is said about their possessing qualities like good judgement, discretion, sagacity and shrewdness, as if these were qualities reserved for worldly men. Ibn Khaldūn clinches the matter by saying bluntly that the *'ulamā'* as a class are not suited to administration and management of affairs; and this is true, although in reality the *'ulamā'* need to be suited to these tasks more than other people.

Unlike other religions, Islam lays down laws not merely for the spiritual but also for the temporal life. Who, for example, among the kings and rulers of the world could surpass the early caliphs in statecraft and administration? Abū Ḥanīfah is undoubtedly in a class by himself among the *'ulamā'* in that he was skilled in worldly matters in addition to being an expert in religious affairs. That is why his school of jurisprudence is better fitted to government and public affairs than any other school. Most of the great ruling dynasties in Islamic history were, therefore, followers of Abū Ḥanīfah.

Although the Imam established no connections with the caliphal court, his relations with the public were such that he was by himself a political institution, and performed his duties of leadership with a wisdom and intelligence that would do credit to an administrator. Unlike the religious leaders who were his contemporaries, he taught his pupils not to be dependent on the generosity of the rich for the fulfilment of their worldly needs, but to fend for themselves, as he did for himself. I have studied the full list of his pupils and have found among them many who, after graduating from his college, attained to positions of importance under the government and discharged their functions with eminent ability and honesty. Qāḍī Abū Yūsuf, who was minister of justice under Hārūn al-Rashīd and whose good management gave his department an organisation which not only was unprecedented but remained unsurpassed under later regimes, owed all this to the training he had received from the Imam.

The Imam was conscious of the difficulty of combining religious and moral duties with political attachments and therefore always gave his pupils such instructions as would enable them to do well in both spiritual and temporal affairs in accordance with the *āyah* "Grant us bliss in this world and also in the hereafter." Although Qāḍī Abū Yūsuf did not establish any connections with the court during the Imam's lifetime, his inborn ability, fostered by the Imam's training, held out ample promise that he would one day do so.

In view of this, the Imam gave him a written set of instructions designed to be guidelines in all important religious and secular matters. These instructions have been reproduced in certain books. Unfortunately, their length prevents me from reproducing them in full. I, therefore, content myself with giving a digest of them with some excerpts.

The instructions, at the outset, treat relations with the ruling monarch. "Go rarely to see him," says the Imam, "and beware of him as if he were fire. Never go to court except for some specific purpose, lest you lose the respect you enjoy there. Avoid it especially when there are present people whom you do not know, for since you are not aware of their rank, you might speak to them in a manner inappropriate to their position. If they are higher than you and you do not show due regard for this, it will be considered bad manners. If, on the other hand, they are ordinary people and you show them too much respect, you will lower yourself in the king's eyes. Should the king offer you the post of *qāḍī*, do not accept it without making sure that he approves of your exercising your personal judgement, lest you should have to act against it under official pressure. Never accept a position which you are not fit to hold."

Although a lot of emphasis has been laid in the instructions on showing due respect to the king, at the same time complete freedom has been enjoined in expressing the truth. "If," say the instructions, "you find someone guilty of improper innovation in matters of Sharī'ah, point out his error, so that others are discouraged from following his example. Never mind if the man is powerful or wealthy, for in declaring the truth, Allah will support you, since He is the guardian and protector of the faith. Even if it is the king himself whom you find doing something improper, do not hesitate to call his attention to it. Tell him frankly that though as his *qāḍī* you are subordinate to him, it is your duty to point out to him his errors. If he pays no heed to this, speak to him in private and explain to him that the action in question is contrary to the Qur'an and Prophetic traditions. If he realises his mistake, well and good; otherwise, pray to Allah to save you from the evil that is in him."

There are useful tips, too, about the daily tasks of life. "Consider the acquisition of knowledge your primary task. After you have completed it, turn to acquiring wealth by legitimate means, for knowledge and wealth cannot be acquired simultaneously. Thereafter, marry, but only when you are sure that you will be able to shoulder the responsibility of looking after a family. Do not marry a woman who has children by a former husband. Mix sparingly with the common people and the rich; the latter might think that you expect something from them and might be led by this to offer you bribes. Strictly avoid going to the bazaar, sitting with shopkeepers, eating in the street and the mosque, drinking at public watering places or drinking water served by water carriers and the like. When someone seeks a ruling from you, confine yourself to answering his question and do not add anything unsolicited. Do not discuss questions of belief with the common people. Treat your pupils with such sincerity and kindness that strangers are led to think they are your own children. Avoid engaging in debate with the common people and people of inferior rank.

"When you visit a city other than your own, conduct yourself towards the men of learning there in such a way that they do not look on you as a rival. When you discourse on learned subjects, speak after due reflection and say only that of which you can produce sufficient proof. In debating be courageous and steadfast; if you have the slightest fear in your heart, you will not be able to keep your thoughts collected, and your tongue will stammer. Never get involved in discussion with people who do not know the rules of debate or who become unpleasant.

"During a debate never get angry, and laugh little, for laughter can hurt your adversary's susceptibilities. Do everything in a calm and collected manner and with dignity. Unless a person accosts you face to face, do not reply to him, for accosting from behind is a habit peculiar to animals.

"While walking, do not look right or left. When you go to a *ḥammām*, pay more than the common people. Never do any shopping yourself; let your servants do it for you. Leave your domestic management in the hands of trustworthy servants so that you have enough time for your proper duties. Never reside in the vicinity of the royal court. Let everything you do or say demonstrate your indifference to worldly matters and personal interests: keep this up even in poverty.

"Never deliver a sermon to gatherings of common people, for in addressing such gatherings one is often compelled to tell lies. If you permit any of your pupils to take a *fiqh* class, attend his lectures in order to form an estimate of his ability. Should he make a mistake, point it out at once, otherwise those present might think that what he had said was correct. In subjects other than *fiqh* you need not personally attend classes taken by your pupils, but should depute your trusted friends or pupils to bring you a report.

"Let piety and faithfulness mark every action of yours. Have the same relations with Allah inwardly as you profess outwardly. As soon as you hear the *adhān* get ready for saying your prayer. Reserve three or four days a month for fasting. After every prayer recite a *waẓīfah*. Never miss reading the Qur'an. Do not incline much to the world. Go frequently to a graveyard. Abstain from pleasure seeking and amusement. If you see any defects in your neighbours, try to hide them. Avoid the company of heretical innovators. Do not be imam at prayers unless asked to do so. When people come to see you, converse with them on scholarly subjects: if they are scholars, they will gain something; if not, they will at least learn to respect you."

One of the Imam's pupils, 'Abd al-'Azīz b. Rawād, having been summoned by the caliph, came to the Imam for advice. He said that he intended to deliver a sermon before the caliph, but did not know what to say and how to say it. "Say," counselled the Imam, "Commander of the Faithful, there can be only three objects of worldly pursuits, namely, honour, territory and wealth. You have all three. Turn now to piety and virtuous deeds so that you acquire the good things of the other world."

Some of the Imam's wise sayings are worth recording here.

"Who can be a greater waster than a man whom even learning has not been able to keep away from sin and depravity?"

"A person who discourses on religion without remembering that he will be questioned by Allah on what he says knows the value of neither religion nor his own mind."

"If the *'ulamā'* are not Allah's friends, then Allah has no friends in the world."

"Whoever hankers after royal power before he is ripe for it meets with humiliation."

"Knowledge never sinks into the mind of a person who acquires it for worldly purposes."

"Faith is the highest act of worship, and faithlessness the greatest sin. One who adheres to the highest worship and avoids the greatest sin can hope for salvation."

"A man who learns Ḥadīth but does not deduce from it answers to religious questions is like a chemist who has medicines in his shop but does not know which to prescribe for what disease."

"Discoursing on learned themes before a man who has no taste for learning is torturing him."

"What an error to amass sins for one's friend (that is, one's soul) and wealth for one's enemies (that is, one's heirs)!"

Somebody having asked the Imam what could aid one in learning *fiqh*, he answered, "Peace of mind." "How can one acquire it?" asked the man. "Reduce your attachments," replied the Imam, "How can one reduce one's attachments?" asked the man further. "Take what is essential and leave what is not," counselled the Imam.

Somebody asked the Imam one day what he thought of the battles between 'Alī and Mu'āwiyah. "My mind," replied the Imam, "is always full of fear about things on which I shall be questioned on Judgement Day. I am sure that this is not one of them. So I do not think much about it."

It would not be right to conclude from this that the Imam had no personal opinion to express on the subject. He has himself said somewhere else, "If we did not have 'Alī's example before us, we would not have known how rebels should be dealt with." Al-Shāfi'ī also made a similar statement. However, it is idle to treat matters of this kind as of essential importance to Islam and to pile up controversies about them; and this apparently is what the Imam was hinting at.

A man wanting to join the Imam's classes came with a letter of recommendation. On the letter being given to him, the Imam said, "Where knowledge is concerned there is no question of recommendation. It is the *'ulamā's* duty to impart what they know to others."

The governor of Kūfah asked the Imam once why he kept away from him. The Imam replied, "A loaf of bread and a few yards of ordinary cloth acquired peacefully are better than luxury bought with self-humiliation."

The Imam occasionally used to write verse, not as an exercise in artistic creation, but merely as a vehicle for moral instruction. Here is a translation of two of his couplets:

> A man, while he is alive, needs a decent house to live in respectably. If he has such a house, he should be grateful and endeavour for a house in the next world.

The Imam's intelligence and quick-wittedness are proverbial, so much so that even where a brief description is given of him, these qualities are invariably mentioned. Al-Dhahabī has written only a brief note on him, but even so could not omit saying, "He was one of the most intelligent of Adam's children." His mind worked so quickly in solving the most complicated problems that the observers were astounded. It often happened that a problem was posed to an assembly of *'ulamā'*, including Abū Ḥanīfah. Some of the *'ulamā'* were his compeers in learning and also knew the answer to the problem, but it was Abū Ḥanīfah alone who gave a reply suited to the circumstances.

Once, a man, getting angry with his wife, said to her on oath, "I am never going to speak to you until you speak to me." The woman was his match in temper, so she repeated the same words on oath. When their tempers cooled, they were both sorry for what they had said. The man went to Sufyān al-Thawrī and related the incident to him. Sufyān ruled that the only course open was for the man to atone for his oath. Disappointed, the man approached Abū Ḥanīfah. The Imam said, "Go and talk to each other as much as you like. There is no question of atonement." When Sufyān al-Thawrī got to know of this, he was very angry and, going to Abū Ḥanīfah, reproached him for giving incorrect answers to people's questions. The Imam sent for the man and made him reiterate his story. Then he turned to Sufyān and "said, "I repeat what I said earlier." "Why?" asked Sufyān. "When the woman," replied Abū Ḥanīfah, "repeated her husband's words, she took the initiative in speaking to him. So the husband's condition was fulfilled."[5] Sufyān al-Thawrī could not but agree. "Things that occur to you on the spur of the moment,"' said he to Abū Ḥanīfah, "are beyond the ingenuity of common men."

A man celebrated at Kūfah the marriages of two of his sons together, with much pomp and ceremony. Eminent citizens, including Mis'ar b. Kidām, al-Ḥusayn b. Ṣāliḥ, Sufyān al-Thawrī and Abū Ḥanīfah, attended the *walīmah* feast. In the midst of the feast the host rushed in, looking distracted, and said, "A horrible thing has happened." "What has happened?" asked some of the guests. "Through bungling on the part of the womenfolk," replied the host, "the brides got exchanged, so that each of them slept with the other's bridegroom. What am I to do now?" "A similar thing happened during Amir Mu'āwiyah's reign," said Sufyān. "It was held that this kind of mix-up does not affect the marriage contract. All that is necessary is for the husbands to give the *mahr* to their wives." Mis'ar requested Abū Ḥanīfah to express his opinion. The Imam asked for the husbands to be produced before him. When they came, he took them aside one after another and asked each whether he would like the woman who had spent the night with him to be his wife. Both of them answered in the affirmative. The Imam thereupon advised each of them to divorce the woman to whom he had been married and get married to the woman with whom he had slept.

Although Sufyān's answer also was correct from the point of view of *fiqh*, because this was a case of "cohabitation in error," in which the marriage tie does not get dissolved, the Imam in giving his ruling kept expediency in view. He realised that it would be impossible for the men and the women to forget what had happened and that the memory would keep hurting their pride and sense of honour. Even if they did agree under compulsion to retain the marriage tie, there would never be between the men and the women that sense of belonging to each other completely, which is the real purpose of marriage. Again, the *mahr* would be reduced because if there is a divorce before consummation, only half the *mahr* is payable.

Al-Layth b. Saʿd, a famous imam of Egypt, relates that he had heard so much about Abū Ḥanīfah that he longed to meet him. On a pilgrimage to Makkah, he found a crowd collected, and sitting in the midst of it was a man whom people were questioning one after another on religious matters. One of them, going forward, said to the man, "O Abū Ḥanīfah!" When Abū Ḥanīfah turned to him, the man said, "I have a bad-tempered son who keeps divorcing the women to whom I get him married and setting free the slave girls I give him. Tell me what to do with him." "Take him to the slave market," replied the Imam promptly, "and buy for him a slave girl whom he himself chooses. Then have him married to her. He will not then be able to set her free, since she will not be his property. Even if he divorces her, you will lose nothing because she will continue to be your slave." Saʿd says that he was more surprised by the Imam's ready wit than by the answer.

Al-Rabīʿ, caliph al-Manṣūr's chamberlain, was hostile to Abū Ḥanīfah. One day, when the Imam was summoned to court, al-Rabīʿ was in attendance. Addressing al-Manṣūr, he said, "Commander of the Faithful, this man contradicts your well-revered ancestor [ʿAbdullāh b. ʿAbbās]. Your ancestor said that if a man took a vow and uttered the phrase '*inshā' Allāh*' a day or two later, the phrase would be regarded as forming part of his vow, and it would not, therefore, be incumbent on him any longer to fulfil the vow. Contrary to this, Abū Ḥanīfah gives the ruling that if the phrase '*inshā' Allāh*' was spoken along with the vow, it would be considered part of the vow, otherwise it would be utterly meaningless and ineffectual." "Commander of the Faithful," rejoined Abū Ḥanīfah, "Al-Rabīʿ thinks that the oath of allegiance to you that people take is ineffectual." "How is that?" asked al-Manṣūr. "He supposes," replied the Imam, "that people after swearing allegiance to you in your court say '*inshā' Allāh*' when they go home and thus absolve themselves from their oath, so that they are no longer liable to any legal penalty for breaking it." Al-Manṣūr burst into laughter and said to al-Rabīʿ, "You cannot trick Abū Ḥanīfah." Later, when they were leaving the court together, al-Rabīʿ said to the Imam, "You very nearly got me put to death today." "It was your intention to get me put to death," said the Imam, "I only defended myself."

One day a number of Khārijites invaded the Imam's house and, catching hold of him, said, "Say you abandon *kufr*." The Imam promptly said, "I abandon your *kufr*." The Khārijites maintain that by committing a sin a man becomes a *kāfir*, which amounts to saying that sin and *kufr* are identical. What the Imam meant was that he repented of what they thought to be *kufr*. Somebody later on went to the Khārijites and told them that the Imam had befooled them. So the Khārijites came back to the Imam and asked him to explain why he had tricked them with a verbal quibble. "Is it your conviction or merely a conjecture that I have done so?" inquired the Imam. "No, it is only a conjecture," replied the Khārijites. "In that case," said the Imam, "you should beg Allah's forgiveness, because Allah has Himself said, 'Verily, some conjectures are sins.'"

One day, when the Imam was sitting in a mosque surrounded by his pupils, a group of Khārijites rushed in. Frightened, the pupils started running away. The Imam, however, stopped them, told them to have no fear and asked them to resume their seats. The leader of the Khārijites went up to the Imam and said, "Who are you people?" "People seeking refuge," replied the Imam. "Allah says, 'If any polytheist seeks refuge, give it to him, so that he may listen to Allah's *kalām*, and then escort him to a place of safety.'" The Khārijites considered every Muslim not belonging to their sect to be a *kāfir* deserving to be put to death. This group had come with the intention of getting Abū Ḥanīfah to state his form of belief, charge him with *kufr* and assassinate him. But they were disarmed by the verse quoted by the Imam, which imposed an obligation on them to protect his life and the lives of his pupils. So the leader said to his men, "Recite the Qur'an for them to hear and then escort them to their homes."

Abū al-'Abbās, who held a high position in al-Manṣūr's court, was the Imam's enemy, always intent on harming him. One day, when the Imam presented himself at court for some piece of business, Abū al-'Abbas also happened to be present. He confided to his friends that he was going to see to it that the Imam did not leave the court alive that day. Turning to the Imam, he said, "Abū Ḥanīfah, it sometimes happens that the Commander of the Faithful orders us to put somebody to death without our knowing whether or not the man is guilty and merits being put to death. In such cases ought we to carry out the order or refuse to do so?" "Are the caliph's orders in your opinion right or wrong?" inquired the Imam. Who could have the boldness to affirm in al-Manṣūr's presence even the possibility of any of his orders being wrong? So Abū al-'Abbās was compelled to say that the caliph's orders were right in his opinion. "Then it was unnecessary for you to ask for my views," said Abū Ḥanīfah.

Once, a man declared that if he had a bath that day after intercourse with his wife, that would have the same effect as if he had pronounced the formula of divorce against his wife three times. A little later he said that if he missed any prayer that day, his wife would stand divorced. Later, still, he said that if he did not have intercourse with her that day, that would mean that he had divorced her. Some people came to Abū Ḥanīfah to get a ruling from him about these utterances of the man. His ruling was this: "Let him have intercourse with her after his *'aṣr* (afternoon) prayer. As soon as the sun sets, let him have his bath and then say his prayer. In this way he can fulfil all the conditions—having intercourse with his wife during the day, not missing any prayer and not having his bath in daytime."

One day a man came to the Imam and said, "I kept some money somewhere in my house, but do not remember exactly where. I now need the money badly. Please tell me how I can find it." "Brother," protested the Imam, "I do not find this kind of problem mentioned in *fiqh*. Why have you come to me for advice?" But on further entreaty by the man, he advised him to pray throughout the night. The man, accordingly, went home and started praying. He had prayed for a little while when he suddenly remembered where he had put the money. So he ran to the Imam and told him of the efficacy of his advice. "Of course," commented the Imam. "Satan could not brook the idea of your praying for a whole night. So he made you remember at once where you had put your money. However, you ought to have prayed throughout the night by way of giving thanks to Allah."

On another occasion, a man sought the Imam's help in finding some articles he had buried in some part of his house, which he could not recall. "If you don't remember the spot," remarked the Imam, "how can I?" The man started crying. So the Imam went to his house with some of his pupils. "If this house were yours," said he to them, "where would you hide things for safety?" They made three or four guesses. The Imam ordered the spots guessed by them to be dug up, the third of which yielded the buried articles.

For all his solemnity and dignity, the Imam occasionally liked to crack a joke. Here are a few witty remarks made by him. One day he said to his barber, who was trimming his hair, "Pluck the grey hairs." "Hairs plucked," said the barber, "grow again and thicker than before." "If that is so," ordered the Imam, "then pluck all the black hairs so that they grow again and thicker." Hearing of this repartee, Qāḍī Sharīk remarked, "Abū Ḥanīfah did not abandon arguing by analogy even in talking to his barber."

There lived in the Imam's lane a miller who was a fanatical and who had, therefore, named his two donkeys Abū Bakr and 'Umar, respectively. One day one of the donkeys kicked the miller so hard in the head that he died. Hearing of this, the Imam said, "It must be the donkey whom he had named 'Umar." On inquiry, the guess was found correct.

There was a fanatical Shi'ite at Kūfah who used to say that the caliph 'Uthmān was a Jew. The Imam went to him one day and said, "You were on the lookout for a husband for your daughter. I know a man who is rich and at the same time pious. He prays throughout the night and is a *ḥāfiẓ* of the Qur'an." "Who could be better than he," said the man, "as a husband for my daughter? Please fix up the marriage." "But there is one thing," said the Imam. "He is of the Jewish faith." The man was furious and exclaimed, "What? You advise me to marry my daughter to a Jew!" "What does it matter if he is a Jew?" rejoined the Imam. "If the Messenger of Allah himself gave his daughter to one whom you call a Jew, why should you have any objection to a Jew for a son-in-law ?" Miraculously enough, the man was so deeply moved by this that he abjured his erroneous belief.

Notes

1. Some of the Imam's debates have been reported by the historian al-Khaṭīb in his *Ta'rīkh Baghdād* and by Imam al-Rāzī in his commentary on the *āyah* "And He taught Adam all the names." They have been reported more elaborately in the *'Uqūd al-Jumān*. Excerpts from them are also available in some other books.
2. Ibn al-Hammām mentions this dialogue in *Fatḥ al-Qadīr*, and there are references to it in *Ḥujjah Allāh al-Bālighah* also.
3. This debate has been reported by al-Khaṭīb in *Ta'rīkh Baghdād* and by Abū al-Maḥāsin in *'Uqūd al-Jumān* with slight variations.
4. Ibn Khallikān, *Wafayāt al-A'yān*.
5. Al-Rāzī narrates this incident in his *Tafsīr al-Kabīr*.

Second Part
The Imam's Writings

8

Abū Ḥanīfah's writings

There are three books attributed to Abū Ḥanīfah, namely, *al-Fiqh al-Akbar*, *al-'Ālim wa al-Muta'allim* and *Musnad.*

Al-Fiqh al-Akbar is a brief treatise on dogmatics, dealing with the same questions, and more or less in the same order, as *al-'Aqā'id* of al-Nasafī and other writings on the subject. It has been published and is available everywhere. Many commentaries have been written on it, such as those of Muḥyī al-Dīn Muḥammad b. Bahā' al-Dīn (d. 953 H), Mawlā Ilyās b. Ibrāhīm al-Sīnūbī, Mawlā Aḥmad b. Muḥammad al-Maghnīsāwī, al-Ḥakīm Isḥāq, Shaykh Akmal al-Dīn and Mullā 'Alī al-Qārī, the last-mentioned being the most popular. Manuscripts of some other commentaries are also to be found here and there. Al-Ḥakīm Isḥāq's commentary was versified by Abū al-Baqā' Aḥmadī in 918 H and *al-Fiqh al-Akbar* itself by Ibrāhīm b. Husām, popularly known as Sharīfī.

Al-'Ālim wa al-Muta'allim is a small treatise in the form of question and answer. I have, however, not seen it.

Of the *Musnad*, there were several versions, which were collected in a single volume by Abū al-Mu'ayyad Muḥammad b. Maḥmūd al-Khawārizmī (d. 665 H). Here is an extract from his Preface:

> I heard a number of ignoramuses in Syria say that Imam Abū Ḥanīfah was not well versed in Ḥadīth, which,

according to them, explained why there was no book by him on the subject. This was a challenge to my sense of loyalty, in answer to which I decided to compile together all the *musnads* which have been composed by different *'ulamā'* on the basis of traditions narrated by Abū Ḥanīfah. These are as follows:

(1) the *Musnad* of al-Ḥāfiẓ Abū Muḥammad 'Abdullāh b. Muḥammad b. Ya'qūb al-Ḥārithī al-Bukhārī, better known as 'Abdullāh al-Ustādh
(2) the *Musnad* of Imam Abū al-Qāsim Ṭalḥah b. Muḥammad b. Ja'far al-Shāhid
(3) the *Musnad* of al-Ḥāfiẓ Abū al-Ḥasan Muḥammad b. al-Muẓaffar b. Mūsā b. 'Īsā
(4) the *Musnad* of al-Ḥāfiẓ Abū Nu'aym al-Aṣbahānī
(5) the *Musnad* of Shaykh Abū Bakr Muḥammad b. 'Abd al-Baqī Muḥammad al-Anṣārī
(6) the *Musnad* of Imam Abū Aḥmad 'Abdullāh b. 'Adī al-Jurjānī
(7) the *Musnad* of Imam al-Ḥāfiẓ 'Umar b. Ḥasan al-Ushnānī
(8) the *Musnad* of Abū Bakr Aḥmad b. Muḥammad b. Khālid al-Kulā'ī
(9) the *Musnad* of Imam Abū Yūsuf al-Qāḍī
(10) the *Musnad* of Imam Muḥammad
(11) the *Musnad* of Ḥammād b. Imam Abū Ḥanīfah
(12) the *Āthār* of Imam Muḥammad
(13) the *Musnad* of Imam Abū al-Qāsim 'Abdullāh b. Abī al-'Awwām al-Sa'dī.

There are other *musnads* besides those listed by Abū al-Mu'ayyad, such as those of al-Ḥāfiẓ Abū 'Abdullāh Ḥunayn b. Muḥammad b. Khusrū al-Balkhī (d. 523 H), al-Ḥaṣfakī (a commentary on which was written by Mullā 'Alī al-Qārī), al-Māwardī and Ibn al-Bazzāzī (d. 827 H). Commentaries were also written on these *musnads*.

People who consider writings an essential ingredient of the Imam's greatness cite the above-mentioned works. The truth, however, is that it is extremely difficult to establish the Imam's authorship of them. It is true that a system of *fiqh* based on his teachings was compiled during his lifetime, references to which are to be met with in the *'Uqūd al-Jumān* and other books. But what is most probable is that that compilation was lost. The names of thousands of books of that period occur in biographical memoirs, but not more than two or three are extant in the libraries of the world. Even the great books of Ḥadīth and *fiqh* known to have been written by the Imam's contemporaries, Sufyān al-Thawrī, al-Awzā'ī, Ḥammād b. Salamah, Hushaym, Ma'mar, Jarīr b. 'Abd al-Ḥamīd and 'Abdullāh b. al-Mubārak, no longer exist.

We cannot but agree with al-Rāzī's statement in *Manāqib al-Shāfi'ī* that no book of Abū Ḥanīfah has survived. Al-Khawārizmī's *musnad* can be called the Imam's only derivatively. Al-Khawārizmī lived in the seventh century of the Hijrah, and the *musnads* he has compiled date back mostly to the third or fourth century or even to later periods. Ḥammād and Qāḍī Abū Yūsuf, on the other hand, were the Imam's contemporaries, and their *musnads* can undoubtedly be ascribed to him. But it is noteworthy that nobody except al-Khawārizmī has mentioned these *musnads*, which argues against their authenticity, for a book of Ḥadīth cannot be regarded as authentic unless established by well-known authorities. We can perhaps take Shāh Waliullāh's verdict on this issue as decisive. He writes thus in the *Ḥujjah Allāh al-Bālighah*: "Books of the fourth period are those whose authors tried after the lapse of a long time to collect narratives which were not extant in books of the first two periods and were to be found only in little-known *musnads* and collections. These authors tried to give prominence to such narratives, although they had either been transmitted by persons on whom the *muḥaddithīn* do not rely, as, for example, loquacious preachers, innovators and weak transmitters, or were annals of the sayings of the Companions and Successors; Jewish legends; sayings of philosophers and preachers, which the transmitters had mixed up with the sayings of the Prophet (ṣ); doubtful citations from the Qur'an or Ḥadīth which had been paraphrased by people not conversant with the subtleties of the art of narration and ascribed to the Prophet (ṣ); inferences drawn from the Qur'an and Ḥadīth and presented as Prophetic traditions; or, finally, bits of different traditions strung together into single passages. Traditions of these kinds are to be met with in *Kitāb al-Ḍu'afā'* of Ibn Ḥibbān, *al-Kāmil* of Ibn 'Adī and books of al-Khaṭīb, Abū Nu'aym, Jawzaqānī, Ibn 'Asākir, Ibn al-Najjār and al-Daylamī. Al-Khawārizmī's *musnad* belongs more or less to the same category."

Shāh Waliullāh, however, goes on to say, rather meticulously, that *musnads* attributed to the Imam's disciples are neither mentioned in history books nor extant. *Musnads* written much later than the Imam's time, however, are extant, but it is highly doubtful if the traditions recorded in them can be traced back to the Imam by an unbroken chain of authoritative transmitters. What is more, some of the *musnads* contain internal evidence of unreliableness. In al-Ḥaṣfakī's *Musnad* there are many traditions attributed to the Imam and described as having been heard by him from the Companions, whereas research by *muḥaddithīn* does not establish that the Imam heard traditions from any of the Companions. Al-Khawārizmī has included even the *al-Āthār* of Imam Muḥammad in Abū Ḥanīfah's *musnads.* True, most of the narrations in that book were made by the

Imam, and the readers are, therefore, at liberty to call it either Abū Ḥanīfah's *Musnad* or *al-Āthār* (memorable sayings) of Imam Muḥammad. But it is to be remembered that Imam Muḥammad has in this book quoted sayings and traditions of other leading masters also, which makes it more appropriate to ascribe the book to him.

Al-Fiqh al-Akbar has been ascribed to the Imam by Fakhr al-Islām al-Bazdawī, 'Abd al-'Alī Baḥr al-'Ulūm and those who have written commentaries on it. Nevertheless, I find it difficult to accept this. The style in which the book is written had not yet come into existence at the time it is said to have been written. It is a regular text with the brevity and orderliness characteristic of books of a later period. Again, there occur in it the words *jawhar* and *'arḍ*, which are philosophical terms that had not yet come into use. It is true that Greek books were translated into Arabic in the time of al-Manṣūr the 'Abbāsid, but that happened towards the end of the Imam's life. It is improbable that these philosophical terms gained so much currency immediately after the translations as to be used in common writings. Philosophical terms found entry into religious literature only after they had became part and parcel of Arabic through frequent use and had become indispensable even in ordinary discourse. That, however, happened after the Imam's time.

So much from the point of view of textual criticism. Even from the point of view of historical criticism, it is not established that Abū Ḥanīfah was the author of *al-Fiqh al-Akbar.* There is no mention of the work in writings of the second and third centuries, The earliest book in which, as far as I know, *al-Fiqh al-Akbar* is mentioned is Fakhr al-Islām al-Bazdawī's *Kitāb al-Uṣūl,* which was written in the fifth century. The Imam had thousands of disciples, most of whom were masters in their own right; and each of these in turn had thousands of disciples. It is highly improbable that if there had existed a work by the Imam, not one of the hundreds of thousands of his direct and indirect disciples should have made a reference to it. There is no mention of *al-Fiqh al-Akbar* in any of the well-known books on dogmatics and allied subjects, such as the *Ṣaḥā'if*, *Sharḥ al-Maqāṣid*, *Sharḥ al-Mawāqif* and *al-Milal wa al-Niḥal*. All the commentaries on the book were written in or after the eighth century.

Furthermore, Abū Muṭī' al-Balkhī, the *rāwī* of the book, is not acknowledged as an authority on traditions and the appraisal of traditions. In biographical works by *muḥaddithīn*, severely critical comments are made on him. Although I do not fully endorse those comments, a book of doubtful credence having no evidence of its existence beyond the word of Abū Muṭī' al-Balkhī cannot pass the test of the principles of Ḥadīth.

What seems to me probable is that a treatise written by Abū Muṭī' al-Balkhī and embodying his own ideas on questions of belief came in the course of time to be attributed to the Imam. This conjecture is supported by the fact that al-Dhahabī, speaking of Abū Muṭī', in his book *al-'Ibar fī Akhbār man Ghabar*, describes him as the "*Ṣāḥib al-Fiqh al-Akbar*," which clearly suggests that he considered Abū Muṭī' the author of that work.

I further believe that the present text and composition of *al-Fiqh al-Akbar* belong to a period much later than that of Abū Muṭī'. This is not something unparalleled. *Al-Jāmi' al-Ṣaghīr*, a work by Imam Muḥammad, was given its present form by Abū Ṭāhir al-Dabbās, who lived in the fourth century. There is, however, a difference. The present text of *al-Jāmi' al-Ṣaghīr* is the original text, but its arrangement has been changed. On the other hand, the text of *al-Fiqh al-Akbar* appears from its style to belong to a later period.

Although I have allowed my personal opinion and judgement to intrude into this discussion, I have related all the facts known to me. I do not insist on the reader accepting my version of them; but my conclusion from the facts is that no work by Abū Ḥanīfah is extant today.

9

Beliefs and *kalām*

As I have already mentioned, Abū Ḥanīfah was very much attracted to *kalām* in the early part of his educational career. Towards the close of the period of the Companions many new sects arose. Ma'bad al-Juhanī introduced the doctrine of *qadr*. Wāṣil b. 'Aṭā', who was a great scholar of Arabic literature and *kalām* and a disciple of al-Ḥasan al-Baṣrī, laid the foundation of *i'tizāl*. Jahm b. Ṣafwān founded the Jahmiyyah sect. Several sects of the Khārijites had already come into existence. All these sects were propagating their doctrines in Abū Ḥanīfah's time, and the whole Islamic world rang with religious controversies.

The Imam also participated in the controversies for the sake of repudiating the new-fangled doctrines. There can be no doubt that with his extraordinarily keen intellect, he made some subtle contributions. But as his interest in *kalām* soon yielded place to occupation with the problems of *fiqh*, there is no record available of his debates on *kalām*. However, there are a few tenets all along attributed to him. These bear the stamp of his penetration, originality and wide reach of intellect. We mention some of these, which are very controversial questions among the *muḥaddithīn*.

To begin with, the Imam does not regard duties and actions as part of faith. It is superfluous today to discuss this point, for even a man of common intelligence today knows that faith means belief, which is a state of mind, while duties and actions are overt exercises of the human organs, the two categories being disparate and incapable of combining or forming part of each other. In the Imam's time, however, this was a very debatable point, to which most scholars of the positive disciplines, some original thinkers among them, were opposed.

Up to the time of the Companions, the surface of Islamic beliefs remained smooth and undisturbed. The Arabs were not interested in philosophical hair-splitting and abstruse questions. But about the middle of the Umayyad period, the decline of military power and the development of culture created an interest in intellectual speculation. Debates started about *jabr* (compulsion) and *qadr* (predestination), *tashbīh* (comparing Allah to man) and *tanzīh* (keeping Allah pure), *'adl* (divine justice) and *jawr* (divine tyranny).

The debates were initiated by people who either were of *'ajamī* (non-Arab) origin or had come under the influence of *'ajamī* thought. Religious circles, which consisted mostly of Arabs, reacted violently to these new voices, and scholars of Ḥadīth and *fiqh* came into the arena to contend against their heresies. For that purpose they had to adopt some attitude, whether positive or negative, towards the new questions raised; but some of them were carried by their combative ardour beyond the limits of moderation.

For example, the Mu'tazilite doctrine that the Qur'an was the word of Allah that came into being with the apostleship of the Prophet of Islam was countered by some *muḥaddithīn* with the proposition that even the pronunciation of the Qur'an was eternal and uncreated. Al-Dhuhalī, who was one of al-Bukhārī's teachers and who has been cited as the authority for many of the traditions narrated in al-Bukhārī's *Ṣaḥīḥ*, got so angry with al-Bukhārī during a discussion on the doctrine that he had him expelled from his class and even went to the length of making it known that anyone associating with al-Bukhārī would not be permitted to attend his classes.[1] Al-Bukhārī believed in the *qidam* (eternity) of the Qur'an, but held that its *qirā'ah* (mode of recitation) was *ḥādīth* (temporal), whereas al-Dhuhalī maintained that it also was eternal.

Extreme views of a similar kind were held on certain other questions too, which it is unnecessary to describe in detail here. In all the debates in which he took part, Abū Ḥanīfah concerned himself with the kernel of the question at issue, combining a rational with a factual approach. One of these questions was the relationship between faith and works.

The Murji'ah held that faith and works were two different things and that, given perfect faith, works were of no importance. According to them, if a person sincerely believed in divine unity and the prophethood of Muḥammad, but was remiss in performing his duties, he was exempt from punishment. Although the first part of this proposition was correct, the *muḥaddithīn* mixed up the two parts and totally opposed the proposition. Their opposition gathered strength from the support that it received from a superficial "interpretation of some passages of the Qur'an on the subject. This was a question of personal opinion, and if it had stopped at that, it would not have mattered very much. Unfortunately, however, these worthies went to the extreme of branding those who disagreed with them as sinners and infidels. Sharīk, when Abū Yūsuf appeared in his court as a witness, declared that he was not willing to accept the evidence of anyone who did not consider the performance of prayers part of faith.

Abū Ḥanīfah always tried to arrive at the truth of a doctrine, irrespective of what person or sect held it. When this debate was reported to him, he declared that, according to him, faith and works were two separate things, on a different footing from each other. On this, many people called him a Murji'ite, but he was happy to be called that rather than slur over the truth. Indeed, this title was conferred on all the *muḥaddithīn* and *fuqahā'* who were at one with Imam Abū Ḥanīfah on this issue. The *muḥaddith* Ibn Qutaybah has in his famous book *al-Ma'ārif* listed the names of many of these, including Ibrāhīm al-Taymī, 'Amr b. Murrah, Ṭalīq b. Ḥabīb, Ḥammād b. Sulaymān, 'Abd al-'Azīz b. Abī Dāwūd, Khārijah b. Muṣ'ab, 'Amr b. Qays al-Māṣir, Abū Mu'āwiyah al-Ḍarīr, Yaḥyā b. Zakariyyā and Mis'ar b. Kidām, all of them imams of Ḥadīth and *riwāyah*, hundreds of traditions narrated by whom have been cited in al-Bukhārī's *Ṣaḥīḥ*. Some superficial observers of today, who are scandalised at the fact that some traditionists have called Imam Abū Ḥanīfah a Murji'ite, would be shocked to see Ibn Qutaybah's list. The *muḥaddith* al-Dhahabī, speaking of Mis'ar b. Kidām in his *Mīzān al-I'tidāl*, writes, "*Irjā'* is a school of thought subscribed to by many great scholars, and adherents of this school should not be denounced." This was the same *irjā'* which was Imam Abū Ḥanīfah's creed.

This doctrine, though apparently not very imposing, had far-reaching implications. That was why Abū Ḥanīfah professed it freely and frankly. A logical corollary of holding works to be part of faith was the proposition that a man devoid of works could not be a *mu'min* (believer), which was what the Khārijites maintained. Although most *muḥaddithīn* did not consider such a man to be an infidel, that was only because they overlooked the corollary, despite its being inevitable.

Imam al-Rāzī, a great supporter of Imam al-Shāfiʿī, discussing in his *Manāqib al-Shāfiʿī* the charge often made against al-Shāfiʿī that he believed in contradictory things, mentions as an instance the objection that while, on the one hand, he held faith to be a combination of profession and practice, he asserted, on the other, that absence of practice did not turn one into an infidel, although a combination could not remain in existence as such if one of the things combined was absent—which, al-Rāzī goes on to say, was why the Muʿtazilah, who believed that works were a part of faith, also maintained that without works faith could not exist. He answers the objection by saying that the substance of faith is confession and affirmation, while works are the consequences and products of it and that, since things are sometimes metaphorically spoken of in terms of what ensues from them, works have come to be known as faith, from which, according to him, it follows that the absence of works does not necessarily entail the absence of faith. But this is reading into the proposition a meaning not intended by the proponent; and al-Rāzī had to admit this, as is clear from the fact that after giving the answer he adds, "This reply gives the lie to the doctrine."

Al-Rāzī was a follower of the Shāfiʿī school and an ardent supporter of its founder. Nevertheless, being a man of great discernment, he could not but acknowledge that either works had to be regarded as the products, and not an ingredient, of faith or it had to be conceded that one devoid of works was not a *mu'min.*

There is a piece of writing by Abū Ḥanīfah on this subject, the reasoning of which bears testimony to the incisiveness of his intellect, going as it does to the heart of the matter. It was a reply to a letter from ʿUthmān al-Battī, a famous traditionist of the day. The letter, provoked by rumours about the Imam's ideas, was a friendly inquiry. "People call you a Murji'ite," 'Uthmān had written, "and that you consider it permissible for a believer to go astray. These imputations have shocked me. Are they true?" The Imam's reply was long. I will content myself with a few excerpts from it. After praising Allah and the Prophet (ṣ) and thanking 'Uthmān for taking a friendly interest in his welfare and reputation, he begins as follows:

> Allow me to remind you that before the Messenger of Allah was assigned his mission the people were polytheists. He preached to them that there is only one Allah and asked them to believe in his message. The life and property of any who gave up polytheism and adopted Islam became sacred. Then duties were enjoined on those who had embraced the faith. The performance of these duties was termed *'amal* (action, works). It is to this that Allah refers in the words "Those who had faith and performed good deeds; and those who believed in Allah and acted virtuously." There are several *āyahs* of the same kind from which it is clear that the absence of works does not nullify faith, but that the absence of affirmation and belief does.
>
> That affirmation and action are two separate things is also evident from the fact that, while in the matter of affirmation all Muslims are equal, they are graded from the point of view of action. For so far as religion and belief are concerned, they are uniform for all Muslims. Allah Himself says, "I have prescribed the same religion for you as I charged Nūḥ with. What I revealed to you and what I charged Ibrāhīm, Mūsā and 'Īsā with was to preserve the religion and not to be divided in it."
>
> You should know that guidance in faith and guidance in works are two different things. You can give the title *mu'min* to a person who is unaware of duties: such a person is ignorant so far as duties are concerned, but is all the same a believer in respect of affirmation. Allah Himself has made these distinctions in the Qur'an. Would you equate a person

> who refuses to acknowledge Allah and His Messenger with one who, though a believer, is ignorant of practical duties.
>
> Where the duties are specified in the Qur'an, it is said, "Allah has stated this so that you do not go astray," and, in another place, "If one goes astray, let another remind him." Again, Mūsā is reported as saying, "When I did that, I was one of those who stray." In addition to these verses there are many which clinch the matter. In fact, the other verses are even clearer. Did the title *Amīr al-Mu'minīn* given to 'Umar and 'Alī signify that they were the *amīrs* of only those who performed their practical duties? 'Alī called the people of Syria, who were at war with him, *mu'mins.* Could there be a greater sin than killing? Would you consider both the killers and the killed to be in the right? If you vindicate one party, namely, 'Alī and his supporters, what would you say about the other? Ponder over this and try to understand it.
>
> I assert that all people of the *qiblah* are *mu'mins* and that none of them becomes an infidel by omission of works. He who has faith and also performs his duties is without doubt a *mu'min* and destined for Paradise. He who is devoid of both faith and works is an infidel and destined for Hell. He who has faith but omits to act is certainly a Muslim, but a sinful one. It is up to Allah to punish or forgive him.

The way Imam Abū Ḥanīfah proved his thesis cannot be improved on. What better argument could there be to show that duties and faith are two distinct things than that Islam at the outset preached faith but prescribed no duties? The Qur'anic verses cited by the Imam furnish manifest proof that his contention was correct, for in all the verses *'amal* has been joined to *īmān* by a copulative particle, which could not have been done if the former were considered to be a part of the latter. The copulative "*fa*" in the verse "*man yu'min billāhi fa ya'mal ṣāliḥan*" finally settles the issue.

There are certain Qur'anic verses and traditions on the basis of which this reasoning could be challenged, but they are not enough to prove the contrary. The *ḥadīth* mostly relied on is the one which says that a *mu'min*, being a *mu'min*, cannot commit fornication or theft; but this way of expression was only a rhetorical device intended for emphasis, just as one may say about a person that, being a gentleman, he cannot do such and such a thing, which only means that the acts in question do not befit a gentleman. There is no doubt that fornication and theft do not befit a man of faith; and that is all that the *ḥadīth* means. Otherwise in Abū Dharr's *ḥadīth* it is clearly stated, "Whoever believes that there is no god but Allah is destined to go to Paradise, even if he is a fornicator and thief."

A second question on which Abū Ḥanīfah expressed himself clearly but has not been correctly understood is as to whether faith can increase or decrease. The Imam is reported to have said, "Faith neither increases nor decreases." There is no doubt that this is a saying of his, but it has been misinterpreted, not only by *muḥaddithīn* and Shāfi'īs but even by some Ḥanafīs.

There can be increase or decrease in faith from two points of view. The first of these is the point of view of quality. From that point of view it may be said that faith can become more or less intense or that, in other words, faith means certainty of belief, of which there are degrees. When Ibrāhīm asked Allah how He brought the dead back to life, Allah said, "You do not yet believe." Ibrāhīm replied, "I do believe, but want satisfaction of mind."

In a number of verses Allah has clearly spoken of increase in faith. One such statement is "*Zādathum īmānan*" (It increased their faith). However, the Imam neither affirms nor denies the proposition in this sense, nor was it a moot point in his time. His assertion that faith neither increases nor decreases was intended in another sense, and in that sense it is correct.

Those who regard works as part of faith hold that faith increases and decreases quantitatively: a person particular about works is more faithful than a sinner. The *muḥaddithīn* clearly make this claim and advance various arguments in support of it. Al-Qasṭalānī writes in his commentary on al-Bukhārī's *Ṣaḥīḥ*, "Faith is increased by righteous deeds and decreased by sin." The *muḥaddithīn* as a class express the same opinion in different contexts. It is in the quantitative sense that Imam Abū Ḥanīfah denies increase or decrease in faith. Since he does not believe works to be a part of faith, he holds that the quantity of works cannot affect the quantity of faith; and this is the correct position. There is a *ḥadīth* that says, "Abū Bakr enjoys precedence over you people, not because he prays much and fasts much, but because of that which is in his heart."

Thus the Imam does not deny that faith can increase or decrease qualitatively, but that it can increase or decrease quantitatively, and this is a corollary of his assertion that works are not part of faith.

The Imam also maintains that faith does not vary in content and that in respect of beliefs all Muslims are equal, for the articles of faith are the same for all of them. The Companions and common Muslims alike believe in divine unity and prophethood If there is any difference between them, it is in the intensity of their belief. The Imam described this, while replying to 'Uthmān al-Battī, in these words: "The dwellers of heaven and earth have the same religion." In support of this he cited the Qur'anic verse "We have prescribed for you the same religion as Nūḥ was charged with."

The Imam's opponents have vehemently accused him of maintaining that his faith was equal to that of Abū Bakr al-Ṣiddīq. It has not been established authoritatively that he ever made such a claim, but even if he did, it does not matter very much. Who can deny the kind of equality that he claimed? What is surprising, indeed, is that the critics failed to understand a simple thing like this. Al-Khaṭīb al-Baghdādī has written many pages to repudiate the claim, without appreciating the real significance of it. He has taken umbrage to the mere fact of the Imam's claiming equality for common Muslims with the Companions, having failed to understand that, although the latter were on the whole infinitely superior to the former, there are many points of equality between the two.

Although on all such questions Imam Abū Ḥanīfah had personal opinions of his own, he never branded the opposite opinions as heresies or deviations. Instances of such liberality are rare in Islam after the first century. Nothing has done more harm to Islam than the mutual denunciations of holders of differing opinions. Differences of opinion had, it is true, cropped up as early as in the time of the Companions. On the question of the Prophet's Ascension, for example, while 'Abdullāh b. 'Abbās and many other Companions believed that the Prophet (ṣ) had actually seen Allah, 'Ā'ishah vehemently opposed this. She also refused to believe that the dead had heard the Prophet (ṣ) speak, just as Amir Mu'āwiyah denied the Prophet's bodily journey to Heaven.

But such differences of opinion in those days did not lead the holders of the opinions to denounce each other as infidels and heretics. A man said to 'Abdullāh b. 'Umar, "There are some people who misinterpret the Qur'an and call us infidels. Are they or are they not themselves infidels?" "Nobody can be called an infidel," replied 'Abdullāh, "until he says that there are two Gods."[2] After the Companions such differences gained in intensity and gave rise to sharply divided factions. There are many questions of belief and law on which no decisive Qur'anic pronouncement is available, such pronouncements as exist being mutually contradictory, which necessitated deduction and the reconciliation of contradictions. This occasioned the exercise of individual judgement, which in turn gave rise to a variety of opinions. Undoubtedly some of these opinions were wrong, but it did not follow from this that they were heresies.

The pity of it was that minds enthused by religious fervour and closed by self-righteousness were unable to tolerate differences of opinion and pitched themselves vehemently against all disagreement. The result was that verdicts of unbelief were bandied about, the care exercised in passing them being in inverse proportion to the religious zeal of those who passed them. Things gradually reached such a pass that every sect took recourse to invented traditions for proving the charge of aberration and deviation against other sects. One of the traditions invented was a prophetic one to the effect that there would arise seventy-three sects in the Muslim *ummah*, of which only one would be destined for Paradise. In order to fulfil the prophecy seventy-three names of sects were fashioned, along with separate traditions in respect of each of them, for example "The Qadariyyah are the Magians of this *Ummah*."

This intolerant sectarianism rent asunder the fabric of Muslim society, deforming all its features—religion, morals, government, culture, civilisation. In the midst of this all-pervading destruction, there was only one constructive voice, that of Abū Ḥanīfah, declaring aloud, "Of the people of the *qiblah*, there is none whom we consider an infidel." Not much attention was paid to this declaration at the time, but with the passage of time it found increasing credence until it became one of the valuable principles of the science of *kalām*, although it is to be regretted that it was not acted on very much, so that the din of verdicts of heresy never entirely died down.

The Imam had formed this opinion after much reflection, research and practical experience. He was a contemporary of many famous founders of religious schools and had met almost all of them. The Khārijites had their headquarters in Baṣrah, which was quite close to the Imam's hometown. Wāṣil b. 'Aṭā' and 'Amr b. 'Ubayd, founders and propagators of the Mu'tazilah, were natives of Baṣrah. Then there was Jahm b. Ṣafwān, after whom the Jahmiyyah sect is known. The Imam had met them and acquainted himself with their ideas. Of the sayings attributed to these sects, some were mere fabrications, some had been misinterpreted and some were absurd without being heretical. It was because of this that the Imam declared all adherents of the *qiblah* to be believers. He perceived that all the statements which had aroused a furore and which had become the touchstone of faith were mere verbal quibbles and technical jargon.

The most vexed question was that of the eternity of the Qur'an, to which people were attaching almost as much importance as they were attaching to the declaration of divine unity. Many great religious scholars have said that there were two men who saved Islam during extremely critical times, namely, Abū Bakr al-Ṣiddīq, who exterminated the apostates of Arabia after the Prophet's death, and Aḥmad b. Ḥanbal, who during the reign of Ma'mūn al-Rashīd persisted in denying the createdness of the Qur'an. In fact, Aḥmad b. Ḥanbal takes precedence because Abū Bakr had the Companions to support him, while Ḥanbal was alone.

When somebody is described as reliable and authoritative in books of biography, the greatest proof adduced in support of this is that he regarded calling the Qur'an created as unbelief, although this is merely a point of verbal debate. Those who regarded the Qur'an as created and non-eternal had in mind its words and their pronunciation, both of which were articulated by the Prophet (ṣ) and represent the Qur'an to the common people. Those who regarded it as eternal understood it to be the *kalām* (speech) of Allah in the sense in which speaking is one of His attributes. There are many statements on this question ascribed to Abū Ḥanīfah, all of them based on this distinction. For example, answering a question put by a man, he said that the Qur'an was non-eternal because it was not Allah, and nothing but Allah is eternal.[3]

To sum up, statements of this kind, not being based on the text of the Qur'an, cannot be a criterion of faith or lack of faith. The wisdom of Abū Ḥanīfah consists in the fact that he prevented the sphere of Islam, whose breadth was described in the words "Whoever utters the words 'There is no god but Allah' enters Heaven," from being narrowed down. It is a pity that his opinion was not given due weight. Had it received the consideration it deserved, we should not have heard al-Ghazālī, Muḥyī al-Dīn b. 'Arabī, 'Abd al-Qādir al-Jīlānī, Ibn Taymiyyah and Abū Ṭālib al-Makkī described as unbelievers by the *fuqahā'*.

Notes

1. Al-Ḥāfiẓ Ibn Ḥajar narrates this in detail in his *Fatḥ al-Bārī*.
2. Imam Muḥammad, *al-Āthār*, p, 65.
3. Abū Hilāl al-'Askarī, *Kitāb al-Awā'il*.

10

Tradition and principles of tradition

It is wrong to say, as some people have, that Abū Ḥanīfah was not well versed in Ḥadīth. The fact nevertheless remains that he is not commonly known as a *muḥaddith.* There were hundreds of men in the early generations who distinguished themselves in both original thinking and traditional learning, but whose fame has survived only in their main field of achievement. That Abū Ḥanīfah enjoys no eminence in Ḥadīth is quite understandable: he has no work on that subject to his credit. What is surprising is that even Mālik and al-Shāfiʿī are not known as *muḥaddithīn* and that their works on Ḥadīth have not gained anything like the popularity enjoyed by the six *Ṣaḥīḥs.*

Aḥmad b. Ḥanbal is better known in Ḥadīth than these three, but is less known than them in the sphere of reasoning and personal judgement. Al-Ṭabarī, himself both a *muḥaddith* and a *mujtahid*, has not included Aḥmad b. Ḥanbal's name in his list of *mujtahids.*[1] Qāḍī ʿAbd al-Barr in his *Kitāb al-Intiqā' fī Faḍā'il al-Thalāthah al-A'immah al-Fuqahā'*, which is a biographical dictionary of *mujtahids*, contents himself with mentioning Abū Ḥanīfah, Mālik and al-Shāfiʿī. Al-Rāzī writes in the *Manāqib al-Shāfiʿī*, "After Imam al-Shāfiʿī no *mujtahid* was at all born." Although many scholars are agreed that

Aḥmad b. Ḥanbal was perfect in *ijithād*, there is no consensus on this.

The fact of the matter is that *mujtahid* and *muḥaddith* are two altogether different categories. A *muḥaddith* scrutinises all kinds of narrations—sermons, stories, sayings about excellences, biographical information. A *mujtahid*, on the other hand, concerns himself mainly with those traditions from which a rule of law can be deduced. For this reason, *mujtahids* cite far fewer traditions than *muḥaddithīn*. *Al-Muwaṭṭa'*, in which all the traditions quoted by Mālik have been collected, hardly contains a thousand traditions, which include also the sayings of the Companions and their Successors.

Al-Shāfi'ī several times admitted to Aḥmad b. Ḥanbal that *muḥaddithīn* (among whom he evidently included the latter) were better acquainted with traditions than legal theorists like him. This admission, it should be noted, was made by one about whom Qāḍī Yaḥyā b. Aktham, the teacher of al-Tirmidhī, used to say regretfully that if he had paid full attention to Ḥadīth, he would have made it possible for all other sources of traditions to be dispensed with.[2] Al-Ḥāfiẓ Ibn Ḥajar in his *Tawālī al-Ta'sīs*, which is a short but useful memoir on al-Shāfi'ī, concludes his discussion of al-Shāfi'ī's masters with the following words: "He did not meet many *shuyūkh* as is the wont of most Ḥadīth scholars, as he was preoccupied with *fiqh*."

The same thing accounted for the small number of Abū Ḥanīfah's *shuyūkh*. Unfortunately, some people have stretched this to mean that the Imam is poor in his citation of traditions. This, however, is not a new idea: it was entertained in the past by some people and still persists. To be just to those who entertain it, it must be admitted that the commonly known facts about the Imam provide, on a superficial view, a basis for it. Not only has he left no work on Ḥadīth, but even in the *Ṣaḥīḥs* there is no mention of him except for a tradition or two attributed to him. Especially important is the fact that he is generally known as a thinker, which has created the impression that he did not have much to-do with Ḥadīth.

It must be admitted that Abū Ḥanīfah's knowledge of military campaigns, stories of notables and biography was limited, but that is equally true of Mālik and al-Shāfiʿī. However, the denial of the Imam's profound learning and penetration so far as religious commandments and beliefs are concerned is nothing but purblindness. That there is no collection of his writings on Ḥadīth and of the traditions narrated by him does not prove that his knowledge of Ḥadīth was poor.

There was no Companion who spent more time with the Prophet (ṣ), whether in company or in privacy, than Abū Bakr al-Ṣiddīq: nobody could have greater knowledge than he did of the Prophet's sayings and doings. And yet the number of authentic traditions recorded on his authority in all the books of Ḥadīth taken together does not exceed seventeen.[3] Can anyone assert that he had only this small number of traditions to relate? Next to Abū Bakr al-Ṣiddīq ranks ʿUmar al-Fārūq. To him are ascribed only fifty traditions, of which some are not fully authenticated. Very much the same is the case with ʿUthmān and ʿAlī. As against these figures, Abū Hurayrah is credited with 5,346 traditions, Anas with 2,286, ʿAbdullāh b. ʿAbbās with 2,660, Jābir with 2,540 and ʿAbdullāh b. ʿUmar, who was only a youth during the Prophet's lifetime, with 2,630. If the number of traditions were the only criterion, we should have to admit in respect of the first four caliphs that they either had extremely weak memories or were not interested in the Prophet's sayings and doings.

If the authors of the six *Ṣaḥīḥs* have cited no more than a few traditions from Abū Ḥanīfah, the other imams of *fiqh* have suffered the same, if not a worse, fate at their hands. There is, for example, not a single tradition cited in the *Ṣaḥīḥs* from al-Shāfi'ī, whom great traditionists like Aḥmad b. Ḥanbal, Isḥāq b. Rāhwayh, Abū Thawr, Ḥumaydī, Abū Zar'ah, al-Rāzī and Abū Ḥātim acknowledge as a rich repository of traditions. In fact, al-Bukhārī and Muslim have not cited any tradition from al-Shāfi'ī even in their other works. Al-Rāzī has tried to explain away this indifference on the part of al-Bukhārī and Muslim, but has not been able to advance a single convincing reason. Leave alone the *Ṣaḥīḥs* of al-Bukhārī and Muslim, al-Tirmidhī, Abū Dāwūd, Ibn Mājah and al-Nasā'ī have cited very few traditions in the chain of transmission which al-Shāfi'ī's name occurs.

The truth is that the criterion fixed by the *muḥaddithīn* for judging reliability and correctness of deduction ruled out thinkers and men of vision. Al-Qasṭalānī, in his commentary on al-Bukhārī's *Ṣaḥīḥ*, quotes al-Bukhārī as saying that he had never recorded a tradition narrated by a man who did not declare that faith consisted of both profession and action.[4] If the statement was correctly reported, what chance did Abū Ḥanīfah have of being admitted to the sanctum of the traditionists?

Al-Bukhārī mentions al-Shāfi'ī in his *Ta'rīkh al-Kabīr*, but with an indifference which al-Rāzī, curiously enough, regards as something to be thankful for, because it was better than including him among weak transmitters of traditions. Here is what al-Rāzī writes while describing al-Shāfi'ī's good qualities, "Imam al-Bukhārī mentions Imam al-Shāfi'ī in *Ta'rīkh al-*

Kabīr, and writes in one of the chapters that Muḥammad b. Idrīs b. ʻAbdullāh Muḥammad al-Shāfiʻī al-Qurashī died in 204 H. But he does not mention him in the chapter on *ḍuʻafā'* (weak transmitters), although he knew that al-Shāfiʻī had narrated many traditions. If he had been a weak transmitter, al-Bukhārī would have included him in the chapter on weak transmitters."

Somebody asked Aḥmad b. Ḥanbal his opinion of al-Awzāʻī, who was a recognised *mujtahid* and enjoyed the same esteem in Syria as Mālik and al-Shāfiʻī enjoyed in Arabia and Iraq. He replied, "Weak in tradition and weak in judgement."[5]

The qualities that *mujtahids* may pride themselves on are incisiveness of vision, power of inference, the capacity to identify questions and find answers to them and skill in deriving commandments. But these are defects in the eyes of a group of traditionists. Abū Jaʻfar Muḥammad b. Jarīr al-Ṭabarī writes in his memoir of Abū Yūsuf, "A group of traditionists have refrained from making use of traditions quoted by him for the reason that he was swayed by his personal opinions and used to draw secondary commandments from commandments already derived. Besides, he was a courtier of the caliph and a *qāḍī*."[6] If deriving commandments is an offence, then Abū Ḥanīfah was undoubtedly a worse offender than Abū Yūsuf.

It is worth considering why Abū Ḥanīfah and his followers were called *ahl al-ra'y* (those who relied on opinion). In this matter many people have accepted a popular notion without due inquiry. Let us, to begin with, try to find out how the title came to be invented and to what class of people it was originally applied. As far as I have been able to ascertain, the first man to be given the title was Rabīʻah al-Ra'y, who was a teacher of Mālik and a *shaykh* of Ḥadīth. *Ra'y* has become a part of his name and is used as such in books of history and dictionaries of names. He was a famous *muḥaddith* and *faqīh*, who had met many Companions. Al-Dhahabī writes thus about him in the *Mīzān al-I'tidāl*: "The authors of all the books (i.e. the six *Ṣaḥīḥs*) have benefited from his reasoning." 'Abd al-'Azīz al-Mājishūn writes, "I have met no man who had more traditions by heart than Rabī'ah."

At that period and afterwards there were many people who were known as *ahl al-ra'y*. The traditionist Ibn Qutaybah has in his *Kitāb al-Ma'ārif* a chapter on *ahl al-ra'y*, and under the chapter heading gives the names of Ibn Abī Laylā, Abū Ḥanīfah, Rabī'ah al-Ra'y, Zufar, al-Awzā'ī, Sufyān al-Thawrī, Mālik b. Anas, Abū Yūsuf, and Muhammad b. al-Ḥasan. As Ibn Qutaybah died in 276 H, it appears from this that at least until the third century of the Hijrah these men were known as *ahl al-ra'y*. With the exception of Zufar they are all traditionists, and especially Mālik, Sufyān al-Thawrī and al-Awzā'ī are too famous as such to need any commendation.

What really happened was that people engaged in teaching Ḥadīth became divided into two groups. One group consisted of those who concerned themselves with collecting traditions and narrations. These dealt with traditions simply as narrations, so much so that they did not even distinguish between abrogating and abrogated traditions. In the second group were men who examined traditions with a view to deducing from them commandments and decisions. When they could not find a clear text, they took recourse to reasoning by analogy. Although the two groups partially combined the two types of approach, they were distinguished by the one which was the more pronounced in their work. Thus, the first group came to be known as *ahl al-riwāyah* or *ahl al-ḥadīth*, and the second as *ahl al-ra'y*.

Why Mālik, Sufyān al-Thawrī and al-Awzā'ī were called *ahl al-ra'y* was because, side by side with being traditionists, they were original thinkers and founders of schools of law. But since they ranked *inter se* at different levels in the two kinds of pursuit, they were sometimes distinguished by one being called *ahl al-ra'y* and another *ahl al-ḥadīth*, which really meant more of the one or the other in comparison with each other. For example, the title *mujtahid* or *ahl al-ra'y* suited Abū Ḥanīfah more than it did Mālik. Aḥmad b. Ḥanbal was once asked by al-Naḍar b. Yaḥyā what he had against Abū Ḥanīfah. He replied, "*Ra'y.*" "Does not Imam Mālik act on opinion?" asked Nadar. "Yes, he does," replied Aḥmad b. Ḥanbal, "but Abū Ḥanīfah relies more on opinion." "Then," observed Nadar, "both of them should be blamed according to the degree of their reliance on opinion." Aḥmad b. Ḥanbal had no answer to this and remained silent.[7]

Before Abū Ḥanīfah *fiqh* was not a systematised discipline. When he started systematising it, he came up against a number of questions on which there was no authentic tradition, not even a pronouncement by a Companion. He, therefore, had to make use of reasoning by analogy. Not that this had not been done before: even some of the Companions had given rulings by analogy, which we shall discuss in detail later on. But in their time, the life of the community had not become complex enough for situations to arise which needed judgement by analogy. In his effort to reduce *fiqh* to a system Abū Ḥanīfah found it necessary to devise rules for analogy along with using it. This underlined in the public mind his association with personal opinion and analogy, which accounts for the fact that in history books the words "imam of *ahl al-ra'y*" are generally found written along with his name.

There was another reason for the Imam's acquiring fame as an *ahl al-ra'y*. The common run of traditionists made no use of *dirāyah* (critical scrutiny) in dealing with traditions and narrations. Abū Ḥanīfah was the first to do so, and he framed guiding principles and rules for it. He rejected a large number of traditions for the reason that they did not come up to his critical standards. Since *dirāyah* and *ra'y* are very close to each other in meaning, almost synonyms, the common people were unable to distinguish between them. This strengthened the Imam's reputation as one who relied on personal opinion.

After this preliminary discussion let us take up the fundamental question of Abū Ḥanīfah's standing in Ḥadīth. To this question are relevant those facts of his scholarly career which are established by authentic accounts. In the first part of this book I have narrated the history of the Imam's study of Ḥadīth on the authority of certain books which form the groundwork of the art of biography. Recalling that history, let us consider what can be the standing in Ḥadīth of a man who started studying it at the age of twenty, when he had attained full maturity of understanding, and pursued it for a number of years; who learnt traditions from eminent masters of the subject at Kūfah; who for years attended Ḥadīth classes in Makkah; who was awarded a certificate of high proficiency by the *shaykhs* of Madīnah; and whose teachers were men like 'Aṭā' b. Abī Rabāḥ, Nāfi' b. 'Umar, 'Umar b. Dīnār, Muḥārib b. Dithār, al-A'mash al-Kūfī, Imam al-Bāqir, 'Alqamah b. Murthad, Makḥūl al-Shāmī, al-Awzā'ī, Muḥammad b. Muslim al-Zuhrī, Abū Isḥāq al-Sabī'ī, Sulaymān b. Yasār, 'Abd al-Raḥmān b. Hurmuz al-A'raj, Manṣūr b. al-Mu'tamir and Hishām b. 'Urwah—all of them pillars of Ḥadīth, whose narrations have enriched the *Ṣaḥīḥs* of al-Bukhārī and Muslim.

Let us next consider the Imam's disciples[8] Yaḥyā b. Sa'īd al-Qaṭṭān, an imam of the arts of rebuttal and appraisal; 'Abd al-Razzāq b. Hammām, on whose *al-Jāmi' al-Kabīr* al-Bukhārī has largely drawn; Yazīd b. Hārūn, who was one of Aḥmad b. Ḥanbal's teachers, Wakī' b. al-Jarrāḥ, whom Aḥmad b. Ḥanbal used to describe as one whose equal he had not met in *isnād* and *riwāyah*; 'Abdullāh b. al-Mubārak, who has been acknowledged as the *Amīr al-Mu'minīn* of Ḥadīth; and Yaḥyā b. Zakariyyā' b. Abī Zā'idah, whom 'Alī b. al-Madanī (al-Bukhārī's teacher) used to call the culminating point of learning. These men were not merely nominally the Imam's disciples, but had sat at his feet for years and were proud of the fact. 'Abdullāh b. al-Mubārak used to say that if Allah had not helped him through Abū Ḥanīfah and Sufyān al-Thawrī, he would have been just an ordinary man.[9] Wakī' and Yaḥyā b. Abī Zā'idah had associated for such a long time with the Imam that they were commonly known as friends or companions of Abū Ḥanīfah. Is it imaginable that men of such rank who were themselves acknowledged masters of Ḥadīth and *riwāyah* would bow to an ordinary man?

Apart from these things, the fact of Abū Ḥanīfah's being one of the supreme *mujtahids* is one which has never been denied during the last twelve centuries except by two or three persons. The word *mujtahid* has been defined as follows by scholars of Ḥadīth like al-Baghawī, al-Rāfi'ī and al-Nawawī: "A *mujtahid* is one well versed in the Qur'an, Ḥadīth, the early schools of law, lexicology and analogical reasoning, that is to say, one who knows all or practically all Qur'anic passages, established traditions from the Prophet (ṣ) and sayings of the early generations pertaining to legal problems, has the necessary lexical learning and is acquainted with all the methods of analogical reasoning. If a man is deficient in any of these things, he cannot be called a *mujtahid* and should conform to one or other of the recognised schools of law."[10]

On the basis of this definition, Ibn Khaldūn, discussing *mujtahids* in the section on Ḥadīth writes, "Some unjust detractors say that some of these *mujtahids* were not well up in Ḥadīth and that this is why narrations on their authority are few and far between. But this is an erroneous idea, which cannot, in any case, be true of the great imams. Sharīʿah is derived from the Qur'an and Ḥadīth and, therefore, a person poor in Ḥadīth ought to try to make up the deficiency so that he can deduce rules of religion from correct principles." Ibn Khaldūn writes further, "That Imam Abū Ḥanīfah was one of the great *mujtahids* in the discipline of Ḥadīth is proved by the fact that his school of law enjoys credit among *muḥaddithīn* and is discussed by them, whether by way of acceptance or by way of rejection."[11] Ibn Khaldūn has also assigned reasons for the fact that the number of traditions cited on the Imam's authority is small. I propose to deal with this subject at some length.

Many of the *muḥaddithīn* have acknowledged Abū Ḥanīfah's high standing in Ḥadīth. al-Dhahabī, the most outstanding figure among the traditionists of later periods wrote a book on the *ḥuffāẓ* of Ḥadīth (those who had committed traditions to memory). He explains in the preface that the book consists of biographical accounts of the men who were repositories of Prophetic traditions and whose personal judgement is relied on in confirming, rejecting, correcting and pruning traditions. In the book al-Dhahabī has not included a single man who was not a great expert of Ḥadīth. Thus, speaking incidentally of Khārijah b. Zayd b. Thābit, he writes, "I have not mentioned him among those who had traditions by heart, because there are very few traditions reported to have been narrated by him." But he writes a note on Abū Ḥanīfah and includes him among the *ḥuffāẓ* of Ḥadīth. What could be a greater acknowledgment of the Imam's status as a *muḥaddith*?

Abū al-Maḥāsin al-Dimashqī al-Shāfi'ī has entitled one of the chapters of his *'Uqūd al-Jumān* as follows: "Chapter Twenty-three, showing that he (Abū Ḥanīfah) was rich in traditions and a leader of *ḥuffāẓ*." Abū Yūsuf, whom Yaḥyā b. Ma'īn called a master of Ḥadīth and whom al-Dhahabī lists among his *ḥuffāẓ*, writes, "We used to discuss legal questions with Imam Abū Ḥanīfah ... After he had expressed a definite opinion, I would go from his class to the *muḥaddithīn* of Kūfah and learn from them traditions pertaining to the question at issue on the day. Then I would go back to the Imam and repeat the traditions to him. He used to accept some of them, while about the others he used to say that they were not authentic. If I asked him how he could say that, he would reply, 'I know all that is known in Kūfah.'"[12]

The testimony given above is enough to prove Abū Ḥanīfah's high standing in Ḥadīth. The truth, however, is that the Imam is not what he is because of that. There were many other men who knew traditions by heart. If he had a few hundred teachers in Ḥadīth, there were some imams of earlier times who had had thousands. If he had attended the centres of Ḥadīth learning in the holy cities, there were many others who had had the same advantage. What distinguished Abū Ḥanīfah among his contemporaries was something else, something of greater importance. That something was the critical appraisal of traditions and the grading of them as authorities for rules of law. The discipline of Ḥadīth made much progress after Abū Ḥanīfah: traditions existing pell-mell were collected, the *Ṣaḥīḥs* were compiled, and principles of Ḥadīth were formulated, which made of it a scientific discipline and on which hundreds of valuable books were written. With the development of the human mind and as an outcome of experience many refinements have since been made. But the examination, appraisal and grading of traditions have not moved a step beyond the point to which Abū Ḥanīfah advanced them,

To understand the full significance of this achievement, it is necessary to examine it in its historical perspective, that is to say, against the background of the beginnings and development of Ḥadīth, and especially how the system of narrations came into being and what changes it underwent from period to period.

The system of transmission and narration started during the Prophet's lifetime in a simple and natural manner. The first thirteen years of the Prophet's mission were a time of troubles, during which the Companions were too busy defending their lives to engage in transmitting and narrating traditions. For that reason there were very few injunctions: nothing was prescribed as a duty except prayer, for more duties would have constituted an insupportable burden. Even the prayers prescribed were small in number and short, namely, the afternoon, evening and night prayers, each consisting of only two *rak'ahs.* The Friday prayer and the two 'Īd prayers were not prescribed at all. Fasting was enjoined in 2 H, that is, in the thirteenth year of the prophetic mission. As to when *zakāh* was laid down as obligatory, there is a difference of opinion. One of the opinions, that of Ibn al-Athīr, is that it happened in 9 H. Hajj was prescribed in the same year. In short, for a number of years, prayer remained the only obligatory duty; there were neither any directions about other duties nor any traditions about such directions.

The Companions did not evince much curiosity about commandments and legal problems. The Qur'an itself says, "Do not inquire about things, which, if revealed, would not please you." 'Abdullāh b. 'Abbās used to say, "I have not seen a group of men better than the Companions. During the whole prophetic mission, they put questions only about thirteen points, which have all been mentioned in the Qur'an."[13] Similar statements are reported to have been made by certain other Companions.

Even in regard to problems that actually arose, narration was not common. The Companions would themselves pose them to the Prophet (ṣ), so that there was no need for intermediaries to narrate the Prophet's pronouncements. The recording of traditions was not permitted. There is a tradition in Muslim's *Ṣaḥīḥ* which says, "Do not record anything on my authority except what is in the Qur'an, and if anyone records anything on my authority that is outside the Qur'an, it should be erased."

After the Prophet's death the first caliph, Abū Bakr, had, to begin with, to deal with a general revolt of the Arabs and after that became busy with expeditions against the Roman and Persian Empires, with the result that during his brief reign much could not be done about the propagation of traditions. 'Umar, although his seven years' reign was a period of internal peace and tranquillity, expressly discouraged the multiplication of traditions.

Al-Dhahabī writes in the *Ṭabaqāt al-Ḥuffāẓ* that 'Umar, from a fear that narrators might ascribe incorrect traditions to the Prophet (ṣ), always used to tell them to narrate as few traditions as possible.[14] While sending a delegation of Anṣār to Kūfah, he instructed them as follows: "In Kūfah you will meet a group of people who recite the Qur'an in a voice full of emotion. On hearing of your arrival they will come to you, eager to listen to traditions of the Prophet (ṣ) from you. Be careful not to narrate to them too many traditions."[15]

Similarly, when sending a number of Companions to Iraq, 'Umar went part of the way with them to see them off. "Do you know," he asked them, "why I am accompanying you part of the way?" "In order to honour us," they replied. "That is so," said 'Umar, "but there is also another reason. I want to tell you that the people of the country to which you are going are fond of reading the Qur'an. Try not to entangle them in traditions, but narrate very few traditions from the Prophet (ṣ)." When the Companions arrived at Qurẓah, the inhabitants came to see them and requested them to narrate traditions; but they declined to do so, excusing themselves by saying that they had been forbidden by the caliph.[16] Abū Hurayrah, asked by Abū Salamah whether he used to narrate traditions as freely in 'Umar's time as he was then doing, replied, "No, for if I had tried, 'Umar would have had me whipped."[17]

During the twenty-one years of the caliphates of 'Uthmān and 'Alī, the narration of traditions gained popularity. The Companions had scattered all over the Islamic world, the life of the community was becoming more and more complex and new problems were arising. These factors combined to give free rein to the narration of traditions. The rebellion that ended the life of 'Uthmān divided the community into warring camps, whose hostilities plagued the reign of 'Alī from the very outset. Among the weapons employed in the fratricidal strife were spurious traditions, thousands of which were invented, to be multiplied as time went by.

In the introduction to al-Bukhārī's *Ṣaḥīḥ*, the story is told of what 'Abdullāh b. 'Abbās said to Bashīr al-'Adawī, who had come to relate a tradition to him. Finding that 'Abdullāh was not listening to him attentively, Bashīr said, "Ibn 'Abbās, I am relating a tradition from the Messenger of Allah, but you are not paying any attention to me." "There was a time," replied 'Abdullāh, "when as soon as I heard the words 'Said the Messenger of Allah' uttered by someone, I looked up and gave ear to him. But since people have given up distinguishing between good and bad, I listen only to those traditions of which I have personal knowledge."

Leave alone oral traditions, forgery started in written ones too. Muslim relates how 'Abdullāh b. 'Abbās, while copying out a decision of 'Alī, left out several passages here and there, exclaiming, "By Allah, 'Alī can never have given such a decision."[17] On another occasion, 'Abdullāh b. 'Abbās, shown a piece of writing attributed to 'Alī, deleted the larger part of it.

One of the factors that encouraged the fabrication of traditions was that no system had as yet been devised of narration along with a chain of authorities. Anybody could say, "Said the Messenger of Allah," and merely by making that declaration become exempt from the necessity to prove his authorities. Al-Tirmidhī, in *Kitāb al-'Ilal*, quotes Imam Ibn Sīrīn as saying, "In the early days people did not ask for authorities. It was only when discord arose that this began to be done so that traditions from the orthodox might be accepted and those from the heterodox rejected." But unreliable traditions were not confined to the heterodox and innovators. The result was that the precaution proved ineffectual, and wrong traditions went on being propagated.

With the advent of the Umayyads the narration of traditions received a new fillip. As the number of Companions dwindled, their value in the public eye increased. Much progress had been made in culture, and the community had been greatly enlarged by the addition of new peoples converted to Islam. Apart from the enthusiasm natural to them as neophytes, there was no better method for these peoples of gaining influence with the conquerors than to distinguish themselves in religious learning. Thus motivated, they soon excelled the Arabs themselves as scholars of Islam. In every nook and corner of the Islamic dominions, schools of Ḥadīth and *riwāyah* were opened, so that their number ran into thousands.

But the increase in the propagation of traditions brought with it a gradual decline in the standard of their correctness and reliability. So large was the circle of narrators that it included people with different habits, different persuasions and different races. Innovators found entry into it and freely spread their heretical ideas. The worst thing of all was that, although more than a century had passed since traditions had begun to be narrated, no system of recording them had been devised.

These factors led to a piling up of fabricated and wrong traditions to such an extent that when al-Bukhārī at a later period tried to isolate authentic traditions, he selected only 7,397 out of hundreds of thousands that were current: this number is further reduced to 2,761 after eliminating repetitions.

Hundreds of thousands of traditions were deliberately invented. According to Ḥammād b. Zayd, the Zanādiqah alone fabricated fourteen thousand.[18] ʻAbd al-Karīm al-Waḍḍāʻ (= fabricator) himself admitted that he had four thousand to his credit.[19] There were quite a few pious worthies who, with good intentions, invented traditions to serve as guides to moral excellences. Zayn al-Dīn al-ʻIrāqī rightly complains, "These traditions did a lot of harm because they were accepted and became current owing to the piety and reputed trustworthiness of their authors."

Next to wilful invention were things like misinterpretation, misunderstanding and careless reporting, which resulted in thousands of imaginary sayings being involuntarily attributed to the Prophet (ṣ). It was the custom of some traditionists to give an explanation of traditions along with narrating them. As they did not clearly mark off the explanatory additions, the listeners were often misled into thinking that they were part of a *ḥadīth marfū‘* (i.e. a tradition containing a statement about the Prophet (ṣ)). It is surprising that many leading imams of Ḥadīth were given to this slipshod practice. About al-Zuhrī, one of Mālik's masters and an eminent traditionist, al-Sakhāwī writes, "Similarly, he added explanations of his own to traditions, but left out the words indicating that they were explanations." The same was the case with Wakī‘. He sometimes introduced his explanations with the word *ya‘nī* (that is to say), but more often did not do so, thus leaving his listeners in doubt. Numerous other examples of this are mentioned in biographical annals and works on the principles of tradition.

Another great source of confusion was the habit, indulged in by many leading traditionists, of concealing defects which tended to throw into doubt the continuity of the chain of transmission. This does not exhaust the list of malpractices and slovenly methods to which Ḥadīth was subjected: these can be found described in detail in works on Ḥadīth.

To sum up, the collection of narrations that passed for traditions in Abū Ḥanīfah's time contained for the most part invented, erroneous, weak and ambiguous narrations. Al-Bukhārī and Muslim were not yet there to select sound traditions from this tangled mass. Abū Ḥanīfah's preoccupation with *fiqh* did not permit him to undertake this work, but he did the next best thing, which was to devise a system of criticising narrations and lay down rules and regulations for it. His standard of criticism has been considered extremely rigorous, so that the *muḥaddithīn* have given him the title *mushaddid fī al-riwāyah* (stringent in narration), and this is one of the reasons, and perhaps the main reason, why of all traditionists he has narrated the smallest number of traditions. Ibn Khaldūn writes, "Why Abū Ḥanīfah has so few traditions is because he imposed strict conditions on narration and transmission."

The first general idea that the Imam formed about Ḥadīth was that there were very few traditions that were sound or sufficiently well authenticated. This radical idea, as was only to be expected, was vehemently opposed, but he felt compelled to stick to it—and he was fully within his rights in doing so. He had met most of the masters of Ḥadīth in his time and profited from what they had to give him, had for years attended the important schools of Ḥadīth in the holy cities and, finally had for a long time studied the personal characteristics, habits and methods of the narrators at Kūfah, Baṣrah and the holy cities. These things together invested him with the competence to make a personal judgement in the matter.

A cautious attitude to traditions was in a way inherited by Abū Ḥanīfah, through his masters in Ḥadīth and *fiqh* from ʿAbdullāh b. Masʿūd, on whose narrations and derivations the Ḥanafī school of law is by and large founded. For all his greatness as a *muḥaddith*, ʿAbdullāh b. Masʿūd has to his credit only a small number of narrations, the reason for which is that he had a very strict standard of acceptance. Al-Dhahabī writes of him, "He was selective and stringent in narration and narrated only (authentic) traditions." This was also characteristic of Ibrāhīm al-Nakhaʿī, who was ʿAbdullāh b. Masʿūd's pupil and Abū Ḥanīfah's teacher, both at one remove, which was why he was called *Ṣayrafī al-Ḥadīth*. Despite the fact that he had attended various educational institutions, Abū Ḥanīfah's store of knowledge and way of thinking were essentially derived from this line of teachers; and it was, similarly, to its influence that he owed the idea of subjecting traditions to scrutiny, which his personal experience and peculiar, intellectual temperament strengthened.

The idea, although it failed to meet with popular acceptance, did not fail to exert its influence in determining the future development of Ḥadīth. Its influence is clearly visible in the principles of personal judgement laid down by Mālik and al-Shāfi'ī, who came into the field later than Abū Ḥanīfah. The conditions prescribed by Mālik for narrations closely resemble Abū Ḥanīfah's, which is why they are often spoken of together as stringent narrators (*mushaddid fī al-riwāyah*). Ibn al-Ṣalāḥ writes in *Muqaddamah*, "According to the *mushaddidīn*, only those narrations are admissible in argument which the narrators have themselves preserved in their memories; and this is quoted from Mālik and Abū Ḥanīfah." We have it on the authority of many *muḥaddithīn* that the first version of Mālik's *Muwaṭṭa'* contained 10,000 traditions, but that on further research he reduced their number to 600 or 700. Al-Shafi'ī, for his part, has expressed views similar to those of Abū Ḥanīfah.

Al-Bayhaqī quotes the reply given by al Shāfi'ī to Haram al-Qurashī's request to dictate traditions proved to go back to the Prophet (ṣ). "In the opinion of knowledgeable people," said al-Shāfi'ī, "there are very few authentic traditions. The traditions quoted by Abū Bakr al-Ṣiddīq from the Prophet (ṣ) do not exceed seventeen in number, while those quoted by 'Umar b. al-Khaṭṭāb, despite the fact that he survived the Prophet (ṣ) by many years, have not been established to be even fifty. Similar is the case with ʿUthmān. As regards ʿAlī, although he used to induce people to learn traditions, there are very few traditions narrated by him. That was because he was not satisfied about the authenticity of any more than those. Most of the traditions attributed to him pertain to the caliphates of ʿUmar and ʿUthmān. From the other Companions a large number of traditions have been narrated, but knowledgeable people do not regard them as established on sound authority."[20]

It should not be concluded from these facts that Abū Ḥanīfah rejected traditions altogether, as did the Muʿtazilah, or that he accepted only ten to twenty all told. His disciples have quoted hundreds of traditions from him. In Muḥammad's *al-Muwaṭṭa'*, *Kitāb al-Āthār* and *Kitāb al-Ḥujaj*, which are in common use as collections of traditions, there are scores of traditions quoted from the Imam. However, the traditions quoted by him as acceptable are smaller in number than those quoted by other *muḥaddithīn* as such, which is explained by his rigorous standards. Some of the conditions he enforced were the same as are accepted by the generality of *muḥaddithīn*, while others were exclusive to him or were shared with him only by Mālik and a few other *mujtahids*.

One rule belonging to the second of the above categories is that only a tradition heard by the narrator with his own ears and fully remembered by him up to the time of narration is admissible in argument. This rule looks quite simple and should on the face of it be acceptable to everyone; but it has far-reaching ramifications, which the generality of *muḥaddithīn* do not agree with. Their objection is that restrictions of this kind unduly limit the scope of traditions. I do not deny that the objection is valid, but leave it to the reader to judge whether it is better to exercise care in accepting traditions or to allow them unlimited scope. I will deal with the ramifications and subsidiary issues in some detail to make clear what led Abū Ḥanīfah to prescribe his rigorous conditions.

There was many a master of Ḥadīth who used to lecture to assemblies of as many as ten thousand, at which relay men were posted here and there to repeat the master's words for the people sitting far away from him to hear. Such people heard only the relay men and not the master himself. The question arises whether they could truthfully claim to have heard the traditions from the master himself. Many Ḥadīth authorities think that they could, but Abū Ḥanīfah thinks that they could not, and some doctors of Ḥadīth, such as Abū Na'īm, al-Faḍl b. Dakīn and Zā'idah b. Qudāmah, agree with him. Ibn Kathīr gives this verdict: "The rational view is the one held by Abū Ḥanīfah, but the other view makes for practical convenience."[20]

What dictated caution to Abū Ḥanīfah was the fact that the practice of narrating the meaning of traditions rather than their actual words was quite common up to his time. This involved the risk of alteration at every stage of transmission. In any case, a tradition heard through an intermediary could not be as accurate as one heard direct from the narrator himself. Undoubtedly, the system of engaging relay men was unavoidable in large assemblies. Nevertheless, it could not be fair to put on the same level a man who had heard a tradition directly from a master himself and one who had heard it from an intermediary. The relay men were often negligent and unintelligent, which increased the risk of misreporting.

An even more careless practice indulged in by some *muḥaddithīn* was to use the words *akhbaranā wa ḥaddathanā* (i.e. "they informed us and related to us") in their popular sense. Al-Ḥasan al-Baṣrī on many occasions says, "Ḥaddathanā

Abū Hurayrah" (i.e. "Abū Hurayrah related to us"), although he never met Abū Hurayrah. He explained it by saying that when Abū Hurayrah narrated such and such traditions, he was present in the city where the narration took place. Similarly, other masters of Ḥadīth would use the word *ḥaddathanā* in connection with Companions, intending it to convey that the people of the cities where the Companions had narrated the traditions in question had heard them. The *muḥaddith* al-Bazzār writes that al-Ḥasan al-Baṣrī claimed to have heard traditions from persons whom he had never met, explaining it by saying that his people had heard the traditions from those persons.[21] This was a kind of circumlocution which cast doubt on the authenticity of the traditions, for if the narrator had not heard a tradition from a master himself, he had obviously heard it from some intermediary. Since he had not disclosed the intermediary's name, it was not possible to know whether he was reliable or not, and one could only take it on trust that he was. Abū Ḥanīfah ruled this as an improper practice, and many other authorities on Ḥadīth subsequently agreed with him.

Another defective method countenanced was that of narrating fragments of traditions heard from some master and recorded casually. So much latitude was allowed in this that it was considered permissible to narrate even traditions of which the narrator remembered neither the words nor the sense. Abū Ḥanīfah, while he allowed this method to be followed, imposed the condition that both the words and the sense must be intact in the narrator's memory. The condition, though it did not meet with general acceptance, was endorsed by Mālik and many other authorities, as the *muḥaddith* al-Sakhāwī states. It ceased to be of much importance in the time of al-Bukhārī and Muslim, because by then verbatim narration had become the common practice. But in Abū Ḥanīfah's time it was certainly necessary, as the practice then prevailing was for a paraphrase of traditions to be narrated rather than their actual words, which made it practically impossible for traditions to be transmitted accurately, unless the narrators fully remembered their words, time, context and so on.

Whether giving a paraphrase of a *tradition* instead of repeating its actual words is permissible is a controversial question of great importance, and so is the allied question whether a paraphrase is admissible in argument. The questions, though debated from the earliest times, are still undecided. Al-Shāfi'ī writes, "Some *Tābi'īn* heard a *ḥadīth* from several Companions. The sense was one and the same, but the words were different. A Companion whom they consulted expressed the opinion that, since the sense remained unaltered, the variation in the words was immaterial."

Al-Shāfi'ī does not mention the names of the *Tābi'īn*. So it is not possible to judge the credibility or accuracy of the story. Nevertheless, it is an undeniable fact that some Companions did think narration of the meaning of a tradition to be permissible and that they themselves acted accordingly. As against this, however, some Companions as, for example, 'Abdullāh b. Mas'ūd, insisted on literal faithfulness. Al-Dhahabī writes thus about him in the *Tadhkirah al-Ḥuffāẓ*, "He was strict in the matter of narration and used to warn his pupils against carelessness in preserving the words intact."

'Abdullāh b. Mas'ūd, whenever he narrated the sense of a tradition, used these introductory words: "The Prophet (ṣ) said this or something like it or something resembling it or something which was more or less this."

Similarly, Abū al-Dardā', after relating a *ḥadīth*, used to say, "This or something like it."[22] Probably it was the same kind of caution which made the caliph ʿUmar forbid the narrating of traditions: he must have realised how difficult it was to remember the words and what a big risk of alternations was involved in permitting the transmission of the sense only.

The question was not settled one way or the other even after the time of the Companions. The Successors were divided into two groups on it, the first of Abū Ḥanīfah's line of teachers belonging to the one that permitted the paraphrasing of traditions, In the course of time, this became the unanimous view. Thus, in books on the *uṣūl* (roots or principles) of Ḥadīth transmission of the sense of traditions is described as a commonly recognised method. Of the *mujtahids*, only Mālik is opposed to it. Although a group of traditionists, including Muslim, al-Qāsim b. Muḥammad, Muḥammad b. Sīrīn, Rajāʾ b. Ḥayah, Abū Zarʿah, Sālim b. Abī al-Jaʿd and ʿAbd al-Malik b. ʿUmar, adhered to verbatim narration, the generality of them subscribed to the permissibility of paraphrase. Indeed, with their fondness for profusion in narrating traditions, they could not do otherwise.

There is no doubt that many Successors, and even many Companions, narrated traditions in paraphrase, so that, if the restriction imposed on this were to be enforced, there would be hardly anything left from which to deduce directions and rules of law. At the same time, it must be admitted that retaining the original form of a tradition in a paraphrase is next to impossible. Connoisseurs of the finer points of language know that no two words are completely identical in meaning and that even so-called synonyms differ from each other in some shade of meaning or other. No paraphrase can, therefore, be a perfect substitute for the original words. Even so, synonyms could serve to retain or reproduce something of the original sense of a tradition. But supporters of paraphrastic narration go so far in their liberality that they do not insist even on synonyms. No one could better understand than the Companions the Prophet's way of using words. Themselves masters of language, they had the opportunity, because of constant association with the Prophet (ṣ), of studying his manner of speaking, his favourite turns of phrase and the senses in which he used different words. Notwithstanding this, books of Tradition provide many instances of failure on their part to convey his intention with accuracy.

Ibn Mājah quotes Abū Mūsā al-Ash'arī as narrating the following tradition from the Prophet (ṣ): "When a dead man is mourned in these words, he is tortured (in his grave)." Somebody is said to have told the Lady 'Ā'ishah that Ibn 'Umar used to relate this tradition and 'Ā'ishah, it is reported, commented as follows: "I do not say that Ibn 'Umar lied, but he was certainly mistaken. What really happened was this. A Jewess died, and her relations mourned her. The Prophet (ṣ), hearing of this, remarked, 'Her relations are weeping for her and she is being punished in her grave.'" According to a variant of this tradition, 'Ā'ishah recited the Qur'anic *āyah* "No one will be punished for others' sins," by which she intended to convey that a person could not be answerable for another person's acts, so that if the relations of the dead Jewess mourned, it was no fault of hers and she was not punishable for it. The point involved is this that, while the Prophet (ṣ) had simply mentioned as a fact that the Jewess was being punished, the transmitter ascribed the fact to her relations' mourning by adding the words "The dead are punished for the wailing of the living."[23]

Similarly, there is a tradition that during the Battle of Badr the Prophet (ṣ), standing over a well, spoke the words "Have you found the promise of your Lord to be true?" The people around him remarked, "You speak to the dead!" He replied, "What I said they have heard." But when the incident was related in this way to 'Ā'ishah, she said that the words actually spoken by the Prophet (ṣ) were "These people have got to know that what I invited them to is right." What a difference there is between the two utterances and what different implications they have for the question whether the dead can hear!

If Companions could commit errors of this kind, it can well be imagined what must have happened when people of the second or third generation narrated traditions. It is interesting that supporters of paraphrastic narration have listed a number of instances of words which, according to them, can be interchanged without affecting the sense at all. But these so-called synonyms do not stand close examination, for they clearly differ from each other in meaning. To quote one example, the traditionist al-Sakhāwī says that the words "*Uqtulū al-aswadayn al-ḥayyata wa al-'aqraba*" (i.e. "Kill two black things, namely, the snake and the scorpion"), occurring in a *ḥadīth*, could well be replaced by the words "*Amara bi qatlihimā*" (i.e. "He ordered their killing") without affecting the sense. But there is an obvious difference between "*uqtulū*" and "*amara bi al-qatl.*"

Appreciating the difficulties described above, Abū Ḥanīfah adopted a middle course. As regards traditions paraphrastically narrated before his time and already current among traditionists, there was no choice but to accept them, otherwise practically the whole corpus of traditions would become useless. The Imam, therefore, accepted them, but imposed the condition that the transmitters were jurists, that is to say, people who could understand the meaning and implications of the words. This no doubt left room for alteration of the sense, but saved the paraphrastic narrations from being rendered null and void, since, as the majority of traditionists have clearly stated, the credibility of traditions is to be determined by the degree of probability and, therefore, in the absence of any cogent reason for rejecting them altogether, paraphrastic narrations could be made use of in legal inferences.

The Imam declared even those paraphrastically narrated traditions as acceptable whose transmitters were reliable, even if not jurists; but he assigned a lower rank to them and considered a closer scrutiny necessary in their case. The other imams agreed with this approach. The *Alfiyyah al-Ḥadīth* lays down, "Literal narration is necessary for one who does not well understand the words argued about. But opinions vary as regards one who does, with the majority agreeing that the latter is not restricted to the actual words." Abū Ḥanīfah confined this latitude to Companions and Successors, and al-Ṭaḥāwī quotes him, on an unbroken chain of authorities, as saying that only those traditions should be narrated which the narrator remembers as fully at the time of narration as he did immediately after he had heard them.[24] Mullā ʿAlī al-Qārī, after citing this quotation, opines that Abū Ḥanīfah considered narrating the sense of traditions permissible.

Mālik and some other traditionists agreed with Abū Ḥanīfah in imposing this restriction. "It has been said," states *Fatḥ al-Mughīth*, "that paraphrastic narration of traditions is not at all permissible. A group of traditionists, jurists and followers of al-Shāfiʿī principles holds this view, and according to al-Qurṭubī this is, really speaking, the view of Imam Mālik too." But the common run of traditionists could not be expected to subscribe to it, and so a large number of them opposed it, describing Abū Ḥanīfah as "stringent in narration."

However, it is only fair to concede that the restriction was really necessary. According to a tradition, the Prophet himself said, "May Allah prosper the man who conveys what he has heard from me exactly as he heard it." No argument can overrule this saying of the Prophet (ṣ). It is possible that this tradition had not come to the knowledge of those Companions who thought verbatim transmission unnecessary. Those Companions about whom it is established that they had heard it, including 'Abdullāh b. 'Abbās, who is its transmitter, adhered to verbatim transmission. The tradition had become commonly known by Abū Ḥanīfah's time, and there was no reason for him not to act on it.

Abū Ḥanīfah's greatest achievement in the field of tradition lay in the formulation and practical application of the principles of rational criticism (*dirāyah*). The work done by our scholars in one branch of Tradition, namely, narration, has no parallel in the history of learning, but it is regrettable that they did not pay much attention to elaborating a system of scientific criticism. We have it from Ibn Ḥajar that some books were written on the subject, but they are so scarce and unknown as to be virtually non-existent.

The principles of Ḥadīth have developed into a regular discipline and big books have been written on them, but these contain very little about the principles of criticism, although these principles constitute an essential counterpart to narration. It goes to the signal credit of Abū Ḥanīfah that at a time when even the rudiments of criticism did not exist, he discovered subtle points of the kind mentioned above. One meets with isolated glimmerings of the principles of criticism in the history of Ḥadīth during the period of the Companions, and it was these which showed Abū Ḥanīfah the way. But they got lost to the public view in the crowd of general religious problems.

The soundness or unsoundness of narrations does not always depend exclusively on the trustworthiness or untrustworthiness of their transmitters. It often happens that, although all the transmitters in a chain of cited authorities are reliable, the incident narrated is not on the face of it believable. There are hundreds of examples of this in Ḥadīth. It is, therefore, necessary that traditions should be appraised, not on the basis of their transmitters alone, but in the light of the principles of rational criticism.

Dirāyah (rational criticism) involves the judging of events described in traditions with reference to the facts of human nature, the peculiarities of the time, the circumstances of the persons to whom the events are ascribed and the common laws of probability. If a tradition does not stand up to any of these criteria, its genuineness must be considered doubtful or, in other words, it should be considered probable that the facts have been altered in the course of transmission.

Ibn al-Jawzī, a high-ranking *muḥaddith*, thus lays down the broad principles of *dirāyah*: "If you find a tradition to be contrary to reason or to the principles of transmission, you may dismiss it as a fabrication and need not inquire into the trustworthiness of its transmitters. Similarly, you may regard as a fabrication any tradition which is falsified by common perception and observation, or which is repugnant to the Qur'an, to a *ḥadīth mutawātir* (i.e a tradition supported by too many persons to be doubted) or to *ijmāʿ qaṭʿī* (i.e. a conclusive consensus of competent opinion) and which does not admit of *ta'wīl* (allegorical interpretation), or in which there is a threat of severe punishment for a minor sin or promise of a great reward for a small good deed. Narrations by preachers and street-corner orators abound in traditions of this sort."[25]

I reproduce below some of the principles of *dirāyah* formulated by Abū Ḥanīfah.

(1) A tradition contrary to reason is not worthy of credence.[26] This is a principle to which Ibn al-Jawzī gives precedence over all other principles of criticism. By his time Islamic learning had reached its zenith and philosophical ideas were in the air. But in Abū Ḥanīfah's time it was anathema to talk of reason in connection with religion. When he first framed this principle and applied it to traditions, he was severely criticised. His refusal to accept traditions on the ground that they referred to impossible events shocked the common people, for whom the only touchstone of correctness and credibility was the personality of the narrator. The principle was in due course incorporated in the principles of Ḥadīth, but transmitters seldom acted on it, with the result that scores of hyperbolic and fantastic traditions are now part of the popular store of knowledge.

There is a tradition that, while reciting Sūrah al-Najm, the Prophet (ṣ) uttered the words "These idols are very venerable and their intercession (with Allah) may be hoped for." These words, the tradition says, were put into the Prophet's mouth by Satan, with the result that, after he had finished reciting the *sūrah*, Jibrīl appeared to him and inquired where he had got them from, because he (Jibrīl) had not communicated them to him. This tradition was declared wrong by some *muḥaddithīn*, such as Qāḍī 'Iyāḍ and Abū Bakr al-Bayhaqī, in accordance with Abū Ḥanīfah's principle, but a large body of *muḥaddithīn* still accepts it. There was no one more distinguished among the *muḥaddithīn* of later ages than Ibn Ḥajar, and even he forcefully supports the tradition, saying that, since its transmitters are reliable, it cannot be rejected.

Then there is the tradition about a prayer by the Prophet (ṣ), having made the sun arise immediately after it had set because 'Alī had missed his evening prayer. The *muḥaddith* Ibn al-Jawzī was daring enough to call this tradition a fabrication, but he was violently opposed by Ibn Ḥajar and Jalāl al-Dīn al-Suyūṭī. Abū Ḥanīfah was opposed even more violently when he rejected this and similar traditions, but that did not deter him. It should, however, be remembered that the Imam did not use the word *reason* in the broad sense in which it is understood by educated people today and in which sense it devastates many fundamental religious beliefs.

(2) A tradition purporting to be from the Prophet (ṣ) which is about common facts of daily experience, but which does not rank above *akhbār al-āḥād* (i.e. single-authority reports), is suspect. The rationale of this principle is that, since in regard to events experienced by the common people in their daily lives the people at large needed the Prophet's guidance, the fact that the tradition is confined to a single transmitter or one or two transmitters militates against its authenticity.

Most commentators have stated that Abū Ḥanīfah rejected traditions which were repugnant to reasoning by analogy. This statement is not entirely unfounded, but many people have misunderstood it, as a result of which a lot of misconceptions have arisen about the Imam among literalist scholars. These people, without fully considering the Imam's intentions, have formed the opinion that he accorded precedence to analogy over Tradition. But all his recorded sayings rebut this opinion. There are many instances in which he completely abandoned analogy in favour of Tradition on questions of law. Muḥammad b. al-Ḥasan, discussing the question whether loud laughter vitiates *wuḍū'* (ritual ablution), argues on behalf of Abū Ḥanīfah and say, "Analogy is from what is asserted by the doctors of Madīnah. But where a tradition is available, analogy is of no account and the tradition must be followed." Nothing could be clearer than this. The author of the *'Uqūd al-Jumān* quotes, from different sources, several statements of the Imam to the effect that he never admitted analogy in preference to tradition. The conversation between him and Ja'far al-Ṣādiq that we have-quoted earlier also endorses this.

In view of these clarifications some of the critics have made the modified and more specific claim that the Imam rejected traditions which were contradictory to clear analogical deductions (*al-qiyās al-jalī*). 'Abd al-Karīm al-Shahrastānī, speaking of Abū Ḥanīfah and his disciples among Men of Opinion (*aṣḥāb al-ra'y*), says, "These people prefer a clear analogy to single-authority reports (*akhbār al-āḥād*)." Al-Rāzī, in his *Manāqib al-Shāfi'ī*, makes a similar statement several times, using it as an argument for ranking al-Shāfi'ī above Abū Ḥanīfah.

Despite much endeavour, I have been unable to find a clear statement by Abū Ḥanīfah on the relative merits of Tradition and analogy. Nor have those who aver that he preferred analogy to Tradition been able to adduce any statement by him in support of that claim. No doubt the rule that a tradition whose transmitters are not reliable and which is in every way contrary to analogy is not a fit basis for argument has been mentioned among the Ḥanafī principles of jurisprudence, but it is not one of the principles unanimously accepted by Ḥanafī jurists. While 'Īsā b. Ibān and his followers accept it, Abū al-Ḥasan al-Karkhī and others explicitly reject it. Yet the author of the *Musallam al-Thubūt* gives it special prominence. What is surpassingly strange is that the rule is attributed to Abū Ḥanīfah without any proof of his authorship of it. The biggest piece of evidence adduced to justify this attribution is the

Ḥanafī stand on the question of the sale of dry milch animals. It has been sought to be proved that on this question the Imam preferred analogy to a clear tradition.[27] Those who make the attribution do not seem to know that the stand was based on the personal opinion of certain Ḥanafī *'ulamā'* and not on that of the Imam. Al-Rāzī has cautiously avoided mentioning Abū Ḥanīfah and has only mentioned "the Companions of Abū Ḥanīfah" in this connection. But I do not think that even so he was sufficiently cautious, for the opinion was held by some, and not all, Ḥanafī scholars, and so the generalisation implied in his description was not justified.

The correct position is that Abū Ḥanīfah rejected the tradition about the sale of dry milch animals not because he thought it contrary to analogy but because he claimed that it had been abrogated. Al-Ṭaḥāwī has dealt with this in great detail in his *Ma'ānī al-Āthār*. After describing the creed of Abū Ḥanīfah and Muḥammad, he writes, "These people believed that what had been related on this subject from the Messenger of Allah had been abrogated."

I do not propose to expatiate on the subject, and content myself with pointing out that the Imam rejected the tradition in question because he considered it abrogated and not because of his partiality to analogy. What is necessary is to ascertain carefully whether the statements ascribed to him are proved to have been made by him. Later scholars did that, and so must we. When we do that, we find that all these accusations about Abū Ḥanīfah's preferring analogy to Tradition are baseless.

On the contrary, it is clearly established by pronouncements proved on good authority to have been made by Abū Ḥanīfah that he attached no importance to analogy vis-à-vis Tradition. Muḥammad, making the point that if a man fasting in Ramaḍān eats something by mistake, then his fast is not broken and it does not become obligatory for him to make up for it, argues from traditions on the point and says that in cases where traditions exist, opinion is of no account. He goes on to quote Abū Ḥanīfah as saying, "If there were no traditions on the point, I would order making up for the error." It is a different matter that Abū Ḥanīfah's conditions about the proof of traditions are very exacting. Unless those conditions were fulfilled by a *ḥadīth*, he did not consider it valid; and if they were fulfilled, he paid no heed to analogy.

As far as I have been able to ascertain, Abū Ḥanīfah never preferred juristic analogy to Tradition. It is, however, to be remembered that the word *qiyās* (analogy) was used in a very wide sense in his day. In that wide sense, he kept *qiyās* out of his consideration of traditions. There were two schools of thought in Islam from the very beginning in regard to rules of law. According to one, rules of law were not based on expediency or rational considerations, from which it followed that right and wrong were not rational concepts. The other school held that rules of law were all based on expediency, which in the case of some was evident and had been indicated in the pronouncements of the Lawgiver, while in the case of others it was implicit, though we might not be aware of it.

This bifurcation produced two different kinds of effects on Tradition. Some people, on hearing a tradition, inquired only whether or not the transmitters were reliable. If they were, they accepted the tradition without demur. Others, who believed in the rightness and wrongness of legal orders, inquired further whether the rules of conduct or beliefs deducible from the tradition were or were not rational and useful. If they were not, they scrutinised the tradition further still to find out if the transmitters had the requisite intelligence and critical power, whether the narration was verbatim or paraphrastic, what was the occasion for the tradition, who were the people to whom it was addressed, what were the circumstances and other relevant factors. This line of inquiry generally revealed the truth.

The examination of traditions in this manner started as early as the time of the Companions. Ibn Mājah and al-Tirmidhī, in their *Ṣaḥīḥs*, relate an exchange of remarks between Abū Hurayrah and 'Abdullāh b. 'Abbās about a tradition of the Prophet (ṣ) which said, "Use of a thing changed by fire voids ablution." (The opinion of some *mujtahids* that when meat is eaten, it becomes necessary to perform a fresh ablution is based on this pronouncement.) Abū Hurayrah narrated the tradition. On hearing it, 'Abdullāh b. 'Abbās, who was in the audience, observed, "On this basis, even the use of hot water makes a fresh ablution necessaṛy." "Nephew," retorted Abū Hurayrah, "when you hear a tradition from the Prophet (ṣ), you should not bring in analogies." 'Abdullāh b. 'Abbās, however, adhered to his opinion. The objection made by 'Ā'ishah to Ibn 'Umar's narration of the tradition concerning the dead being punished for the wailing of the living proceeded from a similar approach. Several other examples of this are to be found in the annals of the Companions, which, however, need not be cited here.

Such then was the practice of Abū Ḥanīfah, which has been misrepresented by being described as *qiyās.* This is not the place for a detailed discussion of the proposition that rules of law are based on expediency. It has, in fact, been discussed so ably and thoroughly in Shāh Waliullāh's incomparable *Ḥujjah Allāh al-Bālighah* that there is no room left for anyone else to say anything further about it. Suffice it to mention that those scholars of Islam who were masters of both the speculative and factual disciplines (*al-'ilm al-'aqlī wa al-naqlī*), such as al-Ghazālī, 'Izz al-Dīn, 'Abd al-Salām and Shāh Waliullāh, adopted an attitude of inquiry similar to Abū Ḥanīfah's. Abū Ḥanīfah, for his part, considered it essential to examine traditions in the light of rational probability and, whenever confronted with two mutually contradictory traditions, preferred the one which stood the examination.

There are several traditions which Abū Ḥanīfah hesitates to accept because they fail to satisfy the criterion of rational probability. He assigns as a reason for this what is called in his terminology an *'illah khafiyyah* (i.e. a hidden weakness or motive). Traditionists distinguish one kind of *ḥadīth* to which they give the name of *mu'allal*, defining it as a *ḥadīth* which, though it apparently fulfils all the conditions of soundness, is not admissible in argument. They take much pride in identifying traditions of this kind, claiming this to be a rare kind of intuition or inspiration.

'Alī b. al-Madīnī, one of al-Bukhārī's teachers and a famous *muḥaddith*, says, "This inspiration, and if you ask one endowed with it why he calls a particular tradition *mu'allal*, he will not be able to advance any reason."[28] The *muḥaddith* Abū Ḥātim, when asked his opinion about a number of traditions, described some as *mudraj* (interpolated), some as *bāṭil* (false), some as *munkar* (disowned) and some as *ṣaḥīḥ* (faultless). "How do you know this?" asked the questioner. "Did the transmitters confide it to you?" "No," replied Abū Ḥātim, "this is all my intuition." "So you claim occult knowledge," remarked the questioner. "Ask other experts; if they agree with me, you will perhaps be satisfied." The man was satisfied when Abū Zar'ah, whom he consulted, confirmed Abū Ḥātim's opinion.[29]

Some *muḥaddithīn* say that this intuition is something which is given to imams of Ḥadīth unsolicited and which they cannot reject—a kind of psychological phenomenon from which there is no escape for them. This statement is true. Constant application creates in them a special talent or acumen which enables them to judge at once whether a saying attributed to the Prophet (ṣ) can or cannot be his. Similarly, faithful observance of the directions of Sharī'ah and diligent study of their meaning and purpose endows one with the power to distinguish whether or not a particular direction was given by the Prophet (ṣ). The exploring of these meanings and purposes is, however, not the task of the *muḥaddith*, but that of the *mujtahid*.

Naturally enough, the Ẓāhirites objected to Abū Ḥanīfah's characterising some traditions as *mu'allal* for recondite reasons and suspected him of rejecting traditions in the light of reason and personal opinion. If by applying themselves merely to the textual study of narratives, traditionists can develop a flair which enables them to reject traditions apparently fulfilling all the conditions of soundness, there is no reason to think that a man who has dived deep into the intents and purposes of legal directions cannot acquire a similar gift of discernment. Of course, rejecting traditions on the basis of personal judgement is a sensitive and highly responsible task that can be accomplished only by one who is a very great scholar, traditionist and original thinker and endowed by Allah with special gifts. Who could combine these qualities in himself better than Abū Ḥanīfah did?

The most valuable contribution made by Abū Ḥanīfah to Ḥadīth is the grading of traditions and the derivation of legal directions from them in accordance with it. The primary source of legal directions is the Qur'an which nobody calls in question. Next to the Qur'an is Ḥadīth. Between the two there is no essential difference, the one being *waḥy matlū* (written revelation) and the other *waḥy ghayr matlū* (unwritten revelation), but there is a difference between them in regard to proof. If a tradition is definitively and unchallengeably proved to be as authentic as the Qur'an is, it ranks with the Qur'an as a source of law. Traditions, however, vary in respect of degree of proof, and this variation must be taken into account in deducing legal directions from them.

The classification of traditions by traditionists into *ṣaḥīḥ* (sound or correct), *ḥasan* (good), *ḍaʿīf* (weak), *mashhūr* (well-known), *ʿazīz* (restrictedly disseminated), *gharīb* (rare) and so on is deficient in this that it does not grade them as sources of legal orders; it is only *ḍaʿīf* traditions that they regard as unreliable, ranking all the other kinds as equally admissible in argument. Nor was it necessary for them to do such grading, since deduction of legal orders and directions was no part of their task. But Abū Ḥanīfah was called on to undertake it as a pioneer in the systematisation of *fiqh*. He accordingly divided traditions from the point of view of proof into the following three grades:

(1) *Mutawātir*: that is, a tradition whose narrators at every stage of its transmission were too numerous for any room being left for the possibility that a lie became established by continual repetition; or, in other words, a tradition initially heard from the Prophet (ṣ) by innumerable persons and transmitted by a succession of innumerable persons down to the last narrator.

(2) *Mashhūr*: a tradition whose narrators, at all stages other than the first, are as numerous as in the case of a *mutawātir* tradition.

(3) *Āḥād*: a tradition which is neither *mutawātir* nor *mashhūr*.

So graded, traditions have, in Abū Ḥanīfah's opinion, different bearings on legal directions. A rule of law derived from a *mutawātir* tradition is mandatory and fundamental. One derived from a *mashhūr* tradition is not mandatory, but it can further define an absolute command of, the Qur'an and thus supplement it. An *āḥād* tradition, since its authenticity is only presumptive, does not in any way affect a clear direction given in a Qur'anic text. Obvious as this distinction is, it is surprising that al-Shāfi'ī and some other traditionists do not agree with it. Al-Bayhaqī and some others describe a number of debates said to have taken place between al-Shāfi'ī and Muḥammad b. al-Ḥasan, in which, according to them, the latter was defeated. I believe that these debates are purely imaginary, unsupported as they are by any reliable evidence. Nevertheless, they prove that the distinction just described can be rightly attributed to Abū Ḥanīfah.

The strongest criticism levelled against the distinction is that Abū Ḥanīfah and his disciples were themselves unable to observe it consistently. Shāh Waliullāh, in the *Ḥujjah Allāh al-Bālighah*, relates a dialogue on this subject between al-Shāfi'ī and Muḥammad. "Is it your opinion," asked al-Shāfi'ī, "that *al-khabar al-wāḥid* (single-person report) cannot supplement the Qur'an?" "Yes, it is," replied Muḥammad. "The Qur'an," said al-Shāfi'ī, "permits a will in favour of an heir. Why then do you consider it impermissible on the basis of a tradition?"

Shāh Waliullah has probably quoted this story from al-Bayhaqī's *Manāqib al-Shāfi'ī*, which is full of fictitious stories of this kind. The fact is that, according to the Ḥanafīs, the Qur'anic dictum about wills in favour of heirs was repealed not by a tradition but by another verse of the Qur'an itself, namely, the one about appointment of heirs. This view, it may be added, is not confined to the Ḥanafīs but held by all exegetes except a few.

Many other controversial issues have been raised on this subject, which I refrain from discussing. I will, however, deal in some detail with the controversy raging round single-person reports and their effect on Islamic beliefs, since it is mainly on this aspect of the matter that some *muḥaddithīn* disagree with Abū Ḥanīfah.

The majority of the masters of Ḥadīth consider single-person reports to be of doubtful authenticity. The dissenting group is led by Ibn al-Ṣalāḥ, but even he does not recognise all varieties of single-person reports as definitive. He classifies traditions into the following seven kinds:

i. those on which al-Bukhārī and Muslim agree,
ii. those accepted by al-Bukhārī alone,
iii. those accepted by Muslim alone,
iv. those quoted by neither al-Bukhārī nor Muslim, but satisfying the conditions prescribed by them,
v. those satisfying only al-Bukhārī's conditions,
vi. those satisfying only Muslim's conditions and
vii. those satisfying neither al-Bukhārī's nor Muslim's conditions, but accepted by other traditionists.

Of these, Ibn al-Ṣalāḥ characterises the first kind as definitive, saying, "This kind is absolutely correct and all theoretical knowledge has to be in accord with it." As regards traditions quoted by either al-Bukhārī or Muslim alone, he includes them in the same category except for those invalidated by al-Dāraquṭnī and others. Although Ibn al-Ṣalāḥ's view has found acceptance, especially in recent times, among superficial students, there is no doubt that it is fallacious and illogical, and imams of Ḥadīth are averse to it. Thus, al-Nawawī, after quoting Ibn al-Ṣalāḥ in his commentary on Muslim's *Ṣaḥīḥ*, writes, "What the Shaykh (i.e. Ibn al-Ṣalāḥ) says in this context is contrary to the view of the majority of authorities, which is that those traditions of the *Ṣaḥīḥayn* which do not attain to the rank of *tawātur* are only of presumptive validity, since they are single-person reports, and it is an established rule that single-person reports at most create a presumption of truth. In this matter, al-Buhkārī, Muslim and all others are on the same footing." Ibn al-Ṣalāḥ's view has been rejected by other doctors of Tradition also. But instead of taking their opinion on trust, let us ourselves examine whether single-person reports create certainty or only a presumption of truth.

When a *muḥaddith*, no matter what his standing, says that a tradition is *ṣaḥīḥ* (correct or sound), he implies certain subsidiary statements, namely that the tradition is *muttaṣil* (having an unbroken chain of transmitters), that its transmitters are reliable and possessed of exact minds, that there is no lacuna in the transmission and that the tradition is free from all damaging weaknesses. All these are matters of presumption and individual judgement, falling short of certainty. Just as a jurist may deduce a point of law from the Qur'an or Ḥadīth and think that he has made a correct deduction, of which, however, there is no guarantee, since his premises are merely his own suppositions, so may a traditionist. In calling a tradition sound, a traditionist relies on his presumptions and individual judgement. If a traditionist or a number of traditionists claim a tradition to be sound and another traditionist does not recognise it as such, all that the latter is guilty of is being opposed to the other traditionist's or traditionists' principles of verification, rules of deduction and chain of transmission—in short, their suppositions and judgements.

The rules of verification and criticism fixed by traditionists for judging the soundness of traditions are all rules for the exercise of personal judgement I and discretion, which is why they vary greatly from one traditionist or group of traditionists to another. Literalists regard Ḥadīth as a narrative and factual and not a rational and speculative branch of learning. But anyone who has pondered over the principles of Ḥadīth can easily detect the fallacy in this way of thinking. It is at this that Abū Ḥanīfah hints in the following dictum: "This is a matter in which we have our own opinion and do not rely on a single-narrator report, nor do we say that it is obligatory for everyone to accept it." Some people have erroneously limited this broad statement to *fiqh*, being presumably unaware of the fact that a *mujtahid* is concerned less with points of law than with their sources.

It is because the principles of Ḥadīth are indeterminate and discretionary that traditionists differ about the soundness or unsoundness of particular traditions. A tradition declared by one traditionist to be absolutely sound, authentic and obligatory may be dismissed by another as weak or even invented. The *muḥaddith* Ibn al-Jawzī, for example, has included in his list of weak traditions a number of traditions recognised by other *muḥaddithīn* as sound and good (*ḥasan*), going to the length of not sparing even some traditions contained in the *Ṣaḥīḥs*. Al-Sakhāwī thus comments on this: "Ibn al-Jawzī has put down as weak even some *ḥasan* and *ṣaḥīḥ* traditions included in the *Ṣaḥīḥs* of al-Bukhārī and Muslim, not to speak of other compilations." Ibn al-Jawzī undoubtedly overstepped the line, but his was merely an error of judgement in that he declared as wrong a correct judgement made by al-Bukhārī and Muslim. Differences of opinion about the soundness or unsoundness of traditions arising from disagreement about basic principles could easily provide enough material for a thick volume.

The first essential condition for a *marfūʿ* tradition is that it should be proved to go back to the Prophet (ṣ) without any missing link; but most of the recognised methods of proving this unbroken continuity are merely discretionary. Some people consider *marfūʿ* such expressions of the Companions as "This is a *sunnah*," "Thus were we ordered." "From this were we prohibited," "This is what we used to do in the time of the Messenger of Allah," "We did not consider this wrong." Some people have even gone so far as to prefix the words "Thus spoke the Messenger of Allah" to traditions containing any of the above expressions, while narrating them, notwithstanding the fact that the expressions do not provide any positive proof of the claim, but indicate that the traditions are based on the judgement or understanding of the narrators.

"The understanding of a Companion is no argument," says one of the generally accepted principles of Ḥadīth, and on the basis of it some scholars maintain that expressions of the kind in question are not enough to prove that the traditions of which they form part are *muttaṣil* and *marfūʿ*. Al-Shāfiʿī, Ibn Ḥazm, al-Ẓāhirī, Abū Bakr al-Rāzī and other scholars do not recognise a statement by a Companion that a particular action is a Prophetic Sunnah as a *marfūʿ ḥadīth*. In books of biography and Tradition, there are scores of instances in which some Companion or other is reported as having made this statement in respect of what was only his own deduction or conjecture and not a Prophetic tradition, but what most traditionists nevertheless describe as a *marfūʿ ḥadīh*. Following these traditionists, many narrators characterised traditions of this kind in clear terms as *marfūʿ*, thus causing a good deal of confusion. In *muʿanʿan* traditions (i.e. traditions in which the transmitters are connected only by the preposition *'an* (from), for example, *A from B*, without a statement as to whether the transmission was direct, it is very difficult to prove uninterrupted transmission. There are plenty of traditions of this kind.

Al-Bukhārī maintains that if it is proved that the transmitter and the recipient of a *mu'an'an* tradition were contemporaries and had met each other, then the tradition is to be considered *muttaṣil*. But Muslim, although he was a pupil of al-Bukhārī's and generally followed his principles, vehemently opposed the condition that the transmitter and the recipient should have met each other and thought it enough for them to have been contemporaries.[30] Thus, according to al-Bukhārī's ruling, all those *mu'an'an* traditions of Muslim whose transmitters and recipients are not proved to have met each other are *maqṭū'* (with a broken chain of transmission), although Muslim regards them as *muttaṣil* and insists so much on this that he does not stop short of using strong language about those who oppose it.

Leaving aside Muslim's liberalised criterion, even the stricter conditions prescribed by al-Bukhārī for *mu'an'an* traditions do not provide anything more than a presumptive proof of continuity of transmission. From the fact that the transmitter and the recipient were contemporaries and met each other, it does not necessarily follow that communication between them was always personal and immediate. Where the words *ḥaddathanā wa akhbaranā* (this was narrated and reported to us) are present, direct and personal communication is, of course, proved. But where these words are not present and only the expression *'an* (A from B) has been used, there is a strong probability, but no certainty, of transmission without a gap. In books of Ḥadīth and biography, one comes across scores of instances in which two persons who were contemporaries and even associated with each other made some communications to each other through intermediaries. Instances of this wanting in daily life.

The most important problem is that of the appraisal of personalities. The validity of single-person reports hinges on the dependability of their reporters. But judging the character of individuals is a matter of opinion in which there can be no definiteness and finality. A man may be regarded by many people as very reliable, pious and righteous, and by many others as a poor transmitter, unreliable and untruthful. Oddly enough, the two groups of people are often people of an equally high rank whose judgement cannot be questioned. Although al-Bukhārī and Muslim do not often disagree violently, there are a number of transmitters whom the one regards as trustworthy, while the other does not. Al-Nawawī gives the names of some of these transmitters in the introduction to his commentary on Muslim's *Ṣaḥīḥ*, and on the authority of *Kitāb al-Madkhal* of the *Muḥaddith*, al-Ḥākim puts down at 625 the number of transmitters whose narration Muslim admitted and al-Bukhārī did not.

Mīzān al-I'tidāl contains the names of hundreds, or rather thousands, of transmitters in the invalidation (*jarḥ*) and rectification (*ta'dīl*), that is, criticism of whose narrations there are wide divergences, as was only to be expected. Acquaintance with the habits and characteristics of a man which may determine the quality of his narrations can be acquired only after long association with him. It was not possible for the people engaged in invalidating and rectifying traditions to acquire a sufficiently intimate acquaintance with the thousands of men who had narrated them. They had, therefore, to rely largely on conjectures, appearances, reputations and hearsay, which seldom, if ever, enabled them to make any definitive assessments. It is true that the traditionists have framed a set of working rules for handling this task, but the rules are discretionary and have not been unanimously agreed on. In fact, the traditionists themselves occasionally find it necessary to depart from them. Generally speaking, invalidation is given precedence over rectification, but there are a number of transmitters in respect of whom this priority is not observed.

There are detailed invalidating criticisms of Muḥammad b. Bashshār al-Miṣrī, Aḥmad b. Ṣāliḥ al-Miṣrī and ʿIkrimah Mawlā b. ʿAbbās, but these are not reliable. This divergence of views between those engaged in invalidation and those engaged in rectification is surprising in view of the fact that both classes of men are generally experts. Here, for example, are a few widely differing opinions about Jābir al-Juʿfī of Kūfah, a well-known transmitter who claimed to have learnt by heart fifty thousand traditions. Sufyān says that he knows of no one who was a more careful transmitter than Jābir, while Shuʿbah says that he is "the most reliable of men" when he introduces a tradition with the words "*akhbaranā wa ḥaddathanā*." Sufyān al-Thawrī said to Shuʿbah, "If you question Jābir al-Juʿfī, I shall question you." Wakīʿ said, "Doubt anything but the fact that Jābir is reliable." Opposed to these are the opinions of other masters of Ḥadīth that Jābir is obsolete, a liar, a forger. The final summing up of the traditionists about Jābir is that he is untrustworthy.

This does not mean that the art of *jarḥ* and *taʿdīl* is unreliable, but it does show that the media and methods employed in recording facts about personalities were such as can at best warrant a presumption or probability of truth, falling far short of certainty.

What remains to be discussed is the question of the communication of meaning. A tradition may be *muttaṣil* according to the criteria agreed on by all *muḥaddithīn* and *mujtahidīn*, its transmitters may all be reliable and there may be no lacuna in it; yet the manner in which the narrator has communicated its meaning may be open to question. Has he, for instance, taken into account the circumstances and the occasion, and has he made no mistake in understanding and conveying the sense of the tradition? These questions acquire an added importance from the fact that, as is commonly admitted, many traditions have been transmitted paraphrastically. This, indeed, was the only ground on which traditions were rejected in the time of the Companions, who were all evidently reliable and in whose case there was no probability of a gap in transmission.

An incident relevant to this is related in the chapter on *tayammum* in Muslim's *Ṣaḥīḥ*. A man asked the caliph 'Umar what he should do about his prayer if, needing a bath, he could get no water for it. 'Umar advised him not to offer his prayer. The Companion 'Ammār, who happened to be present, narrated a tradition from the Prophet (ṣ) on this question and reminded 'Umar that he was present when the Prophet (ṣ) gave his ruling. "Have the fear of Allah, O 'Ammār," remarked 'Umar. Obviously, 'Umar implied not that 'Ammār had related a false tradition but only that there was a possibility of his conveying the meaning of the Prophet's words wrongly. So 'Ammār said, "If you do not like me to relate this tradition, I shall never do so anymore." I have discussed the subject of single-person reports at such length only because it is the main ground on which *muḥaddithīn* attack Abū Ḥanīfah, although his stand on it was the result of much research and reflection.

The uncertainties and variances of judgement dealt with above are not met with in regard to *mutawātir* and *mashhūr* traditions, but are peculiar to single-person reports, and account for the great difference of opinion about the latter. While the Mu'tazilah refused to recognise them at all, some *muḥaddithīn* went to the opposite extreme of declaring them to be definitive, subject only to the condition that their transmitters were reliable and there was in them no breach of continuity, no lacuna and no weakness.

A third group of *muḥaddithīn*, as a matter of principle, regarded single-person reports to be debatable, but overlooked this in respect of detailed legal questions and problems of belief. Abū Ḥanīfah adopted a middle course, testifying to the fairness of his judgement and the incisiveness of his understanding. He neither rejected single-person reports outright like the Mu'tazilah nor accepted them as definitive like the superficial literalists. His stand was similar to that of some great Companions. 'Umar, 'Ā'ishah and 'Abdullāh b. Mas'ūd on several occasions hesitated to recognise single-person reports because they did not regard them as definitive. When Fāṭimah b. Qays related to 'Umar the Prophet's tradition "No house and no maintenance for her," he said, "We cannot depart from Allah's Book on a report by a woman about which we do not know whether it is true or false."

In *fiqh* there are many rules derived from this dictum. There is, for example, the rule that a single-person report is not enough to establish as a *farḍ* (an absolute duty) a legal direction based on it, for that requires conclusive proof of the truth of the report. It is, however, conceded that such a report may raise a strong presumption and thus prove a legal direction derived from it to be *wājib* (obligatory), *masnūn* (recommended, but not essential) or *mustaḥabb* (approved). It is on this basis that while al-Shāfiʿī considers reading Sūrah al-Fātiḥah in prayers *farḍ*, Abū Ḥanīfah considers it *wājib*. There are many other deductions of a similar nature made from the principle under discussion.

The principle plays an even more important role in *kalām* than in *fiqh*, and it was its application by Abū Ḥanīfah to the former that mainly accounted for the widespread hostility to him. On the basis of it he laid down that no single-person report could prevail against a belief held by all Muslims. For example, the innocence of all prophets is axiomatic with every Muslim. Therefore, according to Abū Ḥanīfah, any tradition to the effect that a prophet committed a major sin was unworthy of credence. Thus the principle provides a way out of many difficulties created by heretics, but unfortunately most traditionists, far from appreciating it, opposed it. Ibn ʿAbd al-Barr, a renowned traditionist, writes thus in his *Kitāb al-Kunā*: "In regard to single-person reports, Imam Abū Ḥanīfah maintained that, if they were repugnant to universally held beliefs, they were not acceptable. Traditionists opposed this, carrying their opposition beyond bounds."[31]

The practical difference between the approaches of the *muḥaddithīn* and Abū Ḥanīfah to traditions contrary to universally accepted propositions lay in this that the former, taking the correctness of the traditions for granted, tried to make them acceptable by means of circumlocutory interpretation, often hardly plausible. The latter, however, tended to hold that, since the traditions were not *mutawātir* or *mashhūr*, there was a likelihood of a mistake or inadvertence on the part of the transmitters, which made their validity doubtful. The difference is well illustrated in the following passage quoted from Fakhr al-Dīn al-Rāzī's *al-Tafsīr Kabīr*: "I told a man that the tradition which says that Ibrāhīm told a lie thrice was not correct since, if accepted, it would prove Ibrāhīm to have been a liar. The man said that the transmitter of the tradition was reliable and could not be regarded as a liar. I replied that the tradition, if accepted, would prove Ibrāhīm to have been a liar and, if rejected, prove the transmitter to have been a liar, adding that preference had obviously to be given to Ibrāhīm."

Al-Rāzī here followed the rule laid down by Abū Ḥanīfah inasmuch as he held that, since the innocence and truthfulness of prophets was a universally accepted proposition, a single-authority report could not overrule it. Deplorably enough, the traditionist al-Qasṭalānī, to name a leading representative of a group, after quoting this passage in his commentary on al-Bukhārī's *Ṣaḥīḥ*, adds the rider: "As the transmitter is reliable, the tradition has to be accepted."

Following the same rule, Abū Ḥanīfah maintains that the words "In the name of Allah, the Beneficent, the Merciful" occurring at the beginning of every *sūrah* of the Qur'an are not part of the Qur'anic text. Al-Shāfi'ī and some *muḥaddithīn* disagree with this, adducing certain traditions in support of their view. Abū Ḥanīfah's reply to this is that the Qur'an is proved by *tawātur*, and not by single-authority reports, and that only that is Qur'an which is proved by *tawātur*. Similarly, according to Abū Ḥanīfah's rule, traditions ascribing to 'Abdullāh b. 'Mas'ūd denial of the *mu'awwadhatayn* (the last two *sūrahs* of the Qur'an, in which Allah's refuge is sought against evil) are not worthy of credence. Ibn Ḥajar, on the other hand, accepts these traditions, recommending that they should be so interpreted as to become acceptable. But what interpretation of this kind is possible? Either one has to admit that the two *sūrahs* are not *mutawātir* or so lower the standard of *tawātur* that even the knowledge of the Prophet's Companions does not remain a necessary condition of it.

Abū Ḥanīfah's rule makes Islam's circle as large as it should be, while the opposite approach narrows it down to an infinitesimal point. For example, it is accepted by everybody that one who believes in divine unity and the apostleship of the founder of Islam is a Muslim according to the Qur'an; and this cannot be overruled by traditions which are not definitive and in which a ruling of unbelief has been given on extraneous grounds. This was the reason why Abū Ḥanīfah never stigmatised the Mu'tazilah, the Qadariyyah, the Jahmiyyah and similar sects as unbelievers and never accepted traditions of the kind which assert that of Islam's seventy-two sects only one is destined for Paradise. But many literal-minded scholars accorded such a high status to traditions of this kind that on their basis they gave verdicts of unbelief against people *ad libitum*, sometimes merely because of dress or personal appearance. Even the followers of Abū Ḥanīfah in later times lost sight of the valuable rule enunciated by him and invented thousands of grounds for denouncing people as infidels, with which books of *fiqh* are replete.

Notes

1. Al-Ḥāfiẓ Jalāl al-Dīn al-Suyūṭī, *Ṭabaqāt al-Mufassirīn*, note on al-Ṭabarī.
2. Al-Ḥāfiẓ Ibn Ḥajar, *Tawālī al-Ta'sīs*, p. 56.
3. Imam al-Rāzī, *Manāqib al-Shāfi'ī*. The figures of the traditions narrated by the first four caliphs recorded by me have been taken from Imam al-Shāfi'ī. *Muḥaddithīn* attribute more traditions to them. But even so, their numbers are not so large as to warrant our saying that they were profuse narrators.

4. Ibn Ḥajar quotes this statement of al-Bukhārī in the introduction to *Fatḥ al-Bārī.*
5. Al-Rāzī, *Manāqib al-Shāfi'ī,* Chapter IV.
6. Ibn Khallikān, *Ta'rīkh,* note on Qāḍī Abū Yūsuf.
7. *'Uqūd al-Jumān.*
8. A detailed account of these is given in the appendix.
9. *Tahdhīb al-Tahdhīb,* note on Imam Abū Ḥanīfah.
10. Shāh Waliullāh, *'Iqd al-Jīd.*
11. It is surprising that, despite this clarification, some narrow-minded people have tried to prove that the Imam was not well acquainted with Ḥadīth on the basis of a parenthetical remark of Ibn Khaldūn, which he has made in words that show that he himself was not convinced of the truth of it.
12. *'Uqūd al-Jumān.*
13. The *Musnad* of al-Dārimī.
14. Al-Dhahabī, *Ṭabaqāt al-Ḥuffāẓ,* note on the caliph 'Umar.
15. *Musnad al-Dārimī.*
16. Al-Dhahabī, *Ṭabaqāt al-Ḥuffāẓ,* note on 'Umar.
17. Ibid.
18. *Fatḥ al-Mughīth,* p. 108.
19. *Ibid.*
20. *Fatḥ al-Mughīth,* p. 118.
21. Ibid., p. 171.
22. Ibid.
23. Abū Ja'far Jarīr al-Ṭabarī, *al-Ta'rīkh al-Kabīr,* p. 1332.
24. Mullā 'Alī al-Qārī, *Sharḥ Musnad al-Imām al-A'ẓam,* p. 3.
25. Ibn al-Jawzī, quoted in *Fatḥ al-Mughīth.*
26. Ibn Khaldūn, in his *Muqqadimah,* attributes this to Abū Ḥanīfah.
27. It is surprising that even eminent *'ulamā'* like al-Ghazālī and al-Rāzī have levelled this charge against Abū Ḥanīfah, adducing as a case in point the tradition about dry milch animals.
28. *Fatḥ al-Mughīth,* p. 98.
29. Ibid.
30. See introduction to Muslim's *Ṣaḥīḥ.*
31. Quoted by Abū al-Maḥāsin, *'Uqūd al-Jumān.*

11
Fiqh

Although the Islamic *'ulūm*, such as exegesis, Tradition, jurisprudence and military science, came into existence simultaneously with the advent of Islam, it was not until they became regular disciplines that they were associated with particular individuals. Their compilation and systematisation took place in the second century of the Islamic era, and those who accomplished this task came to be known as their founders. Thus, Abū Ḥanīfah was rightly acknowledged as the founder of *fiqh* in the same way as Aristotle was called the founder of logic. It was his contribution to *fiqh* that constituted his real lifework. I, therefore, propose to discuss it in detail, but think it necessary, before doing so, to make a brief survey of the development of *fiqh*—when and how it began and where it stood when Abū Ḥanīfah took it up.

Shāh Waliullāh has related the history of *fiqh* in a fine essay, a summary of which will suffice my purpose. Legal directions, he writes, were not graded during the Prophet's lifetime. If he preformed *wuḍū'* (ablution) in the presence of Companions, he did not tell them whether it was a *rukn* (a principle) or *wājib* (obligatory) or *mustaḥabb* (desirable). The Companions contented themselves with imitating him. The same was the case with *ṣalāh* (ritual prayer): the Companions performed it exactly as the Prophet (ṣ) did, without inquiring what in it was *farḍ* (an imperative duty) and what *wājib* (obligatory). "I know of no group of people," says Ibn 'Abbās, "better (i.e. more intelligent) than the Companions of the Messenger of Allah, but during his long association with him, they posed to him no more than thirteen legal problems, all of which are dealt with in the Qur'an." It was only about extraordinary occurrences that people sought rulings from the Prophet (ṣ). It sometimes also happened that the Prophet (ṣ) on his own' initiative expressed approval or disapproval of things done by people. The rulings and opinions were given mostly in public and recorded by someone or other present.

With the territorial expansion and cultural development that took place after the Prophet's death, new situations arose so thick and fast that it became necessary to deduce specific rules and detailed directions from the broad principles that had earlier proved adequate. For example, if a person inadvertently omitted some part of the ritual of prayer, the question arose as to whether his prayer was valid or not. Now, it was not practicable to declare as imperative every one of the actions constituting prayer. Therefore, the Companions had to divide the actions into different grades, such as *farḍ*, *wājib*, *masnūn* and *mustaḥabb.* Differences of opinion, however, arose among them in regard to the criteria to be adopted for this grading. Similar differences arose on many other questions, some of which had not emerged or even been conceived of during the Prophet's lifetime. In deciding such questions, the Companions had to take recourse to deduction, analogy and conjecture, in which they followed different methods. All this resulted in a body of divergent rules and decisions as early as during the period of the Companions.

Among those of the Companions who were acclaimed as *mujtahids* and *faqīhs* for their work in deducing rules of law, there were four leading figures, namely, the caliphs ʿUmar and ʿAlī, ʿAbdullāh b. Masʿūd and ʿAbdullāh b. ʿAbbās. ʿAlī and ʿAbdullāh b. Masʿūd resided mostly in Kūfah, which, thanks to them, became a seat of *fiqh* learning, just as the two holy cities had done earlier owing to the presence of ʿUmar and ʿAbdullāh b. ʿAbbās.

ʿAlī, having been brought up under the Prophet's tutelage, had had more opportunities than anyone else of observing his actions and hearing his utterances. Asked why he related more traditions than any other Companion, he said, "The Prophet (ṣ) used to tell me things whether I questioned him or not." Besides, he was gifted with the intelligence and percipience of an order rare even among the Companions and was acknowledged by them all. ʿUmar is reported to have said, "Allah forbid that we should ever be confronted with a difficulty without ʿAlī being there." ʿAbdullāh b. ʿAbbās, himself a *mujtahid*, used to say, "When ʿAlī gives a ruling on a point, what more do you need?"

ʿAbdullāh b. Masʿūd was a finished scholar of Ḥadīth and *fiqh* and had associated with the Prophet (ṣ) more intimately than most. How intimately is shown by the following statement of Abū Mūsā, quoted in Muslim's *Ṣaḥīḥ:* "We people came from Yemen to Madīnah and stayed there for a few days. During those days, we found ʿAbdullāh b. Masʿūd visiting the Messenger of Allah so frequently that we took him for a member of the Messenger's household." "There is no *āyah* in the Qur'an," ʿAbdullāh b. Masʿūd used to claim, "the occasion of whose revelation I am not aware of." "If I knew," he also used to say, "of a greater scholar of the Qur'an than myself, I would have travelled any distance to meet him." According to a story related in Muslim's *Ṣaḥīḥ*, ʿAbdullāh b. Masʿūd declared at a public meeting that all the Companions acknowledged him as the greatest living scholar of the Qur'an. This claim was denied by no Companion, as testified by Shaqīq, who was present at the meeting and had occasion to meet several gatherings of Companions subsequently.

'Abdullāh b. Mas'ūd held regular Ḥadīth and *fiqh* classes, which were attended by a large number of students, of whom four, namely, Aswad, 'Ubaydah, Ḥārith and 'Alqamah, achieved great frame. 'Alqamah was born during the Prophet's lifetime and had heard traditions from 'Umar, 'Uthmān, 'Alī, 'Ā'ishah, Sa'd, Ḥudhayfah, Khālid b. al-Walīd, Khubāb and many other Companions. In particular, he had associated with 'Abdullāh b. Mas'ūd so regularly and imitated him so faithfully that people often remarked: "Whoever has met 'Alqamah has, so to speak, met 'Abdullāh b. Mas'ūd." The latter himself used to admit that he knew no more than 'Alqamah did. There could be no better proof of his standing as an authority that even Companions used to consult him on legal questions. His only equal among 'Abdullāh b. Mas'ūd's pupils was Aswad.

The mantle of 'Alqamah and Aswad fell, after their death, on Ibrāhīm al-Nakha'ī, who made a considerable contribution to *fiqh*, earning thereby the title *Faqīh al-'Irāq* (the *Faqīh* of Iraq). In Ḥadīth, his standing is shown by the title *Ṣayrafī al-Ḥadīth* (Appraiser of Ḥadīth), which he enjoyed. Al-Sha'bī, acclaimed as *'Allāmah al-Tābi'īn* (Great Scholar among the Successors), said on hearing of his death, "Ibrāhīm has left behind no one who is a greater scholar and *faqīh* than he was." Somebody asked him with surprise, "Are you including even al-Ḥasan al-Baṣrī and Ibn Sīrīn?" "Not to speak of al-Ḥasan al-Baṣrī and Ibn Sīrīn," replied al-Sha'bī, "there is no greater scholar whether in Baṣrah and Kūfah or in Syria and Ḥijāz."

In Ibrāhīm al-Nakha'ī's time, a short collection of *fiqh* rulings was compiled, the sources of which were Prophetic traditions and *fatwās* of 'Alī and 'Abdullāh b. Mas'ūd. This was not a systematic compilation, but Ibrāhīm al-Nakha'ī's pupils committed its contents to memory. The largest stock of these was in the possession of Ḥammād, who was one of Ibrāhīm's leading pupils and who succeeded him in the *fiqh* chair. As mentioned earlier, Ḥammād died in 120 H and was succeeded by Abū Ḥanīfah.

Although the accepted rules of *fiqh* had been collected by Abū Ḥanīfah's time, they existed for the most part in the shape of oral traditions and had not been systematised into a regular discipline. There were no methods of reasoning, no rules for the derivation of orders, no grading of traditions and no principles of analogical deduction. In short, *fiqh* was still a congeries of uncoordinated dicta and rulings that had a long way to go before becoming a system.

History throws no light on what in particular induced Abū Ḥanīfah to take up the systematisation of *fiqh*. The author of the *Qalā'id 'Uqūd al-'Iqyān* quotes a story in this connection from *Anmūdhaj al-Qitāl*. Two men went to a *ḥammām* and, before going in for their bath, deposited something with the keeper for safe custody. The one who came out earlier took the thing from the keeper and went away. Later, the other man, after finishing his bath, demanded the thing, and was told by the keeper that his companion had taken it away. He filed a suit against the keeper in the court of the *qāḍī*, who decided against the keeper on the ground that, as the thing had been entrusted to him jointly by the two bathers, it was incumbent on him to return it to them jointly. The keeper came to Abū Ḥanīfah, who advised him to tell the plaintiff that he would let him have the thing, provided he came together with his companion to take it. This incident, the author of *Anmūdhaj al-Qitāl* suggests, was what made Abū Ḥanīfah decide to take up the compilation and systematisation of *fiqh*. It is possible that the incident did take place, but the real incentive lay elsewhere.

It is a historically established fact that Abū Ḥanīfah turned to the systematisation of *fiqh* around 120 H, that is to say, the year in which Ḥammād died. By that time, Islamic culture had spread to distant lands, and a multitude of situations connected with religious performances and secular affairs had arisen which could not be dealt with without a legal code. Besides, contact with other peoples over the vast Islamic domains had developed education to such an extent that it was no longer feasible to carry on with oral narration of traditions and citation of authorities. It was but natural for people to think of integrating scattered rulings and directions into a regular code.

Abū Ḥanīfah was endowed with an original mind and an extraordinary flair for law. Besides, his extensive experience of trade and public affairs had acquainted him with the legal requirements of the society of his day. The hundreds of legal inquiries he received daily from all parts of the Islamic world made him realise how badly a system of jurisprudence was needed, and this realisation was strengthened by the errors he found judicial officers committing in deciding cases. These then were the factors which decided him to undertake the compilation and systematisation of laws, although it is possible that some incident of the kind just described provided an additional impetus.

It was a gigantic and hazardous project that Abū Ḥanīfah ventured on. Realising, this, he decided not to base it entirely on his personal knowledge and thinking. Accordingly, he selected as his assistants some eminent scholars from among his pupils acknowledged as masters in the branches of learning specially relevant to jurisprudence. For example, Yaḥyā b. Abī Zā'idah, Ḥafṣ b. Ghiyāth, Qāḍī Abū Yūsuf, Dāwūd al-Ṭā'ī, Ḥabbān and Mindal, who were finished scholars of Ḥadīth and *āthār*; Zufar, who was renowned for his logical prowess; and al-Qāsim b. Ma'n and Muḥammad, who were accomplished in literature and Arabic learning. Abū Ḥanīfah formed a board consisting of these men and entrusted to it the work of compiling laws. According to a *muttaṣil* tradition from Asad b. al-Furāt, quoted by al-Ṭaḥāwī, those of Abū Ḥanīfah's pupils who assisted him numbered forty, the most distinguished of them being Abū Yūsuf, Zufar, Dāwūd al-Ṭā'ī, Asad b. 'Umar, Asad b. Khālid al-Tamīmī and Yaḥyā b. Abī Zā'idah. Al-Ṭaḥāwī adds that the scribe was Yaḥyā, who rendered service as such for thirty years.

While it is true that the work took more or less thirty years, that is to say, from 121 H to 150 H, the year of Abū Ḥanīfah's death, it is not true that Yaḥyā was associated with it from the very beginning. Yaḥyā was born in 120 H and could not conceivably have begun to participate in the work when he was an infant. In addition to the members of the compilation board named by al-Ṭaḥāwī, there were al-'Āfiyah al-Azadī, Abū 'Alī al-'Azzī, 'Alī b. Mushir, al-Qāsim b. Ma'n, Ḥabbān and Mindal.

The compilation was done by free discussion. If all members of the board were agreed on a point taken up, their agreed opinion was recorded there and then. Otherwise the point was fully thrashed out, which sometimes took a long time. Abū Ḥanīfah would listen to the discussion and, after summing it up, conclude it with his own opinion. His opinion was generally so balanced that it was accepted by all the others. When, however, a unanimous conclusion could not be arrived at, the various opinions expressed were all recorded. No conclusion was ever recorded unless all the members of the board were present and reached it unanimously.

The author of *al-Jawāhir al-Muḍiyyah* states in his biographical note on 'Āfiyah b. Yazīd, on the authority of Isḥāq, that, if on any occasion 'Āfiyah was late in coming, the Imam would wait for him and would order the decision on the point at issue to be recorded only after he had come and expressed his concurrence. In this way, the work of compilation was completed in thirty years, including the last years of the Imam's life, which were spent in prison.

As described by Abū al-Maḥāsin, the contents of the compilation were divided into chapters on various subjects in the following order: *ṭahārah* (purity), *ṣalāh* (prayer), *ṣawm* (fasting), *'ibādah* (rites of worship), *mu'āmalāt* (secular matters) and *mīrāth* (inheritance).

The compilation gained, during the Imam's lifetime, a popularity difficult to conceive of in the circumstances of the time. As soon as its various parts were ready, one after another they were published throughout the Islamic world. The Imam's school, thanks to the compilation, became a veritable law college whose alumni were appointed in large numbers to judicial and administrative posts, in which they used it as their handbook What is particularly interesting is that even people who claimed to be Abū Ḥanīfah's equals could not do without it. Sufyān al-Thawrī very cleverly obtained a copy of one part, namely, *Kitāb al-Rahn* (the manual on mortgage) and always used to keep it handy. Zā'idah relates that one day, seeing a book near Sufyān's pillow, which he was reading, he looked at it with his permission and found it to be Abū Ḥanīfah's *Kitāb al-Rahn.* "You read Abū Ḥanīfah's books!" he exclaimed with surprise. "I wish I had all of them," replied Sufyān.[1]

It is no less surprising that, although there were many people at that time who claimed to be authorities on law and some of whom were hostile to Abū Ḥanīfah, not one of them dared to criticise the compilation. Al-Rāzī writes thus in *Manāqib al-Shāfi'ī*: "At the time when the *aṣḥāb al-ra'y* (followers of opinion, namely, Abū Ḥanīfah and his pupils) published their opinions and conclusions, the world was full of *muḥaddithīn* and narrators of traditions, but not one of them proved capable of objecting to the things that they said." I have, however, come across one exception to this generalisation. Al-Bayhaqī says that al-Awzā'ī wrote a refutation of Abū Ḥanīfah's *Kitāb al-Siyar*, to which Abū Yūsuf wrote a counter refutation.

It would seem that the compilation was a voluminous one, comprising thousands of *masā'il* (legal propositions). The author of *Qalā'id 'Uqūd al-'Iqyān* states on the authority of *Kitāb al-Ṣiyānah* that the number of the *masā'il* compiled exceeded 1,290,000. Shams al-A'immah al-Kurdarī puts the figure at 600,000. Neither of these figures may be accurate. Nevertheless, there is no doubt that the figure was not less than a few hundred thousands, as can be verified from the surviving books of Imam Muḥammad.

Although there can be no doubt that all the chapters of the *fiqh* compilation were completed during Abū Ḥanīfah's lifetime—there is undeniable proof of this in books of biography and history—unfortunately, the compilation has been irretrievably lost and there is no copy of it in any library of the world. Al-Rāzī clinches this by saying in the *Manāqib al-Shāfi'ī*, "No work of Abū Ḥanīfah's is extant." As al-Rāzī died in 606 H, this means that Abū Ḥanīfah's works disappeared at least six centuries ago. This is nothing surprising in the history of Muslim learning. None of the thousands of books written in Abū Ḥanīfah's age has survived the ravages of time. For example, the works of al-Awzā'ī, Ibn Jurayj, Ibn 'Arūbah and Ḥammād b. Abī Ma'mar were published about the same time as Abū Ḥanīfah's compendium, but not even the names of these works are known today.

There is, however, a special reason for the disappearance of Abū Ḥanīfah's writings. Despite the fact that Abū Ḥanīfah's compendium was well arranged, it was superseded in popular use by the derivative writings of Abū Yūsuf and Muḥammad, which presented the legal questions dealt with by Abū Ḥanīfah in a more perspicuous and detailed manner and with elaborate annotations. A parallel case is that of al-Farrā', al-Kisā'ī, al-Khalīl, al-Akhfash and Abū 'Ubaydah, originators and first systematisers of grammar, whose works were superseded by those of later grammarians and completely vanished.

What survives of the contribution of Abū Ḥanīfah to *fiqh* is embodied in the writings of Muḥammad and Abū Yūsuf, brief accounts of whom will be found in the appendix. In fact, what is known as Ḥanafī *fiqh* is a collection of the opinions of four men, namely, Abū Ḥanīfah, Zufar, Abū Yūsuf and Muḥammad. Abū Yūsuf and Muḥammad differ with Abū Ḥanīfah on many points, but, according to many Ḥanafī jurists, for example, al-Shāmī, they admitted that the dissident opinions expressed by them were those of Abū Ḥanīfah himself, since in many matters he expressed different opinions in different contexts. This is, however, difficult to substantiate and was probably dictated by partiality to Abū Ḥanīfah. Abū Yūsuf and Muḥammad were themselves acknowledged *mujtahids* and had every right to differ with their master. Islam's progress took place only so long as people openly expressed their disagreement with the older masters, uninhibited by the reverence they had for them.

The legal system known as Ḥanafī *fiqh* spread rapidly over the whole of the Islamic world except Arabia, where it could not gain much currency because of the presence of Mālik in Makkah and of other imams in Madīnah. It became the main legal system of the whole territory extending from Sind to Asia Minor and the sole legal system of India, Sind, Kabul, Bukhārā and neighbouring lands. As regards other countries, in some of them it remained current side by side with the Shāfi'ī and Ḥanbalī systems, while in others it was supplanted by them after remaining current for some time. There were special reasons for the latter event. In Africa, for example, after remaining the main legal system until 406 H, it was supplanted by the Mālikī system owing to the patronage of the latter by the government of al-Mu'izz b. Bādīs.[2]

One special factor responsible for the dominance of Ḥanafī *fiqh* is that most rulers of Islamic countries followed it. The 'Abbāsid caliphs, however, were exceptions to this. As long as the rule of their dynasty lasted, they were lords of the pen as well as the sword, or, in other words, considered themselves *mujtahids* in their own right and refused to conform to any system. After the decline of their dynasty, they were no longer in a position either to exert any influence in this sphere or to maintain their independent attitude. Even so, if any of them conformed to any system, it was to that of Abū Ḥanīfah. 'Abdullāh b. al-Mu'tazz, founder of the art of *badī'* and the greatest of 'Abbāsid poets and litterateurs, followed the Ḥanafī *madhhab*.[3]

The dynasties that rose to power with the decline of the 'Abbāsids mostly adhered to the Ḥanafī system. The Seljukians, who ruled for a long time and whose dominions extended from Kashghar to Jerusalem and from Constantinople to the shore of the Caspian Sea, were of the Ḥanafī persuasion.

Maḥmūd al-Ghaznawī, whose name is a household word in India, was a great scholar of Ḥanafī *fiqh*. There is extant a book by him on the subject entitled *al-Tafrīd*, containing about sixty thousand *masā'il*. Nūr al-Dīn Zangī, one of the heroes of Islamic history, who distinguished himself in the holy war at Jerusalem before Ṣalāḥ al-Dīn, one of his servants, conquered it, and who established the first college of Ḥadīth, was, like others in his dynasty, a Ḥanafī, although he respected the Shāfi'ī and Mālikī systems too. Ṣalāḥ al-Dīn was a Shāfi'ī, but there were many Ḥanafīs in his family.[4]

About al-Malik al-Mu'aḍam 'Īsā b. al-Malik al-'Ādil, ruler of a vast territory, Ibn Khallikān writes, "He was high-minded, learned, wise, brave, dignified and profoundly dedicated to the Ḥanafī *madhhab*." The Circassians of Egypt, who established their rule at the beginning of the ninth century of the Islamic era and ruled for 148 years were Ḥanafīs and patrons of the Ḥanafī *madhhab*. Most of the Turkish sultans, who ruled over Turkey for centuries and whose empire is today one of the symbols of Islam's previous power and prestige, have been Ḥanafīs. In India itself, the Pathan kings and the House of Tīmūr were of the same persuasion, and no other system could gain currency in their vast domains.

Some people think that the popularity of the Ḥanafī *madhhab* has been due to state patronage. Ibn Ḥazm, famous imam of literalist scholars, writes, "There were two *madhhabs* which gained currency with governmental support. The first of these was Abū Ḥanīfah's *madhhab*, which flourished because Abū Yūsuf during his term of office as the chief *qāḍī* appointed only Ḥanafīs to judicial posts. The second was Imam Mālik's *madhhab*, which made headway in Spain, thanks to the patronage of Imam Mālik's disciple, Yaḥyā al-Maṣmūdī, who was so close to the caliph that all appointments to judicial posts were made on his recommendation and who got only followers of his *madhhab* appointed."[5] But this is a superficial view.

Abū, Ḥanīfah acquired the status of a *mujtahid* in 120 H, while Abū Yūsuf was appointed to the post of chief *qāḍī* in 170 H, the year of the accession of Hārūn al-Rashīd, during whose reign he attained to eminence. During the interval of fifty years, Abū Ḥanīfah's *madhhab* gained wide popularity, and hundreds of his pupils were appointed as *qāḍīs*. To whom is this success to be attributed? There is no denying that Abū Ḥanīfah's legal opinions gained added popularity because of Abū Yūsuf, but they owed to Abū Ḥanīfah's own efforts the popular acclaim they originally enjoyed. Al-Rāzī admits this despite his opposition to Abū Ḥanīfah: "The *madhhab* of the adherents of opinion gained strength and fame and public esteem. Later, when Abū Yūsuf and Muḥammad were admitted to Hārūn al-Rashīd's court, it gained further strength from the combination of learning and political power."

Apart from this, Abū Yūsuf's influence was confined to the reign of Hārūn al-Rashīd. Who then was responsible for the long-enduring and continued success of the Ḥanafī legal system? It is true that some other imams attained to eminence during their lifetime. For example, al-Awzā'ī became the unchallenged imam of Syria during his lifetime and remained so for a time after his death, so that in that region it was mainly his *madhhab* that was followed. But his influence was limited and shortlived. It is clear from these facts that Abū Ḥanīfah's *madhhab* has some qualities which other *madhhabs* do not have.

There are only four imams whose systems of jurisprudence gained wide currency in the Islamic world, namely. Abū Ḥanīfah, Mālik, al-Shāfi'ī and Aḥmad b. Ḥanbal. Although the popularity of these systems is accounted (or by their own goodness, there is no doubt that the personal influence and importance of their founders had also much to do with it. It is my opinion that the popularity of the systems other than that of Abū Ḥanīfah was largely the out come of the personal advantages enjoyed by their founders. Thus, Mālik was a native of Madīnah, which, having been the centre of the Prophetic mission and the capital of the early caliphs, still had a halo of glory around it. He came of a family of learned men, his grandfather, Mālik b. Abī ʻĀmir, having learnt traditions from prominent Companions, and his paternal uncle having been a *shaykh* of Ḥadīth. His accomplishment in Ḥadīth and *fiqh* was thus a gloss on his legacy of scholarship. The two together won wide fame for him.

Al-Shāfiʻī had even greater personal advantages. A native of Makkah, he was a Qurayshī and Muṭṭalibī on the father's side and a Hāshimī on the mother's. His family had been distinguished for generations. His great-grandfather, Sā'ib, had been the standard-bearer of the Hāshimīs at the Battle of Badr and, having been taken prisoner, had embraced Islam. Nothing could be a better means of gaining popularity and public esteem than this combination.

Abū Ḥanīfah enjoyed no advantage of this kind. Far from being a Qurayshī and a Hāshimī, he was not even an Arab, and none of his ancestors had occupied a position of leadership among the Muslims. Born of a family of traders, he was himself a trader all his life long. His birthplace, Kūfah, although a seat of learning, did not rank as such with Makkah and Madīnah. Added to these was the hostility of a group of traditionists which he unavoidably incurred. In short, he possessed none of the natural means of winning popularity and public acclaim.

That, despite this, his system of jurisprudence gained wider currency in the Islamic world than any other system, is a sure proof of the fact that it suited human needs, and especially the needs of a culturally advancing Muslim society, better than the other systems. It is significant that the other systems were adopted mostly in those countries which had not made much progress in culture. Explaining why Mālik's system gained dominance in the Maghrib and Spain, Ibn Khaldūn writes, "The inhabitants of the Maghrib and Spain were still at the stage of Bedouin primitivism and had not yet made the same progress as the people of Iraq had made. That was why no *fiqh* other than that of Imam Mālik made headway there."

The Ḥanafī system of jurisprudence, which comprises the legal doctrines and enunciations, not only of Abū Ḥanīfah, but also of his prominent disciples, was a great system and, in fact, a great code of laws for its time. In later times Ḥanafī scholars added much to it, not only by way of elaborating details, but also by way of formulating principles. Nevertheless, no greater progress could have been made by any system of jurisprudence or, for that matter, by any discipline in its initial stages than that which the Ḥanafī system made during Abū Ḥanīfah's lifetime. It included not only laws relating to ritual duties but also civil, criminal, penal and revenue laws, laws governing evidence, contracts, inheritance and wills, and laws relating to many other matters. Its comprehensiveness and usefulness can be gauged from the fact that it was in force throughout the empire of Hārūn al-Rashīd, which stretched from Sind to Asia Minor.

The Ḥanafī code, known as *fiqh*, deals with two broad categories of legal subjects, which invest its author with two distinct capacities: (1) rules deduced from Sharī'ah, which may be described as canon law, and (2) rules relating to matters on which Sharī'ah is silent and which are thrown up by the development of social life or to matters referred to in Sharī'ah but not legislated on canonically. In relation to the first category of rules the *faqīh* is a commentator and expounder, and the qualifications he needs in that capacity are command of language, knowledge of texts, power of deduction, ability to rectify inconsistencies and skill in appraising arguments. In relation to the second category of rules, he is a lawgiver and must possess, gifts comparable with those of the world's famous lawgivers. These two capacities are quite distinct from each other. In Islam, there have been many renowned exegetes and commentators on the Qur'an and Ḥadīth who had no ability to frame laws. Similarly, there have been great lawmakers who had no talent for explaining texts of Sharī'ah. know of no other man—whether *mujtahid* or imam—in the whole of Islam's long history who combined in himself qualities of the two orders to the high degree that Abū Ḥanīfah did.

The most valuable contribution that Abū Ḥanīfah made to *fiqh* was distinguishing between canon law and non-canonical rules of law.

Some accounts of the sayings and doings of Islam's Lawgiver related to matters having nothing to do with his prophetic office, but owing to a terminological laxity even these accounts had come to be designated as traditions. This led to the grave and common error of deducing rules of canon law from words and deeds of the Prophet (ṣ) which did not pertain to his office of Lawgiver. Dealing with this subject, Shāh Waliullāh writes as follows: "Whatever has been reported from the Prophet (ṣ) and included in books of Ḥadīth is divisible into two categories: (1) things pertaining to the Prophetic mission, in connection with which was revealed the *āyah* "Adopt whatever the Prophet (ṣ) commands and refrain from whatever he prohibits," and (2) things not connected with the Prophetic mission, in regard to which the Prophet (ṣ) himself said, "I am only a man: whenever I give you a religious command, follow it, but whenever I give you a direction based on my personal opinion, remember that I am only a man."[6]

Included in the second category are traditions from the Prophet (ṣ) in which he made pronouncements on medical questions; actions performed by him habitually and not as acts of worship, casually and not deliberately; traditions narrated by him in accordance with the common beliefs of his people, such as the traditions about Umm Zar' and Kharāfah; and things done or said by him at the dictates of expendiency and which, therefore, it was not incumbent on everyone to follow, such as orders about the deployment of troops and determination of fighting slogans. It was in connection with the last-mentioned that 'Umar said, "What need is there for *ramal* (walking proudly during hajj) now? The people for whose sake we used to do it have been destroyed by Allah." There are many other orders of the Prophet (ṣ) which were similarly based on mere expediency, as, for example, the ruling that a Muslim killing an infidel became the owner of the latter's arms.

Abū Ḥanīfah anticipated Shāh Waliullāh in this fine distinction. Thus, he assigned to the second category traditions relating to such matters as the Friday bath, the going out of women for the two 'Īd prayers, the execution of divorce, the determination of *jizyah*, the levying of tribute and the distribution of booty. Al-Shāfi'ī and others, on the other hand, include such traditions in canonical traditions.

What essentially distinguishes the Ḥanafī school of law from other schools is the fact that all its rules are based on this distinction, and it is this which gives them a breadth and liberality not found in the rules framed by any other school. It is a pity that, clear as the distinction is, the founders of the other schools did not pay heed to it. Indeed, if examples provided by the first four caliphs had not been there to support the distinction, it is probable that even Abū Ḥanīfah would not have ventured to adopt it. Several imams after Abū Ḥanīfah, who were his rivals in *ijtihād*, ignored it. That, however, does not cast any doubt on its soundness and on Abū Ḥanīfah's legal acumen in observing it.

No one could understand the inner meaning of canonical commands better than the first four caliphs. Let us look at their practice. Before 'Umar became caliph, slave girls who had borne children were generally bought and sold. 'Umar stopped this altogether. The Prophet (ṣ) during his journey to Tabūk had imposed *jizyah* on non-Muslims at the rate of one dinar per head. 'Umar fixed it in Iran at different rates, namely, 48, 12 and 6 dinars per head. The Prophet (ṣ) used to give a share of the booty to his relatives. The first four caliphs gave none even to Hāshimīs. In the time of the Prophet (ṣ) and even during Abū Bakr's caliphate three pronouncements of divorce were considered a single pronouncement. 'Umar, when he became caliph, had it proclaimed that three pronouncements would be regarded as constituting an irrevocable divorce. During the Prophet's lifetime no *ḥadd* (definite punishment) had been prescribed for drinking. Abū Bakr prescribed forty stripes, which 'Umar, because of increased drinking during his reign, raised to eighty. These are facts which have been stated in Ḥadīth books and which there is no denying. But does this mean that the first four caliphs defied canonical orders of the Prophet (ṣ), knowing them to be such? If they had done so, they would not have been the "rightly guided caliphs" they are considered to have been, but rivals and adversaries of the Messenger of Allah.

The truth of the matter is that for the Companions, who through associating with the Prophet (ṣ) day and night had developed an intuitive understanding of Sharī'ah, it was easy to distinguish between canonical directions and those about which the Prophet (ṣ) said, "You people know more about your worldly affairs than I do." 'Ā'ishah said on one occasion after the Prophet's death, "If the Messenger of Allah were alive today, he would not have permitted women to go to the mosque." This is a clear proof of the fact that 'Ā'ishah did not regard the permission given to women by the Prophet (ṣ) to go to the mosque as canonical and irrevocable. For had it been so, change of time and circumstances would have made no difference to it.

Abū Ḥanīfah followed the example of the Companions in this matter, and his opinions are generally in accord with the practice of the first four caliphs but people who are unable to discern the fine distinction involved reproach him and even the Companions. Quoting 'Umar on the question of divorce, Qāḍī al-Shawkānī writes, "What was poor 'Umar in comparison with the Messenger of Allah?" But he seems to have forgotten that 'Umar himself was conscious of his inferiority to the Prophet (ṣ) far more than he, al-Shawkānī, could understand.

The greatest contribution made by Abū Ḥanīfah to the first of the two divisions of *fiqh* which we have distinguished above was the formulation of rules of deduction, which made of *fiqh* (until then only a collection of fragmentary rules and propositions) a regular science. In this lay his most valuable and most astonishing achievement—an achievement which no other man was capable of at a time when the religious sciences were still in a rudimentary stage.

It is commonly thought that al-Shāfi'ī was the first to formulate these rules, which are now called *uṣūl al-fiqh* (the roots or principles of jurisprudence). This idea is correct only in so far as reduction of the rules to writing is concerned. Before al-Shāfi'ī set them forth regularly in writing, the rules had been framed by Abū Ḥanīfah, who had thus already laid the foundation of the science of *fiqh*.

The process of deducing legal principles and particular rules had started in the time of the Successors or rather in that of the Companions. The method followed was not, however, scientific, but purely pragmatic and intuitive like the practical reasoning of the common man. Neither any technical terms nor any rules had yet been devised.

Some technical terms came into use towards the end of the Umayyad rule. For example, Wāṣil b. 'Aṭā', the founder of *kalām*, classified rules of Sharī'ah according to their sources, namely, clear Qur'anic texts, universally accepted traditions, the consensus of the community and reason (i.e. analogical deduction). He also established a number of general propositions, such as that generality and particularity are two distinct concepts, that abrogation is possible only in the case of commands and prohibitions and that there can be no abrogation in regard to events and reports.[7] Wāṣil b. 'Aṭā' can be described, on the basis of these propositions, as a pioneer in formulating principles of *fiqh* only in the same way as the caliph 'Alī is reputed to be the founder of grammar because of his having framed a few grammatical rules. However, this was all that had happened up to Abū

Ḥanīfah's time: because of his desire to organise *fiqh* as a regular science, he had to devise his own rules for deducing legal principles.

Although in later times the roots of *fiqh* became the subject matter of a vast science, which addressed itself, along with the older questions, to hundreds of new ones of which there was no sign in Abū Ḥanīfah's time, there is no doubt that he formulated principles relating to all the fundamental questions with which *fiqh* was and is to this day concerned, such as exposition of the four roots, gradation of traditions and deduction of rules from them, exposition and rectification of errors, limits of public consensus, kinds and conditions of analogy, classification of dicta, distinction between the general and the particular, reconciliation of contradictions, and methods of interpretation.

I have already dealt with the principles formulated by Abū Ḥanīfah in respect of traditions. Examples of his principles in regard to other matters are provided by the following pronouncements made by him: "Nothing that is not proved by *tawātur* is part of the Qur'an, and whatever is redundant is abrogated. No addition to the Qur'an is permissible simply on the basis of a single-person report. To construe as absolute what is limited is to add to *naṣṣ* (the Qur'anic text). The generality of the Qur'an cannot be particularised by single-person reports. The general is absolute like the particular. If the particular is posterior in time, it makes the general definitive. If the particular is prior in time, it does not particularise the general. In fact, the general abrogates the particular; and if the narrator is ignorant of history, both become void and some other argument becomes necessary. The meaning of an attribute cannot be argued from. Denial is not a proof of falsification."

Pronouncements of this kind by Abū Ḥanīfah lie scattered in the writings of his pupils and books on the roots of *fiqh* written by al-Shāfiʿī and al-Ḥanafī scholars in a large enough number to provide material for a small book.[8] It is on the basis of these pronouncements that Abū Ḥanīfah is regarded as the originator of a special method of *ijtihād*, and since the principles embodied in these pronouncements are followed by Muḥammad b. al-Ḥasan and Abū Yūsuf, their methods of *ijtihād* cannot be considered to be different from that of Abū Ḥanīfah's, although the three differ on a number of particular questions.

The disagreement of al-Shāfiʿī and other doctors with Abū Ḥanīfah about the principles gave rise to a lengthy and involved controversy, for an account of which there is no room in this small book. Those interested will find it in books on the roots of *fiqh*.

As I have already said, the position of Abū Ḥanīfah in the division of *fiqh* dealing with canon law is that of an exponent and deducer, and there is no doubt that the work done by him as such is unparalleled in the history of Islam and, perhaps, in all history. The followers of other religions that possess revealed books also derive rules of law from those books, but none of them can claim to have raised this to the rank of a regular science based on properly formulated principles.

The second division of *fiqh*, which is law pure and simple, is wider in scope than the first, and in this division Abū Ḥanīfah has a position all his own as a *mujtahid*: indeed, he is the only lawmaker in the history of Islam.

Among the Muslims the framing of laws has always been the preserve of religious leaders, men distinguished for their extreme devoutness and piety. The qualities prized most in religious people are detachment from worldly matters, aloofness, strictness in the performance of duties, unawareness of public affairs and dislike of the followers of other religions. All these are qualities adverse to social progress. People characterised by an excess of these qualities, especially if they are inborn in them, are unable to understand the requirements of a developing civilisation. For all the veneration that such people rightfully enjoy because of their holiness and purity, they can offer little guidance to men and women in the conduct of their mundane affairs. Who can deny the exalted rank of godly men like al-Junayd al-Baghdādī, Maʿrūf al-Karkhī, al-Shiblī and Dāwūd al-Ṭā'ī, but cannot imagine them in the role of legislators.

Even the *mujtahids* who framed personal and public laws under the title *fiqh*, although no anchorites like these holy men, did not know enough about mundane matters to legislate about them. That explains why some of their laws are so rigid and unimaginative as to be difficult of enforcement. For example, al-Shāfiʿī and some other *mujtahids* maintain that no one but a reliable man can be a witness to a marriage, that a neighbour has no right of pre-emption, that it is impermissible to sell gifts, that the testimony of *dhimmīs* is not admissible in any circumstances and that if a Muslim kills hundreds of innocent *dhimmīs*, he is not punishable for this. Laws of this kind are simply not workable.

Abū Ḥanīfah was alone among his contemporaries in combining religious piety with an understanding of worldly needs, and especially the needs of a growing society. Because of the legal references constantly made to him, he had become acquainted with thousands of complicated questions concerning human relations. His consultative council was to all intents and purposes a supreme court, which had decided hundreds of thousands of cases. It virtually had an official status and was consulted by State functionaries. Most of his disciples and associates, who numbered hundreds, were people holding judicial posts. To crown all, he was a born jurist with a flair for the finer points of law and an intuitive appreciation of its operation in human affairs. A good illustration of this is provided by the following incident, narrated by most of the historians who have written about him.

One day, Abū Ḥanīfah called on Qāḍī Abū Laylā and found him engaged in hearing a case. The plaintiff alleged that the defendant had defamed him by calling his mother an adulteress. The Qāḍī inquired of the defendant, who also was present in court, what he had to say in his defence. Abū Ḥanīfah, intervening, said to the Qāḍī that the suit was not yet ready for being heard and advised him to ask the plaintiff if his mother was alive, because, if she was, she should also join the suit and be either personally present or authorise the plaintiff in writing to represent her. On the Qāḍī questioning him accordingly, the plaintiff stated that his mother was dead. The Qāḍī thereupon wished to proceed with the hearing. Abū Ḥanīfah intervened again and suggested that the plaintiff be asked whether he had any brothers and sisters because, if he did, they should also be joined to the suit. There were a number of further questions which Abū Ḥanīfah caused the Qāḍī to put to the plaintiff. After those questions had been answered, Abū Ḥanīfah declared that the case was ripe for hearing and advised the Qāḍī to proceed with the examination of the plaintiff.

It is clear from this account that, but for Abū Ḥanīfah's intervention, the Qāḍī would have proceeded with the case in a manner no better than the rough and ready manner in which the common people settle their disputes. Abū Ḥanīfah desired the case to be heard in accordance with the proper judicial procedure, an essential requirement of which was that all the persons who could claim to be aggrieved by the cause of action should be parties to the suit so that it should not be necessary for the court to adjudicate severally on a number of claims arising from the same facts.

Abū Ḥanīfah's compilation of laws falling within the second division of *fiqh* was a comprehensive code for its time, and although known by the general title of *fiqh*, it comprised laws relating to many subjects, such as contract, sale, revenue, crime and criminal procedure, on which separate laws have been framed in modern times.

Some writers think that in compiling his code, Abū Ḥanīfah took a good deal of help from Roman law, incorporating many of its rules in the rules framed by him. In support of this they advance the following arguments:

(1) Many of the propositions of Ḥanafī *fiqh* are in accord with Roman law.
(2) Roman law was in force in all the lands comprising Syria and, since the civilisation and culture of Syria exerted a good deal of influence on the Muslims, it is very likely that the Muslim lawmakers profited from the law prevalent in Syria.
(3) The number and extent of the laws included in Ḥanafī *fiqh* cannot be explained otherwise than by acquisition from other laws already existing in the civilised world.

This issue can best be decided by a thorough comparative study of the two sets of laws with a view to determining whether what they have in common is what is common to the laws of all peoples or something more. I am not acquainted with Roman law. Even if I were, it would not have been possible for me to find time for the task. I must, therefore, confess that what I am going to say on the subject is nothing better than conjecture. It must, however, be remembered that those who have initiated this debate rely no less on conjecture, for I have yet to come across a writer who can claim to have mastered both Roman law and Ḥanafī *fiqh* and made a comparative study of much of their content.

It cannot be denied that there are in Ḥanafī *fiqh* a number of rules of law which were prevalent in Arabia and Iraq before the advent of Islam; but borrowing from indigenous laws is nothing peculiar to Ḥanafī *fiqh*. Many of the laws considered Islamic and even laid down in the Qur'an were in vogue in pre-Islamic times. Abū Hilāl al-'Askarī has set them out at length in his *Kitāb al-Awā'il*. For example, the regulations laid down by 'Umar about tribute and taxes were the same as had been framed by Anūshirwān the Just, and this was not a pure coincidence. 'Umar deliberately adopted Anūshirwān's regulations, as has been explained in clear words by al-Ṭabarī and Ibn al-Athīr.

In framing laws for a country a legislator generally has before him all the laws and customs already prevalent: he adopts some of them, adapts others and rejects the rest. Presumably, Abū Ḥanīfah did the same. The probability, however, is that he drew more on the laws of Iran than on Roman law, because, in the first place, he was a Persian with Persian as his mother tongue and, in the second place, his native city was Kūfah, which was part of Persian territory.

It has to be conceded that Abū Ḥanīfah must have profited from the laws and customs prevalent in Persia. The question is: how does this affect his status as a lawmaker? Can he properly be called a lawmaker or only a reproducer and compiler? As far as my research goes, the Muslims acquired very little knowledge of other peoples' laws. Lists of translations consist of the names of thousands of books, but they were most of them books of philosophy, medicine and allied disciplines; not a single book of law is mentioned in the lists. In any case, it is an established fact that when Abū Ḥanīfah compiled his code of *fiqh*, no book of law had yet been translated. Therefore, the hypothesis that Abū Ḥanīfah drew on the law books of other nations must be dismissed as baseless. As regards the customs prevailing in the country, they were not fit to be given the title of law, even if reduced to writing.

To sum up, the historical indications available do not at all prove that Abū Ḥanīfah had before him any book of Roman or Persian law on which he could lay the foundation of his *fiqh*. Nor can it be denied that such collections of *fiqh* propositions as existed before his code were not scientific in character. It follows from all this that he was the originator of the science of *fiqh*. He was no doubt helped by popular customs, the laws in force and the rulings of doctors of law, but as no lawmaker in the world has been able to do without help of this kind, the fact does not detract from his stature as a lawmaker.

I will now deal with those special features of Ḥanafī *fiqh* which exalt it above all other systems of *fiqh*.

The first and foremost distinguishing mark of Ḥanafī *fiqh* is that it bases laws on expediency and beneficiality. There have been two schools of thought in Islam from the very beginning in regard to prescriptions of Sharī'ah. According to one of them, they are purely devotional, that is to say, there is no expediency or benefit implied in them. For instance, wine-drinking and debauchery are reprehensible simply because Sharī'ah has prohibited them, while charity and almsgiving are praiseworthy simply because the Lawgiver has enjoined them: intrinsically none of these acts is either good or bad.

Al-Shāfi'ī is inclined to subscribe to this school of thought, and perhaps that is the reason why Abū al-Ḥasan al-Ash'arī, the founder of *kalām* among the Shāfi'īs, based his system on it. According to the second school of thought, all rules of Sharī'ah have their origin in expediency, even though the common people do not understand this in the case of some of them. This doctrine has been the subject of much controversy because of prominent authorities ranging themselves on opposite sides in regard to it. The controversy, however, was not justified, since the expediency and purpose of all important enjoinments have been stated in the Qur'an itself. In rejoinders to the unbelievers, the Qur'an always explains the rationale of its directives. For example, it says that prayer saves one from immoral and forbidden acts; that fasting leads to piety; that jihad is intended to end disruption. There are similar explanations and hints here and there in the Qur'an about other acts commanded by it.

Abū Ḥanīfah subscribed to the doctrine of the rationality and beneficialness of the rules of Sharī'ah and made it a postulate of all his *fiqh* propositions. It is owing to this that of all the systems of *fiqh* the Ḥanafī system is most in accord with rational principles. Al-Ṭaḥāwī, who was both a *muḥaddith* and a *mujtahid*, has written a book on this subject under the title *Sharḥ Ma'ānī al-Āthār*, in which he stresses the necessity of proving *fiqh* propositions with the aid of both Qur'anic texts and rational argument. He deals with every aspect of *fiqh* and, although, exhibiting a creditable impartiality, he disagrees with Abū Ḥanīfah on some questions, he proves by arguments worthy of a *mujtahid* that on most questions Abū Ḥanīfah's stand was in accord with both traditions and reason. Muḥammad b. al-Ḥasan also has employed rational argument on most questions in his *Kitāb al-Ḥujaj* Both these books have been published and are available for anyone interested to consult.

Even Shāfiʿīs and others do not deny that Abū Ḥanīfah's *madhhab* is in conformity with reason. Indeed, it was not to be expected that they would deny this, maintaining as they do that the farther the prescriptions of Sharīʿah are removed from reason, the better. Thus, al-Rāzī, discussing *zakāh*, says that al-Shāfiʿī's standpoint on it is more correct than Abū Ḥanīfah's because it is far removed from reason and analogy, *zakāh* being a purely devotional duty needing no rational justification.

The fact that, unlike his contemporaries, Abū Ḥanīfah favoured the principle of rationality was due to a special reason. The other doctors who applied themselves to the systematisation of *fiqh* began their education with that subject. Abū Ḥanīfah, on the other hand, began his education with *kalām*, application to which sharpened his intellect and increased his power of reasoning. As the Muʿtazilah and others with whom he engaged in debates followed the principle of rationality, he had to do the same in contending with them. This exercise made him realise that every prescription of Sharīʿah was consonant with reason. When he turned to *fiqh* later on, he brought the same approach to bear on its problems. A comparison of the formulations of the Ḥanafī system of *fiqh* with those of other systems clearly shows this approach as the distinguishing feature of the former. Not to speak of mundane matters, even in matters pertaining to worship, which in the view of literal-minded people have nothing to do with reason, the rules framed by Abū Ḥanīfah are eminently rational.

If one tries to determine the benefits aimed at by Sharīʿah in prescribing prayer, fasting, hajj and *zakāh* as obligatory duties and what in the light of the benefits should be the modes of performing these duties, one finds that only the modes established by Ḥanafī *fiqh* are appropriate. Prayer, for example, is the name given to a combination of acts, having different degrees of importance in relation to the real object of prayer (namely, the cultivation of humility, expression of devotion, affirmation of Allah's greatness, invocation of Allah's grace) and in proportion to the extent to which they are respectively effective in achieving that object. Some of the acts are obligatory and indispensable because in their absence the object of prayer is defeated. Each of such acts is called a *farḍ* in the language of Sharīʿah. The other acts only add grace and beauty to the ritual of prayer and their omission does not defeat the object of prayer. Such acts rank lower than acts of the first kind and are called *sunnah* or *mustaḥabb.*

As I have already mentioned, the Prophet (ṣ) did not specify which acts were *farḍ* and *wājib* and which were *sunnah.* There can, however, be no doubt that all the acts involved in prayer are not of equal importance. That is why the *mujtahids* thought it necessary to grade them and give them separate names. Abū Ḥanīfah did the same, but his grading is superior to that of the other imams in that it is more realistic. For example, take the question as to what are the essential ingredients of prayer, that is to say, the acts without which prayer cannot be performed. Now, since in reality prayer consists in the affirmation of submission to Allah and in humbling oneself before Him, therefore all the imams are agreed that *niyyah* (expression of the intention to pray), *takbīr* (saying, "Allah is great"), *qirā'ah* (reciting Qur'anic passages), *rukūʿ* (bending down with hands on knees), *sujūd* (bowing the head on the ground) and so on, which are the best outward forms of submission to Allah and humbling oneself before

Him, are obligatory. The Lawgiver himself has hinted at that and, in fact, clearly stated it in some places.

But some of the imams went beyond that and declared even a particular manner of performing these acts or making these utterances to be *de riguer*, although it was not intended to be so. Abū Ḥanīfah does not consider the manner to have been prescribed strictly. For example, he thinks that the *takbīrh al-taḥrīm* (the formula of glorification of Allah, namely, *Allāhu akbar*) can be uttered in words other than *Allāhu akbar* which have the same meaning, such as *Allāhu a'ẓam* or *Allāhu ajall.* Al-Shāfi'ī thinks that it cannot. Abū Ḥanīfah even maintains that it is permissible to say the *takbīr* in Persian. Al-Shāfi'ī, on the other hand, holds that this invalidates the prayer. According to Abū Ḥanīfah, the duty of *qirā'ah* can be performed by reciting any *āyah* of the Qur'an, while according to al-Shāfi'ī it can be performed only by reciting Sūrah al-Fātiḥah. In Abū Ḥanīfah's opinion, a person incapable of reciting the Qur'an in Arabic may recite it in some other language, but al-Shāfi'ī rules that out as impermissible.

It should not be concluded from this that Abū Ḥanīfah or any other *mujtahid* fixed the essential elements of prayer purely on the basis of reason and analogy. The imams have, on the contrary, adduced pronouncements and hints from traditions in support of these elements, and their arguments are set forth at length in books of *fiqh.* All that I mean to say is that Abū Ḥanīfah's enunciations are supported both by pronouncements and hints derived from traditions and by rational arguments, which shows what an insight he had into the inner purpose and justification of Sharī'ah prescriptions.

These remarks apply equally to questions relating to *zakāh.* The real motive behind *zakāh* is human sympathy and help of the needy. That is why those who most need and deserve sympathy and help, such as beggars, the indigent, officers administering *zakāh*, the grief-stricken, debtors, travellers, soldiers and self-ransomed slaves, have been declared to be special objects of it. But differences arose on the question of dispensation. Al-Shāfiʿī thinks that it is obligatory to give *zakāh* to all these categories of recipients at the same time or that, in other words, if even a single category is left out, the duty of *zakāh* is not fulfilled. Abū Ḥanīfah, on the other hand, holds that although *zakāh* cannot be given to anybody outside these categories the question whether it must be given to all the categories together or may be given to some of them has to be decided with reference to the circumstances. Thus, according to him, the imam or ruler may select some of the categories and leave out the others.

Another question on which Abū Ḥanīfah and the other imams disagree is that of the mode of giving *zakāh* on domestic animals. According to Abū Ḥanīfah *zakāh* on domestic animals may be given either in kind or in cash. Al-Shāfiʿī maintains that it must be given in kind and that, if given in cash, it does not discharge the obligation. This ruling ignores the fact that, so far as the object of *zakāh* is concerned, it is immaterial whether an animal or its price is given away: the Lawgiver himself made no clear distinction between the two.

Besides these propositions, there are hundreds of questions relating to ritual duties (*ʿibādāh*) on which Abū Ḥanīfah's enunciations show that he gave special consideration to the inner purpose and the benefits likely to accrue. I, however, refrain from setting them forth for want of space. This characteristic is even more manifest in Abū Ḥanīfah's treatment of secular matters.

The second distinguishing feature of Ḥanafī *fiqh* is that it is easier to understand and act on than the other systems of *fiqh*.

The Qur'an says repeatedly, "Allah wishes to be gentle, and not strict with you." The Prophet (ṣ) declared, "I come to you with a gentle and easy Sharī'ah." It is Islam's special pride in comparison with other religions that it is far removed from monasticism, that its ritual is not rigorous and that its enjoinments are easy to understand and act on.

Ḥanafī *fiqh* is superior to its rivals on similar grounds.

So well known is the fact that Ḥanafī *fiqh* is easy and liberal that poets and writers often employ it as a proverb. A rather curious example of this is a simile used by Anwarī, an obscene and unbridled poet, in which he speaks of "the liberties allowed by Abū Ḥanīfah." The simile occurs in an improper context, but the point it makes is clear. On any question, whether pertaining to the duties of worship or to worldly transactions, one finds Abū Ḥanīfah's precepts easy and gentle and those of the other imams difficult and harsh. Let me by way of illustration take the rules regarding theft laid down in *Kitāb al-Jināyāt* (the Criminal Code) and *Kitāb al-Ḥudūd* (the Penal Code).

It is agreed by all authorities that the punishment for theft is cutting off the right hand, but the *mujtahids* in defining "theft" have laid down certain conditions without the fulfilment of which this punishment cannot be awarded. What effect these conditions have on the rules relating to theft will be clear from the following comparative table, which will also show how easy and consistent with civilised living is Abū Ḥanīfah's *madhhab* as compared with the other *madhhabs*.

Thefts which, according to Abū Ḥanīfah, are not punishable with the cutting off of the right hand	*Divergent views held by the other imams*
• Theft of an article valued at less than an ashrafī.	• The other imams fix the minimum value at a quarter ashrafī.
• A theft committed jointly by a number of persons.	• Aḥmad b. Ḥanbal thinks each of them is liable to have his hand cut off.
• A theft committed by a non-adult.	• Mālik holds the opposite view.
• Theft of a shroud.	• The other imams hold the opposite view.
• Theft of a wife's of or a husband's goods.	• Mālik holds the opposite view.
• Theft of a father's goods.	• Mālik holds the opposite view.
• Theft of the goods of a near relation, such as a nephew or a brother.	• The other imams hold the opposite view.
• A theft committed by refusing to return a thing taken on loan.	• The other imams hold the opposite view.
• When the thief becomes the owner of the thing stolen by subsequent gift or purchase.	• The other imams hold the opposite view.
• Thefts committed by followers of other religions living under Muslim protection.	• The other imams hold the opposite view.
• Theft of a copy of the Qur'an.	• Al-Shāfi'ī and Mālik hold the opposite view.
• Theft of wood or other perishable goods.	• The other imams hold the opposite view.

A large part of *fiqh* deals with prohibitions and permissions. In this connection there are many precepts of the other imams which, if they were to be acted on, would make life unlivable, while Abū Ḥanīfah's precepts are easy to follow. For example, according to al-Shāfi'ī, the following acts are impermissible: bathing or performing ablution with water heated on dung fire; eating out of clay vessels baked on dung fire; using vessels made of tin, glass, crystal and agate; wearing garments made of wool, sable fur and leather (in which prayer cannot be offered); using vessels, chairs and saddles with silver work on them; and common sales in which there is no declaration of selling and buying. Abū Ḥanīfah considers all these acts permissible.

An important sector of *fiqh* connected with the requirements of society is that which deals with transactions between individuals, and it is here that the practical wisdom of the various *mujtahids* can best be judged. Up to Abū Ḥanīfah's time, the legal directions regarding transactions were too primitive to fulfil the needs of a developed society. There were no rules governing contracts, no written documents, no procedure laid down for the adjudication of disputes and the adducing of evidence. Abū Ḥanīfah was the first to introduce all these. Unfortunately, *mujtahids* who came after him, instead of adding to what he had accomplished, reverted to the old-time rough and ready practices, motivated as they were by a deep-rooted bias for unworldliness. A famous traditionist taunts jurists in the following words: "These people think that when a suit is filed regarding a piece of land, it is necessary to state in the plaint its situation, boundaries and legal position, although in the Prophet's time there was no question of furnishing these particulars." For the traditionist, this is a matter for reproach, but if he had lived in a civilised country and had had something to do with business transactions, he would have known that the things he considers reprehensible are essential to civilised living.

Al-Shāfi'ī does not consider delivery of possession necessary for a gift, does not recognise a neighbour's right of pre-emption, regards the testimony of unknown persons as inadmissible in transactions, requires witnesses to a marriage to be reliable and just and rules out as invalid the testimony of *dhimmīs* in their transactions among themselves. These things may be practicable in countries still in a primitive state, where transactions are simple and of an elementary nature, but not in civilised countries, where transactions are variegated and complex and cannot be conducted without a proper determination of the rights of the parties and the nature of the subject matter. Abū Ḥanīfah, realising this, holds views different from those of al-Shāfi'ī; and it was Mālik's failure to realise it that evoked from Ibn Khaldūn the well-founded remark about his *madhhab*, which I have quoted in an earlier chapter, namely, that it gained currency only in countries which had not made much progress in civilisation.

The sagacity and clearsightedness that Abū Ḥanīfah brought to bear on his formulation of rules relating to secular transactions can properly be gauged only by a detailed examination of some of the chapters into which these rules are divided. But there is no room for that in this short book. I, therefore, content myself with discussing the rules on marriage, which pertain to both the religious sphere and the secular.

The jurists have included marriage among religious duties, but this is only a technical convention. Because of its intimate connection with the life of the community, marriage is largely a social transaction. One reason why I have selected the rules about marriage by way of illustration is that some European writers have described the Ḥanafī law of marriage as barbarous and inhuman. But I hope to prove that not even the most civilised countries of the world today have fairer and more humane marriage laws than those laid down in Ḥanafī *fiqh*. Bentham characterises the Roman law of marriage as a collection of unjust rules. The Ḥanafī law of marriage, as I hope to show, is the very antithesis of an unjust dispensation. This may also, incidentally, correct the misconception that Ḥanafī *fiqh* is derived from Roman law.

Marriage forms a large part of social life. According to a philosopher, it is the binding force of communities, the root of civilisation and the foundation of culture. It can, therefore, well be said that a lawmaker who makes a good exposition of marriage laws has a good insight into the laws that govern civilisation. Although Abū Ḥanīfah was not the author of the marriage laws he expounded, these having been laid down in principle by the Lawgiver himself, the perspicacity with which he expounded them and deduced detailed rules from them is the hallmark of a great lawmaker. The Lawgiver's pronouncements were at times mere aphorisms, at times ambiguous statements, at times broad hints, spelling out no details. As a consequence, wide differences arose among the *mujtahids* about their interpretation and application. The way in which Abū Ḥanīfah worked out the details of the general statements, removed the ambiguities, clarified the hints and framed specific rules was a performance which only his unique gift of *ijtihād* was equal to. No other *mujtahid* is his rival in this field.

The following are the broad heads under which he deals with marriage laws:

(1) the persons between whom marriage is permissible
(2) guardianship for purposes of marriage
(3) stability of the marriage contract
(4) the rights of the parties to a marriage contract
(5) the ritual of marriage

Restrictions on marriage exist in all religions with slight differences. All religions prescribe certain prohibited degrees, which are more or less the same in all of them and all of which are based on rational considerations. Shāh Waliullāh, in the *Ḥujjah Allāh al-Bālighah*, and Bentham, in *Utility*,[9] advance the same arguments to justify the prohibited degrees. As these are in accord with nature and reason and are clearly stated in the Qur'an, all the *mujtahids* are agreed on the principle underlying them, but they disagree on the details not mentioned in the Qur'anic text. One of the latter is the question whether the prohibition is created by illicit sexual intercourse, which is the subject matter of much controversy between Abū Ḥanīfah and al-Shāfi'ī. Al-Shāfi'ī holds that it is not.

For example, a man is not prohibited from marrying a woman with whom his father has had sexual intercourse. In fact, al-Shāfi'ī stretches this to the point of saying that a man may even marry his illegitimate daughter. The argument he advances is that, since illicit intercourse is an illegal act, it cannot turn what is lawful into what is unlawful.

Abū Ḥanīfah holds the opposite view. According to him, the natural effect of blood relationship on the relations between men and women is not confined to marriage, and this is the correct view. The principle underlying forbidden degrees does not come into operation specially as a consequence of marriage. It is patently contrary to the laws of nature to permit marital relations between a man and his own daughter, even if born out of wedlock. This is also true of the concubine of one's father. There are hints about this in the Qur'an, but as I am not concerned with a textual debate, I refrain from citing them.

The second broad head concerns the competence to enter into a marriage contract. This is a very important question, on the decision of which depends the goodness or badness of the institution of marriage to a large extent. According to al-Shāfi'ī and Aḥmad b. Ḥanbal, a woman, even if she has attained to puberty and maturity, is not competent to contract marriage independently and needs a guardian to consent to her doing so. On the one hand, they thus restrict a woman's legal powers and, on the other, gave such vast powers to the guardian that he can give her in marriage even against her will. According to Abū Ḥanīfah, a woman who is a major is competent to contract marriage of her own will and can, in fact, refuse to be bound by a marriage contracted for her by her guardian during her minority.

This divergence of views stems from a difference of outlook on women's rights. In all religions other than Islam women have been assigned a low social status and granted rights in a niggardly manner. Among the Hindus and Christians, they have no right of inheritance, which was the case in Arabia itself before Islam. In many other matters, they are treated as men's inferiors, but Islam gave men and women equal rights, declaring, "Men are entitled to what they earn by their deeds, and women to what they earn by theirs."

Abū Ḥanīfah kept this equality in view in all matters, which is a distinctive feature of his *fiqh*. For example, according to him, in matters like marriage, divorce and release from the marital bond, women's testimony is of equal value to men's, whereas the other imams regard it as unreliable. Even where the latter consider women's testimony admissible, they impose the condition that two women should corroborate each other, al-Shāfiʿī raising the number to four. With Abū Ḥanīfah, a woman's evidence is as reliable as a man's. Abū Ḥanīfah regards women as fit to be appointed *qāḍīs*, whereas the other imams do not. As in these matters, so in marriage, Abū Ḥanīfah concedes to women an independent legal status equal to men's.

Apart from the principle of the equality of the sexes, marriage is a transaction which cannot be dealt with on the analogy of other secular transactions, since it is a relationship which is many-faceted and intended to be lifelong. It is extremely unfair to grant one of the parties to such a relationship no rights at all.

Al-Shāfiʿī relies on literalist arguments to justify his stand, but Abū Ḥanīfah counters them with stronger arguments of the same kind. If al-Shāfiʿī quotes "There is no marriage without a guardian," Abū Ḥanīfah rejoins with "A woman is entitled to contract marriage herself rather than through her guardian. The consent of a woman who has come of age is to be obtained." However, this is not the place to go further into the debate.

The third broad question is about the extent to which it is necessary to make the marriage contract stable and enduring. Marriage can be the foundation of civilised life and the binding force of communities only if it is a firm and lasting relationship, otherwise it is only a means of gratifying an animal appetite. Abū Ḥanīfah has kept this clearly in view in laying down rules about the method of performing marriage, fixing the dower, enforcing divorce and giving effect to *khulʿ* (divorcement by the wife).

Abū Ḥanīfah's most important pronouncement in this connection is that so long as the relations between husband and wife are good, divorce is prohibited. Even where he considers it permissible—that is, when there are compelling reasons for it—he prescribes a procedure which leaves room for rectification and revocation. According to this procedure, there must be three divorces at intervals of one month, so that the husband gets ample time to reconsider his decision and, if he so wishes, rescind it, which, indeed, is *mustaḥabb* (desirable). If there is no reconciliation during this period, and it is established that none is possible, then there has of necessity to be a divorce. After the divorce, the husband has to pay the wife's dower and her maintenance expenses for three months. The idea behind this is that the wife should have means of subsistence until she can find a new husband.

I give below a table showing Abū Ḥanīfah's rules on this subject and those of other imams. How important Abū Ḥanīfah considers the marriage contract to be and how solicitous he is to ensure that it remains inviolate under any circumstances will be clear from the table:

Abū Ḥanīfah's Rules	***Other Imams' Rules***
(1) So long as there are good relations between husband and wife, divorce is prohibited.	(1) According to al-Shāfiʿī, it is permissible even then.
(2) It is forbidden to give three divorces at a time, and whoever does so is a sinner.	(2) Al-Shāfiʿī and Aḥmad b. Ḥanbal think "that it does not matter.
(3) The amount of dower can in no circumstances be less than 10 dirhams. (The idea is to prevent thoughtless divorces, for poor people would not find it easy to pay such an amount.)	(3) According to al-Shāfiʿī and Aḥmad b. Ḥanbal, even a *ḥabbah* is enough (which means that a man may divorce his wife frivolously and subject her to severe hardship.)

(4) Consummation of marriage makes payment of the full dower compulsory.	(4) According to al-Shāfi'ī, it makes only half the dower payable.
(5) Skin diseases, such as leucoderma, are no ground for dissolution of marriage.	(5) According to al-Shāfi'ī, they are.
(6) If a man divorces his wife during his last illness and dies during the *'iddah* (period of probation), the wife is entitled to inherit from him.	(6) Al-Shāfi'ī holds that she is not.
(7) A revocable divorce is no legal bar to sexual intercourse, for the marital connection is not broken by a minor misunderstanding or quarrel.	(7) According to al-Shāfi'ī, it is forbidden as if the divorce were irrevocable.
(8) For the revocation of a divorce an oral declaration is not necessary; any act indicative of reconciliation is enough. (The idea is to facilitate reconciliation and revocation of divorce.)	(8) Al-Shāfi'ī thinks that a formal declaration is necessary.
(9) No witness to a revocation is required, for it may happen in some cases that no witness may be available during the prescribed period, which may be about to expire, and as a result the divorce may become irrevocable	(9) Mālik considers a witness to be indispensable.

In framing rules of law for marriage, it is extremely necessary to fix the rights of men and women in such a way as to ensure justice between them and see that the equality with men which women enjoy in certain matters is not nullified. This is because what a woman expects from marriage is happiness and comfort and not the negation of her inherent rights. It is a specially liberal feature of Islam, not paralleled in any other religion, that it has fixed women's rights in the matter of marriage with magnanimity. Abū Ḥanīfah's rules of marriage are par excellence inspired by this spirit. It is a result of this that the other imams, where they disagree with him, seem to err on the side of injustice.

Let me, by way of illustration, take the question of *khul'*, which is a counterpart of divorce. All the imams are agreed that, just as a man has been given the right of divorce, a woman has the right to get a dissolution of marriage for a consideration, that is, on giving something by way of compensation. There is, however, a difference of opinion as to the form of the consideration. Abū Ḥanīfah holds that, if the fault is the wife's, in that it is her behaviour which is the cause of estrangement, then she should give the husband by way of compensation a sum equal to her dower and that it would be improper for the husband to demand a higher sum. If, however, the fault lies with the husband, then the wife is entitled to release from the marriage bond without paying any compensation, and it would, indeed, be improper on the husband's part to ask for compensation. Al-Shāfiʿī and Mālik, on the other hand, are of the opinion that the husband may claim as much compensation as he likes and compel the wife to pay it, even if he is in the wrong—which is obviously unjust.

The last broad question is that of the rites of marriage. The rites are intended to achieve two objects: first, verification of the parties' consent and, second, giving publicity to the factum of marriage. Abū Ḥanīfah prescribes rites eminently suitable for the achievement of these objects: first, that the parties should utter such words as clearly signify that they consent to the contract and, second, that the contract should be entered into in the presence of two witnesses. These are simple conditions which can be fulfilled in practically any circumstances.

Some other imams, however, prescribe conditions so stringent as to be extremely difficult to fulfil. Al-Shāfiʿī, for example, insists that the witnesses should be just. The definition of "just" that the *mujtahids*, and especially al-Shāfiʿī, give is such as fits hardly one in a thousand persons. With such a condition imposed, a fully legal marriage would be extremely rare, if not non-existent. Furthermore, al-Shāfiʿī and Aḥmad b. Ḥanbal consider it essential for the witnesses to be men; but Abū Ḥanīfah thinks women also to be qualified, which is the more reasonable view. Again, al-Shāfiʿī maintains that a verbal formula specifically pertaining to the marriage contract must be used, although there is nothing to be gained by such a formula and the form of words relating to contracts like gilt, transfer of ownership and so on, should do.

One more distinguishing characteristic of Ḥanafī *fiqh* is the liberal rights it grants to *dhimmīs*, that is to say, non-Muslims living under the protection of an Islamic State. Preservation of the rights of *dhimmīs* finds mention in many of the Lawgiver's own directives, but since these are directives of a general nature and some other pronouncements of his seem to be at variance with them, they were interpreted in different ways. There is, however, no doubt that Abū Ḥanīfah's interpretation of them is the correct one. Islam ruled over vast territories, in which there lived hundreds of non-Muslim groups, the proper preservation of whose rights was a sine qua non of peace and order. No non-Islamic government in history has granted to peoples who were not co-religionists of the ruling race rights as liberal as those granted by Abū Ḥanīfah to *dhimmīs*. Europe, which is proud of its systems of law and justice, may boast of such liberality, but can produce no practical example of it. So far as Abū Ḥanīfah's laws relating to *dhimmīs* are concerned, they were actually in force under all Islamic governments and were an important part of the fundamental rights of the subjects. An outstanding example is provided by the treatment accorded to non-Muslims in Hārūn al-Rashīd's vast empire.

The biggest question in this connection is that of murder and retribution for it. In Abū Ḥanīfah's opinion, the blood of *dhimmīs* is equal in sanctity to that of Muslims. He holds that if a Muslim murders a *dhimmī*, he must be put to death in return, and if it is a case of killing in error, then the same blood money must be paid as is payable by a *dhimmī* for killing a Muslim in error.

Al-Rāzī, in his *Manāqib al-Shāfiʿī*, jibes at the Ḥanafīs, saying that for them the blood of Abū Bakr has the same value as that of a *dhimmī*, so that if Abū Bakr were to kill a *dhimmī*, he would, according to them, be liable to be punished with death. The Ḥanafīs have nowhere put forward this proposition, which has been invented by al-Rāzī himself by way of a reductio ad absurdum. However, I as a Ḥanafī proudly accept it, for under a just regime, king and beggar, the elect and the rejected have the same status, and it is a proof of Islam's broad-mindedness that it puts ruler and ruled on the same footing. Al-Rāzī had no reason to be ashamed of this fact.

Let us look at the precepts and examples of the Companions on this subject. ʿAlī said, "The blood of *dhimmīs* is our blood, and mulct is payable to them as much as to us." All the other Companions, whether *Muhājirs* or *Anṣār*, avowed the same sentiment and acted on it. When 'Umar was wounded, his son 'Ubaydullāh put two unbelievers to death on suspicion. 'Uthmān, as soon as he acceded to the caliphate, sent for the *Muhājirs* and the *Anṣār* and consulted them about this incident. They unanimously declared 'Ubaydullāh deserving of being put to death.

Abū Ḥanīfah's other laws about *dhimmīs* were similarly generous. They were to have the same freedom to trade as was enjoyed by the Muslims and would be liable to taxes in the same way as the Muslims. The *jizyah*, which was a poll tax levied in return for protection, was to be fixed in accordance with each payer's capacity to pay, so that poor *dhimmīs* would be exempt from it, and if a *dhimmī* died without paying the *jizyah* levied on him, it would be written off. Disputes between *dhimmīs* about secular transactions would be settled according to their laws. Thus, to take an extreme case, if a fire worshipper married his own daughter, the Islamic government would accept the marriage as valid, since it was in accord with the laws of his community. The testimony of *dhimmīs* would be admitted in law suits between them. *Dhimmīs* would be free to go into the interior of the Ka'bah, settle at Makkah and Madīnah, enter all mosques without let or hindrance, and build their places of worship anywhere except in new cities founded by Muslims. If they chose to side with the Muslims, in wars against hostile infidels, the Muslim commander could trust them and take all sorts of help from them.

There are many other laws framed by Abū Ḥanīfah in respect of *dhimmīs* which show that in all matters he invested them with rights equal to those of Muslims. In fact, in certain matters he carried this liberality beyond the limits of moderation, as, for example, on the question as to when a *dhimmī* could be considered to have violated his covenant with the Islamic State and forfeited his status as a citizen of it. He maintained that, unless the *dhimmīs* had a fighting force at their disposal and pitched themselves against the government, they did not forfeit their rights of citizenship. For instance, if a *dhimmī* refused to pay *jizyah* or committed adultery with a Muslim woman or spied for infidels or induced a Muslim to abjure Islam or uttered a blasphemy against Allah or the Prophet (ṣ), he rendered himself liable to punishment, but would not be considered a rebel or a traitor and would not forfeit his citizenship rights.

Let us now look at the precepts of the other imams in regard to these matters. According to al-Shāfiʿī, if a Muslim voluntarily killed an innocent *dhimmī*, he would be exempt from retribution except that he would have to pay *diyah* (blood money), which would be one-third (according to Mālik, one-half) of the blood money payable for a Muslim. In regard to trade, al-Shāfiʿī made the discriminatory proposal that, unlike a Muslim, a *dhimmī* would have to pay a new tax every time he carried commercial goods from one city to another. As for *jizyah*, al-Shāfiʿī maintained that it could in no circumstances be less than an *ashrafī* and that no *dhimmī*, whether old, blind, crippled, poor or a hermit, should be exempt from it. In fact, according to one account, al-Shāfiʿī ruled that a *dhimmī* incapable of paying *jizyah* on account of poverty had no right to stay in Islamic territory. The tribute fixed in ʿUmar's time could be increased, but not decreased in any circumstances. The testimony of *dhimmīs* was not admissible, even in disputes between them, on which Mālik agreed with al-Shāfiʿī. A *dhimmī* could not enter the Kaʿbah, nor could he settle at Makkah or Madīnah. As regards entering common mosques, according to al-Shāfiʿī, a *dhimmī* could do so with permission, while, according to Mālik and Ḥanbal, he could not do so in any circumstances. Nowhere in Islamic territory, according to all the imams other than Abū Ḥanīfah, could *dhimmīs* build their places of worship.

As *dhimmīs* could not be trusted, they were to be debarred from serving in the Muslim army. If a *dhimmī* murdered a Muslim or committed adultery with a Muslim woman, he forthwith forfeited all his rights and was to be regarded as a belligerent unbeliever. These rules pertained to Christians and Jews only. As regards idolaters, they could not, according to al-Shāfi'ī, be permitted to reside in Islamic territory, even if they were willing to pay *jizyah*.

So harsh were these dispensations that even the weakest of subject peoples could not be expected to tolerate them, and that was why the *madhhabs* of al-Shāfi'ī and like-minded imams became outdated with the expansion of the Muslim Empire. In Egypt, it is true, the Shāfi'ī *madhhab* was the statutory law for some time. Consequently, during that time, there were frequent rebellions on the part of Christians and Jews.

It must be admitted that in books of Ḥanafī *fiqh*, there are to be met with certain rules about *dhimmīs* which seem to stem from intolerance and undue discrimination. Since these have been set forth in such a manner as to convey the impression that they were framed by Abū Ḥanīfah himself, this has given occasion to non-Muslims to attack the Ḥanafī *madhhab* and, in fact, Islam itself.

In the *Hidāyah*, for example, it is laid down that *dhimmīs* must not emulate Muslims in dress and personal appearance, move about on horseback or carry weapons, and that they must, as a distinctive mark, wear a *zunnār* (sacred thread) and make a mark on the outside of their houses to show that they are non-Muslims. The purpose of these enjoinments, according to the author of the *Hidāyah*, was to humiliate the *dhimmīs*, which was considered necessary.

The *Fatawa-i-Alamgiri* contains directives even harsher than these. All such rules, however, are inventions of later jurists, and Abū Ḥanīfah is not to blame for them. What we have on his authority is only that they should wear *zunnār*[10] and use saddles of a particular kind which resemble in shape the inverted palm of the hand.[11] Abū Yūsuf made a few additions to these rules, namely, that *dhimmīs* should take care not to resemble Muslims in appearance, dress and mount, should wear tall caps, should have a round piece of wood fixed to the front of their saddles and should use shoelaces of a distinctive kind, and that their women should not ride litters. Abū Yūsuf's explanation is that these rules were introduced by the caliph 'Umar, whom he quotes as expressing the wish that the appearance of *dhimmīs* should be different from that of Muslims.

'Umar was undoubtedly the author of these rules, but it is an error to attribute to him any intention of humiliating the *dhimmīs*—an error which many writers of later periods committed. It was a matter of personal taste with 'Umar that he liked the different communities to be distinguishable from each other. For example, he several times sent instructions to his soldiers that they should not give up basking in the sun during winter, never use stirrups in mounting and should always wear garments made of coarse cloth. The purpose behind these instructions was to make sure that the Arabs retained their national characteristics. It was with the same purpose in view that he instructed the *'Ajamīs* (Persians) who had embraced Islam not to lose their indigenous traits. Before the advent of Islam, the *'Ajamīs* used to wear *zunnārs* and tall caps,[12] their saddles resembled modern European saddles and their women never used camels as mounts. It was these characteristics which 'Umar ordered *dhimmīs* to retain. Abū Ḥanīfah and Abū Yūsuf kept his orders intact and, in doing so, were motivated by the same desire to see Muslims and non-Muslims, Arabs and non-Arabs, following their own traditional customs in dress, appearance and transport.

Abū Ḥanīfah is at one with the other imams in prohibiting *dhimmīs* from building their places of worship in Muslim cities, but his object was only to guard against breaches of the peace, for the Muslims, being mostly Arabs and unused to the sound of the prayer gong, might have been annoyed by the *dhimmīs'* practices of worship into creating trouble. The prohibition, in fact, did not affect the *dhimmīs* very much, as there were hardly three or four cities in the whole Muslim world that had been founded by Muslims, the rest of the cities having been founded by non-Muslims, who, of course, were free to build their places of worship in the latter. It actually remained in force only as long as there was danger of communal disturbances. As soon as the danger passed away, it was lifted. Thus, in Baghdad, an Islamic city par excellence, hundreds of churches were built.

One great quality of Abū Ḥanīfah's work as a lawmaker is that on directives derived from *nuṣūṣ* (texts) about which the imams disagree, Abū Ḥanīfah's stand is the most rational and supported by the most cogent arguments. As the word *naṣṣ* is used in connection with both the Qur'an and Ḥadīth, even those directives are called *naṣṣ* which are established on the basis of Ḥadīth and not the Qur'an. I, however, do not propose to discuss them for several reasons.

In the first place, directives of this kind are so innumerable that there is no space in this book for even the smallest cross section of them. If I were to mention a few of them by way of illustration, I might give occasion for the suspicion that I had made a tendentious selection. In the second place, it is not possible for anyone today to settle the issues involved in the manner of a *mujtahid*. The most controversial question about traditions is that of their soundness and correctness, and it is this question which has created sharp divisions between the imams in their juristic dicta. One imam may consider a tradition arguable, while another may not.

The material available in our country is not adequate for the settlement of these differences. The biggest problem is presented by the names of authorities. The books on this subject available in our country, such as *Tahdhīb al-Kamāl* of al-Mizzī, *Tahdhīb al-Tahdhīb*, *Mizān al-I'tidāl*, *Ṭabaqāt al-Ḥuffāẓ* and *Tahdhīb al-Asmā' wa al-Lughāt*, quote sayings of the imams about *jarḥ* (invalidation) and *ta'dīl* (rectification), but without quoting the chain of authorities, with the result that no decision can be made about their authenticity. Apart from this, most of the invalidating comments, including some that have been explained, are ambiguous. These issues could certainly be decided with the help of the writings of the ancients, but I have not been able to get hold of them. Ḥanafī scholars have written a large number of books to prove that the rules of Ḥanafī *fiqh* are derived from valid traditions, and anyone interested in pursuing the subject further may consult them.

Much of this controversy can be settled by reference to the Qur'an, whose authority is beyond question. The only debatable point that then remains is whether deductions from Qur'anic texts have been made correctly or not. The rules of Ḥanafī *fiqh* supported by Qur'anic texts are not small in number, and all these are concerned with important questions of *fiqh*. Reference to the Qur'an thus easily establishes the superiority of the Ḥanafī system of *fiqh* to the other systems and that of Abū Ḥanīfah as a *mujtahid* to the other imams, for *ijtihād* consists mostly in deducing correct propositions from the basic texts.

Although, in the light of what I have just said, it would be enough for my purposes to deal with those of the Ḥanafī rules of law which are supported by the Qur'an, a brief discussion of their relation to Ḥadīth seems called for in order to correct a common misconception about this. Some people think that many of Abū Ḥanīfah's rules are contrary to valid traditions. While a number of these people charge Abū Ḥanīfah point-blank with having deliberately set Ḥadīth at naught, others, more fair-minded, put forward in his favour the condoning fact that up to his time traditions had not been scientifically compiled, with the result that he had no access to many of them.

The charge is not worth rebutting. As regards the explanation, it is simply preposterous. It is true that traditions had not been compiled up to Abū Ḥanīfah's time. But how was it that after they had been compiled, leading traditionists continued to accept Abū Ḥanīfah's enunciations as correct? Wakīʿ b. al-Jarrāḥ, from whom a large number of traditions have been quoted in al-Bukhārī's *Ṣaḥīḥ* and whom Aḥmad b. Ḥanbal used to describe as the man with the best memory that he had ever met, followed Abū Ḥanīfah's rules. Al-Khaṭīb al-Baghdādī in his biographical note on him writes, "He used to give *fatwās* in accordance with Abū Ḥanīfah's dicta."[13] Yaḥyā b. Saʿīd b. al-Qaṭṭān, the founder of the art of *jarḥ* and *taʿdīl*, followed Abū Ḥanīfah on many questions, as he himself admits.[14] Al-Ṭaḥāwī, a *ḥāfiẓ* of Ḥadīth and a *mujtahid*, began as a Shāfiʿī, but later adopted Abū Ḥanīfah's views, although he used to say that he was not a follower of Abū Ḥanīfah's, but only happened to agree with him. Al-Ṭaḥāwī, being a contemporary of al-Bukhārī and Muslim, lived at a time when the compilation of traditions had been completed. Among the scholars of later periods, al-Mārdīnī, al-Zayla'ī, Ibn al-Hummām and al-Qāsim b. Qaṭlūbaghā, men whose breadth of vision is beyond question, were supporters of Ḥanafī thinking.

Then there is the question why some men who are reputed to have known *ḥadīths* by heart agreed with Abū Ḥanīfah on many questions. In the first rank of these was that greatest of *muḥaddithīn*, Aḥmad b. Ḥanbal, whose disciples al-Bukhārī and Muslim were proud to have been and about whom there is the common saying of *muḥaddithīn* "What Aḥmad b. Ḥanbal does not know for a *ḥadīth* is not one," disagrees with al-Shāfi'ī and agrees with Abū Ḥanīfah on many questions. "Leave aside details and minor questions," writes al-Khawārizmī. "So far as fundamental questions of *fiqh* are concerned, Aḥmad b. Ḥanbal is at one with Abū Ḥanīfah and differs with al-Shāfi'ī." I have examined this statement with reference to a large number of such questions and found it to be true. Sufyān al-Thawrī, who is generally acknowledged as an imam of Ḥadīth, was in agreement with Abū Ḥanīfah on many points of law. "By Allah," Abū Yūsuf used to say, "Sufyān follows Abū Ḥanīfah more than I do." There are many rulings of Sufyān to be found in al-Tirmidhī's *Ṣaḥīḥ* which are in accord with Abū Ḥanīfah's and opposed to al-Shāfi'ī's.

The misconception that Abū Ḥanīfah's juristic formulations ran counter to Ḥadīth owes its origin largely to a statement made to that effect by some *muḥaddithīn* as, for example, al-Bukhārī and Ibn Abī Shaybah. The latter wrote a whole chapter in refutation of Abū Ḥanīfah's legal theories, but that does not justify the misconception. Many imams have found fault with each other.

For example, al-Shāfi'ī, who was a faithful disciple of Mālik's and used to say, "There is no book under the sky which is more correct than Mālik's *al-Muwaṭṭa'*," wrote a treatise in rebuttal of Mālik, the thesis of which is that many of Mālik's legal rulings are contradictory to valid traditions. Al-Rāzī has quoted the preface to this treatise in his *Manāqib al-Shāfi'ī*, and I have read it. Al-Layth b. Sa'd, a well-known *muḥaddith*, used to say, "Mālik has gone against Ḥadīth on seventy questions, and I propose to write to him about this." Al-Shāfi'ī himself did not escape this charge, and there was no reason why he should, for his stand is evidently wrong on many questions, for example, *jahr bismillāh* (uttering the *bismillāh* aloud), *qunūt al-fajr* (standing long in silence during the morning prayer), *tawrīth dhawī al-arḥām* (inheritance by distant relatives). The fact, however, is that these are matters of personal judgement, and we cannot on the basis of them condemn a jurist as opposed to the Ḥadīth. It is not necessary that if one *muḥaddith* regards a *ḥadīth* as valid, another should do the same,

Having disposed of the question whether Abū Ḥanīfah deliberately went against Ḥadīth, I come to the question of deduction and reasoning, on which it is seldom possible for the *mujtahids* to be unanimous, following as they do different rules in this behalf. I have gone through al-Bukhārī's *Juz' al-Qirā'ah* and the reference to Abū Ḥanīfah in his *Ṣaḥīḥ*. In both of them he alleges that Abū Ḥanīfah's *madhhab* is opposed to Ḥadīth. But the fact of the matter, as I have found on comparing Abū Ḥanīfah's *fatwā* on the subject with these writings of al-Bukhārī, is that the *fatwā* is opposed not to Ḥadīth but to al-Bukhārī's understanding and judgement.

Abū Ḥanīfah's reasoning about the reading of Sūrah al-Fātiḥah is based on the *āyah* "When the Qur'an is recited, listen to it in silence." Al-Bukhārī says in the *Juz' al-Qirā'ah* that the *āyah* was revealed in respect of the *khuṭbah* (sermon) and is not connected with *ṣalāh.* This is an astounding statement which I could never have believed to have been made by al-Bukhārī had I not read his *Juz' al-Qirā'ah.* It is established by scores of traditions that the *āyah* in question was revealed in connection with prayer. Even if we accept al-Bukhārī's statement as correct, it does not follow from it that the *āyah* does not apply to prayer. It is common knowledge that the fact of an *āyah* having been revealed on a particular occasion does not detract from its general applicability.

While Abū Ḥanīfah rules that *āmīn* must be said in a low voice by both the imam and the *muqtadīs*, al-Bukhārī holds that it should be said aloud, and he bases this view on the Prophet's direction that when the imam pronounces "*wa lā al-ḍāllīn*," the followers should say *āmīn* is concerned, Abū Ḥanīfah does not deny that it being said aloud, and so far as the mere saying of *āmīn* is concerned, Abū Ḥanīfah does not deny that it is enjoined. Abū Ḥanīfah maintains that ablution with date-palm juice, provided that it is not intoxicating, is permitted, al-Bukhārī writes a whole chapter against this, basing his arguments on the *ḥadīth* "All intoxicating liquors are prohibited."

Abū Ḥanīfah holds that it is not necessary for a *muqtadī* to read Sūrah al-Fātiḥah, but al-Bukhārī holds it as necessary and says in his *Jāmi' al-Ṣaḥīḥ*, "The reading (of the *sūrah*) is compulsory for both imam and *muqtadī* during every prayer, whether the prayer is performed at home or during a journey and whether aloud or in a low voice." In support of this, al-Bukhārī puts forward two traditions. One is about a complaint made by the Kūfans to 'Umar against Sa'd b. Abī Waqqāṣ that he did not even know how to perform his prayers, as a result of which 'Umar removed him from office and appointed 'Ammār in his place. The tradition goes on to say that, when 'Umar summoned Sa'd and informed him of the complaint, Sa'd replied, "By Allah, I used to perform my prayers with them exactly in the Prophet's style: in my *'ishā'* prayers, I used to stand for a long time during the first two *rak'ahs* and for a short time during the last two."

How does this tradition prove that the reading of al-Fātiḥah is obligatory? Even if one tries to prove that it is with the help of the interpretation made by Ibn Ḥajar and others, how does it follow from that, that Abū Ḥanīfah contradicted Ḥadīth in this matter? In truth, it is a grave error to think that a *mujtahid* had had no access to traditions bearing on any rule of law. The differences of opinion are the inevitable result of variations in the criteria applied to appraise the soundness of traditions, in the reasons for the deductions made and in the method of ratiocination employed.

Let me now revert from this diversion to my main argument. I claim that the only correct and workable interpretation of those verses of the Qur'an from which rules of *fiqh* have been deduced is the one made by Abū Ḥanīfah. As there are more than a hundred such verses, it is not practicable for me to deal with all of them. I, therefore, content myself with a brief statement of some of them, which will enable the reader to form a general idea.

Abū Ḥanīfah holds that there are four obligatory acts involved in ablution, while al-Shāfi'ī adds to this number two, namely, *niyyah* (intention) and *tartīb* (order of succession), for which Mālik substitutes *muwālāh* (continuity). Aḥmad b. Ḥanbal thinks that before performing ablution it is necessary to say *bismillāh* and that, if this is intentionally omitted, the ablution is invalidated. Abū Ḥanīfah argues that in the relevant Qur'anic verse, only four acts have been stated as obligatory and that, therefore, no act outside these can be such. *Niyyah*, *muwālāh* and *tasmiyah* (speaking Allah's name) find no mention in the verse. As regards *tartīb*, a presumption could be said to have been raised by the occurrence of the conjunction *wāw*, but Arabic scholars have unanimously decided that the conjunction does not connote anything like the order of succession. Al-Rāzī in *al-Tafsīr Kabīr* puts forward a number of arguments to prove that *tartīb* is obligatory, but these are no more than personal constructions of his. His first argument is that in the clause "*faghsilū wujūhakum*," the particle *fa* is intended to signify succession in time, which proves that it is obligatory to wash the face first and that, since in regard to one act an order of succession is established, it should apply to the other acts too. Al-Rāzī's second argument is that the direction about ablution is contrary to reason and that, therefore, it should be carried out in the same order as the direction itself. What these arguments are worth is too clear for there being any need to rebut them.

Abū Ḥanīfah asserts that touching a woman does not vitiate ablution. Al-Shāfi'ī disagrees with this, relying on the following verse: "If you are sick or on a journey or come out of the privy[15] or have touched a woman and you can get no water, then perform *tayammum* (ablution with clean earth)." Abū Ḥanīfah explains that touching a woman is intended to mean having sexual intercourse, in accordance with the common Qur'anic method of not mentioning such matters openly and directly. An interesting thing to note is that the word *mass* used in this verse, which primarily means "touch," has been used in the sense of "sexual intercourse" in the *āyah* "*mā lam tamassūhunna,*" and Shafi'ī himself admits this. To take the word *touching* in its literal and primary sense is, in fact, an error which no native speaker of Arabic could commit. There is also the word *ghā'iṭ* in the verse in question. All *mujtahids* interpret it metaphorically because, taken literally, it would render it necessary for anyone coming from a lower place to a higher to perform ablution.

In holding that touching a woman vitiates ablution, al-Shāfi'ī seems to me to have relied not on the above-quoted verse but on some tradition, and it is probable that the arguments attributed to him were actually advanced by his followers with the object of rebutting the Ḥanafī view. Abū Ḥanīfah maintains that with a single *tayammum*, one can perform several obligatory rites, but al-Shāfi'ī thinks that for every rite a new *tayammum* is necessary. The argument Abū Ḥanīfah advances is that the directive about *wuḍū'* applies equally to *tayammum*, and since a new ablution is not necessary for every prayer, a new *tayammum* is not necessary either. He, however, concedes that those who hold that with a single ablution several prayers cannot be offered can logically apply this rule to *tayammum* as well. He sees no reason for making a distinction between *wuḍū'* and *tayammum* in this regard.

It is Abū Ḥanīfah's view that, if a person who has performed *tayammum* finds water while he is offering his prayer, the *tayammum* becomes void. Mālik and Aḥmad b. Ḥanbal are opposed to this view. The argument Abū Ḥanīfah puts forward is that *tayammum* has been omitted in the Qur'an subject to the condition that water is not available that the permission is cancelled as soon as the condition ceases to be fulfilled.

Abū Ḥanīfah maintains that the *takbīrah al-taḥrīmah* (the formula of glorification) is not an integral part of the ritual of prayer and that it is permissible to say the *takbīr* in Persian. Al-Shāfiʿī and others disagree with this. Abū Ḥanīfah's arguments are that in the verse which is adduced to prove the obligatory nature of the *takbīr*, namely, "*wa dhakara isma Rabbihī fa ṣallā*," there is no mention of any particular language and that, since the *fa* of "*fa ṣallā*" denotes posteriority in time, the prayer has necessarily to follow the *takbīr*, from which it is clear that, although the *takbīr* is obligatory, it is no part of the prayer itself but is a separate act.

In Abū Ḥanīfah's opinion, it is not necessary for a *muqtadī* to recite al-Fātiḥah, while in that of al-Shāfiʿī and al-Bukhārī it is. Abū Ḥanīfah bases his opinion on the verse "*wa idhā quri'a al-Qur'ānu fa istamiʿū lahu wa anṣitū*" (when the Qur'an is recited, listen and remain silent). The direction not to recite al-Fātiḥah can be deduced from this verse, not only in respect of silent prayers but also in respect of loud prayers. In fact, so far as the latter are concerned, the verse is an authentic and imperative text, which cannot be explained away. It is surprising that the Shāfiʿīs have advanced arguments based on traditions against such a clear and unmistakable text, although the traditions contradict each other on this point, there being as good ones in favour of non-recitation as there are in favour of recitation. Al-Bukhārī has written a whole treatise on the subject, in which he has tried to counter the deduction made by Abū Ḥanīfah from the verse in question, but the counter-arguments advanced by him are really surprising.

Let me next take up the Qur'anic verse "There is nothing prohibited for you by Allah except corpses, blood, pig-flesh and that over which some name other than Allah's has been spoken; but it (i.e. the use of even these things) is not a sin for one who is under compulsion (to use them), provided that he is not disobedient and immoderate." There is much divergence of opinion among the *mujtahids* about the points of law deducible from this verse. The correct interpretation of the verse is the one made by Abū Ḥanīfah.

The first controversial point that arises is about the meaning of *corpse*. Abū Ḥanīfah takes the word to mean what it does in common parlance, but al-Shāfi'ī stretches its meaning to include even the wool and bones of dead animals and so declares the use of articles like fur to be prohibited. Mālik permits the use of the wool, fur and skin, but prohibits the use of the bones. Since the meaning adopted by al-Shāfi'ī and Mālik was obviously wrong, their disciples found it necessary to offer explanations. "Bones can be described as dead," says al-Rāzī in *al-Tafsīr al-Kabīr*, "because Allah says in the Qur'an, 'Who will quicken bones?' and only that can be quickened which has died. In the same way, Allah speaks of land as dead." This is a surprisingly naive explanation. Rules of law cannot be deduced from literalist interpretations of this kind. Al-Rāzī, having proved land to be dead on the authority of the Qur'an, should logically have gone on to declare the use of land and earth to be prohibited.

The second point of disagreement is the meaning of *blood*, which Allah has declared as prohibited. Abū Ḥanīfah takes it to mean "spilled blood" and, accordingly, considers the blood of fish to be unprohibited. According to al-Shāfi'ī, all kinds of blood are prohibited without qualification. Abū Ḥanīfah argues in reply that Allah has Himself made exceptions, as, for example, in the verse "*Qul lā ajidu fī mā ūḥiya ilayya muḥarraman 'alā ṭā'imin yaṭ'amuhu illā an yakūna maytatan aw daman masfūḥan*" (Say, "In what has been conveyed to me by revelation, I find nothing forbidden for any eater to eat except carrion or flowing blood") (Qur'an, 6:145). In this verse, the epithet *masfūḥ* (spilled) limits the meaning of *blood.*

The third point of controversy is the meaning of *bāghin wa ʿādin* (disobedient and immoderate). According to Abū Ḥanīfah, it is necessary that there should be no disobedience and immoderation in eating and drinking. Thus, if a person is on the brink of death for want of food and the only food available to him is carrion and pig flesh, then he is permitted to eat them, subject to two conditions: first, that he eats no more of them than is necessary to save his life and, second, that he does not snatch them from some other person similarly in dire need of them.

Al-Shāfiʿī interprets *baghāwah* and *ʿudwān* to mean "rebellion against the ruler" and "sinfulness." Thus, according to Abū Ḥanīfah, if a Muslim in rebellion against his ruler is on the point of death because of starvation, it is permissible for him to eat the quantity of carrion or pork necessary to save his life. According to al-Shāfiʿī, on the other hand, this is permissible only if the Muslim in question is not a rebel. The meaning attached by al-Shāfiʿī to the two words, in the first place, does not fit in with the context and, in the second, is contrary to the principles of Sharīʿah. The permission given by Sharīʿah in cases of necessity is not nullified by the commission of a crime or a sin. For example, lying, although it is a sin, has been permitted when it is necessary to save one's life. Can it be said that a sinner cannot take advantage of this permission? If a Muslim, by being a rebel, forfeits the benefit of the permission to eat prohibited food to save his life for the reason that it is better to let him die, then what was the need for denying him prohibited food alone? He should be debarred from eating permitted food as well.

Apart from these textual questions, Abū Ḥanīfah propounds a hypothetical question on the basis of analogy, on which al-Shāfiʿī joins issues with him. The question is this: if a man is dying of thirst and has nothing to drink but wine, is he permitted to drink it? Abū Ḥanīfah says that he is, while al-Shāfiʿī says that he is not. Al-Shāfiʿī's ruling is surprising in view of the fact that he is not opposed to analogical inference like the literalists Since the situation posed in the question is similar to the one clearly stated in the Qur'an in that the object in both cases is to save life, why should not the same directive apply to both?

No other *mujtahid* has interpreted the Qur'anic injunctions about crimes as correctly as Abū Ḥanīfah has done. Let me take murder for an example. The rules relating to retaliation for murder that were prevalent in pre-Islamic Arabia were extremely iniquitous and barbarous. Islam substituted for them a set of laws which have not been surpassed for fairness.

In pre-Islamic times retaliation was determined with reference to the status of the murderer and the murdered person. A powerful tribe exacted it by killing a freeman of the murderer's tribe for a slave of its own killed, a man of the murderer's tribe for a woman of its own killed, and two men of the murderer's tribe for a man of its own killed. Allah lays down a general rule, according to which the murderer is to be put to death in every case, whether he is highborn or lowborn, man or woman, freeman or slave, Muslim or *dhimmī*. For greater clarity, He abrogated the forms of retaliation prevalent before Islam, thus the verse "Retaliation for those murdered is ordained for you as a duty—a freeman for a freeman, a slave for a slave and a woman for a woman."

In pre-Islamic times, murder could be compounded on payment of monetary compensation, which was called *diyah.* Islam restricted this to cases of suspected murder or involuntary killing and fixed the same *diyah* for Muslims and *dhimmīs.* "It does not become a Muslim," says the Qur'an, "to kill another Muslim except in error; if a man kills a Muslim in error, he shall set free a Muslim slave and pay *diyah* to the relations of the man killed; and if the man killed belongs to a tribe with whom you have a treaty, then you shall pay *diyah* to his relations and also set free a Muslim slave."

Abū Ḥanīfah accepts these unmistakably clear orders of the Qur'an, but al-Shāfi'ī disagrees with him about some of the rules deducible from them—wrongly, I regret to say.

The first point of difference is this that while, according to Abū Ḥanīfah, a freeman may be killed in retaliation for the murder of a slave, al-Shāfi'ī thinks that this is not permissible, and Mālik and Aḥmad b. Ḥanbal agree with him. The Qur'anic text provides no justification for this kind of inhuman discrimination. If al-Shāfi'ī's view is based on the specific statement made in the phrase "a freeman for a freeman," then the equally specific statement made in the phrase "a woman for a woman" could be so interpreted to imply that a man should not be killed for a woman murdered—a position which nobody would accept.

The second point on which al-Shāfi'ī differs with Abū Ḥanīfah is that, while the latter thinks that the same *diyah* is payable for a *dhimmī* as for a Muslim, the former thinks that the *diyah* payable for a *dhimmī* is less than that payable for a Muslim. Al-Shāfi'ī seems to disregard the fact that Allah has used the same words in respect of those to whom Muslims are bound by treaties as He has used in respect of Muslims themselves. It is a proof of Islam's liberality that it has conferred equal rights on Muslims and *dhimmīs.* What a pity that people have misconstrued its liberal directives!

The third point of disagreement is that al-Shāfiʿī considers, and Abū Ḥanīfah does not consider, monetary compensation to be sufficient requital for murder, that is to say, wilful killing, although the Qur'an prescribes retaliation and forbids *diyah*—a dispensation which is in consonance with reason. In pre-Islamic times homicide was a civil wrong which could be redressed with monetary compensation. Islam could not endorse an error of this kind.

The fourth point of disagreement is that according to al-Shāfiʿī it is, and according to Abū Ḥanīfah it is not, essential for the killer to be put to death by the same method as he himself employed, for example, breaking the head with a stone or burning alive. No word in the Qur'anic text suggests anything like this.

The fifth difference of opinion between al-Shāfiʿī and Abū Ḥanīfah is that, while the former considers both retaliation and atonement necessary in case of a murder, the latter considers retaliation to be enough. In the Qur'an atonement is ordered specifically in respect of involuntary homicide and is nowhere mentioned in respect of murder.

Abū Ḥanīfah and al-Shāfiʿī are at variance with each other about some important orders relating to inheritance also. Abū Ḥanīfah's stand is in accord with the clear precepts of the Qur'an. Islam's rules of inheritance, which are different from those of all other legal systems, are inspired by a fine appreciation of human relationships, which is a proof of their being divinely ordained. The principle underlying them is that, in the absence of a bequest, the property of the deceased should devolve on his natural heirs, in proportion to the degrees of their relationship, which is considered, so to speak, an implied bequest. Allied to this is the economic principle that it is better for wealth to be distributed among a large number of persons than be concentrated in the hands of a single person or a few persons. These principles seem to have been overlooked by other religions, with the result that their rules of inheritance leave much to be desired. Under Christian law, the eldest son is practically the sole heir, the other sons getting only some odds and ends. Among Hindus, only sons are entitled to inherit, the father or brother or other relations having no entitlement at all. Islam looked closely and realistically into the claims of various people arising from their relationship to the deceased and, accordingly, fixed three classes of heirs, namely, *dhawī al-furūḍ* (close relations or sharers), *ʿaṣabāt* (residuaries) and *dhawī al-arḥām* (distant kindred). All these classes have been clearly mentioned in the Qur'an, and the *dhawī al-arḥām* have been specially mentioned in the following verses: "For men there is a share in what is left behind by their parents or close relatives; and in all property left behind by parents and close relatives. And of those who are relatives some have greater entitlements than others."

Abū Ḥanīfah in framing his rules of inheritance took all the three classes into consideration, but al-Shāfiʿī and Mālik left out the *dhawī al-arḥām* altogether, so that, according to them, the maternal grandfather, nephews, nieces and so on are entitled to nothing whatever. They committed the error of treating the *dhawī al-arḥām* as a genus and the *dhawī al-furūḍ* and *ʿaṣabāt* as its species. The Qur'an gives many directives about marriage and divorce, on some of which the *mujtahids* disagree with each other. I content myself with mentioning two of the most important.

According to al-Shāfiʿī, a woman, even if she has reached the age of discretion, cannot marry without the consent of her guardian, while according to Abū Ḥanīfah she can. Both of them adduce Qur'anic verses and traditions in support of their points of view. This is no place to discuss the traditions, but so far as the Qur'an is concerned, al-Shāfi'ī bases his claim on the verse "When you divorce your wives and when the probationary period is over, do not prevent them from taking other husbands." Al-Shāfi'ī argues that the words "do not prevent" are addressed to guardians, and he concludes from this that the guardians have the right of prevention. In support of this he refers to the occasion for the revelation of the verse, describing it thus: "Ma'qil b. Yasār gave his sister in marriage to his paternal uncle's son, who divorced her after a few days, but repented after the probationary period had expired and wished to remarry her, to which she was agreeable. Ma'qil, however, went to her and forbade the new marriage." It was then that the *āyah* was revealed.

I could never have believed that al-Shāfi'ī had put on this verse the construction that he has done had I not read it in his book with my own eyes. The first question to consider is whether the verse can have the meaning that al-Shāfi'ī attaches to it. It is accepted by everybody that the word "*ṭallaqtum*" (you divorce them) is addressed to husbands, and once this is accepted, it follows that the words "*ta'ḍulūhunna*" must also be addressed to them. Otherwise, the sentence would become incoherent, running thus: "O husbands, when you divorce your wives and when the probationary period is over, then, O guardians for marriage, do not prevent them from taking other husbands." Thus constructed, the sentence is undoubtedly ungrammatical and illogical because in the adverbial clause, the husbands are addressed, but in the main clause, they are forgotten and it is the marriage guardians who are addressed. This is no way of speaking.

Al-Rāzī, although a follower of al-Shāfi'ī, clearly admits in *al-Tafsīr al-Kabīr* that "this interpretation is quite wrong:

Allah cannot speak in this incoherent manner." Even if we accepted al-Shāfiʿī's interpretation, his reasoning would not be complete, for it is not conceivable that persons prohibited from doing a thing should at the same time be permitted to do it.

Let me now briefly explain the background of the *āyah*. It was customary for men in pre-Islamic times to prevent their divorced wives from remarrying because of aversion to the idea of their former wives cohabiting with other men. It was to abolish this evil custom that the *āyah* was revealed, and its correct translation is as follows: "O husbands, when you divorce your wives and when the probationary period is over, do not prevent them from marrying their husbands (that is to say, the men whom they wish to marry)" (Qur'an, 2:232). This is the meaning that Abū Ḥanīfah attaches to the *āyah*, and he argues from it that women have an independent right to contract marriage. This argument is confirmed by the word "*yankiḥna*," because in this word the act of marrying has been ascribed to women and not to marriage guardians.

The second question at issue relates to three divorces. All the four *mujtahid* imams agree that if a man pronounces three divorces at the same time, the divorce becomes finally effective and ceases to be revocable. They, however, disagree with one another as to whether giving divorce in this manner is lawful and permissible. Al-Shāfiʿī thinks that it is and that Allah has permitted it. Abū Ḥanīfah considers it prohibited and unlawful, and he also regards a man who gives this kind of divorce as a sinner.

His argument is that the method of divorce indicated by Allah is based on the *āyah* "Divorce is twice; then there is either stopping nicely or revoking or repudiating graciously." It is only by the method laid down in this *āyah* that divorce can be given lawfully. Some people have raised an objection to Abū Ḥanīfah's stand, saying that if it is not legally permissible to give three divorces at a time, then what is the sense in "repudiating," that is to say, giving effect to the divorce, especially when Abū Ḥanīfah himself admits that the latter is permissible? This involves a fine point, which this is not the occasion to discuss. However, I may point out that it is one thing for an act to be prohibited and another for it to be effective. For example, it is prohibited for a man to gift his property to his children in unequal shares; yet if an unjust man does so, his gift will be effective.

In concluding the discussion, let me make it clear that I do not claim infallibility or finality for Abū Ḥanīfah's legal pronouncements. He was, after all, only a *mujtahid* and not a prophet, and was therefore liable to commit errors, which, in fact, he actually did. This is why many of his close disciples have disagreed with him on many questions. On the period of *riḍā'ah*, on the apparent or real effectiveness of the *qāḍī's* decree, on murder by analogy, on the question of the maximum punishment prescribed being necessarily awardable for prohibited degree marriages, Abū Ḥanīfah's *madhhab* does not admit of a reasonable interpretation. The same is true in the case of many other questions. My purpose, however, has been to show that Abū Ḥanīfah was as correct in his opinions as it is possible for a *mujtahid* to be.

Notes

1. *'Uqūd al-Jumān.*
2. Ibn Khallikān, *Ta'rīkh*, on Ibn Bādīs.
3. Ibid., on 'Abdullah b. al-Mu'tazz.
4. *Al-Jawāhir al-Muḍiyyah*, on Nūr al-Dīn Zangī.

5. Quoted by Ibn Khallikān in his note on Yaḥyā al-Maṣmūdī.
6. *Ḥujjah Allāh al-Bālighah.*
7. Abū Hilāl al-'Askarī, in his book *al-Awā'il*, attributes these dicta to Wāṣil b. 'Aṭā'.
8. It should, however, be remembered that all the principles stated in books on the roots of *fiqh* cannot be claimed to be Abū Ḥanīfah's pronouncements. Shāh Waliullāh has written a fine essay on this in his *Ḥujjah Allāh al-Bālighah*, but he denies the authorship of Abū Ḥanīfah even in respect of some pronouncements established on authentic testimony to be Abū Ḥanīfah's.
9. Shiblī was presumably referring to *An Introduction to the Principles of Morals and Legislation* by Jeremy Bentham. [Tr.]
10. Imam Muḥammad, *al-Jāmi' al-Ṣaghīr.*
11. See Qāḍī Abū Yūsuf, *Kitāb al-Kharāj.*
12. It was the same kind of cap that the caliph al-Manṣūr compelled his courtiers to wear. The historians say that he did so in imitation of the Persians.
13. Ibn Jazlah, *Mukhtaṣar Kitāb Ta'rīkh Baghdād*, note on al-Wakī' b. al-Jarrāḥ.
14. Al-Ḥāfiẓ Ibn Ḥajar, *Tahdhīb al-Tahdhīb*, note on Abū Ḥanīfah.
15. The word in the verse is *ghā'iṭ*, which means a depression, and is secondarily used for a privy or toilet.

Appendix
Abū Ḥanīfah's disciples

Although in Asian countries there is generally a close relationship between a teacher and his pupils, sometimes the names of particular pupils become inseparably associated with their teacher's name for various reasons. As I have stated in the first part of this book, the circle of Abū Ḥanīfah's pupils was so wide as to be conterminous with the caliph's domain. Abū al-Maḥāsin al-Shāfiʿī has listed the names and origins of 918 men who were Abū Ḥanīfah's pupils in one way or another. Some of these are so important that brief biographical notes on them are a necessary complement to an account of Abū Ḥanīfah's life and work.

There were forty specially devoted pupils of Abū Ḥanīfah's who collaborated with him in the codification of *fiqh*. Since this was Abū Ḥanīfah's life work, the omission to give some account of these men would leave his biography incomplete. Not only are these men intimately connected with the history of Abū Ḥanīfah's own work, but their greatness provides a measure of the greatness of Ḥanafī *fiqh* as well as a proof of Abū Ḥanīfah's high rank. Al-Khaṭīb al-Baghdādī in his account of Wakīʿ b. al-Jarrāḥ reports a conversation about Abū Ḥanīfah which shows how, in the opinion of men who mattered, the greatness of his pupils reflected lustre on him. On one occasion, reports al-Khaṭīb, when some men of learning were assembled around Wakīʿ, somebody remarked that Abū Ḥanīfah had committed an error on a certain question. "How could Abū Ḥanīfah commit an error?" retorted Wakīʿ. He had eminent men to assist him—in analogy, Abū Yūsuf and Zufar; in Ḥadīth, Yaḥyā b. Zā'idah, Hafṣ b. Ghiyāth, Ḥabbān and Mindal; in lexicography and the Arabic language, al-Qāsim b. Maʿn; in devotion and piety, Dāwūd al-Ṭā'ī and al-Faḍayl b. ʿIyāḍ. How could one with such men by his side commit an error? Even if he were going to commit one, would these men let him do so?"

If, as is generally thought, the greatness of his pupils redounds to the glory of a teacher, then in the whole history of Islam no teacher enjoys more reflected glory than Abū Ḥanīfah. He could rightly claim that some of his pupils were the teachers of great imams and *mujtahids.* For example, al-Shāfiʿī used to say about Muḥammad that he had acquired a "camel-load of learning" from him.[1] This is the same Muḥammad who is a well-known pupil of Abū Ḥanīfah's and who spent his whole life vindicating his master. Indeed, some of Abū Ḥanīfah's pupils, especially Abū Yūsuf and Muḥammad, were scholars of such high rank that if they had claimed to be *mujtahids* in their own rights, hundreds of thousands of people would have accepted their claim and become their followers.

The religious sciences in the ascendant during Abū Ḥanīfah's time were *fiqh*, Ḥadīth, *asmā'* and *asmā' al-rijāl.* It is to be noted that the leading authorities in these sciences were all Abū Ḥanīfah's pupils, and not so merely in name, but in actual fact, having sat at his feet for years, which they were proud to acknowledge. Probably nobody will deny this so far as *fiqh* is concerned, but some people may wonder in regard to Ḥadīth, for most of Abū Ḥanīfah's pupils who attained to fame as such were *faqīhs*, those of them who are known as *muḥaddithīn* being famous in their own right and not because they were Abū Ḥanīfah's pupils.

In my notes on the various pupils dealt with in this appendix, I shall make specific mention of the disciplines which they studied under Abū Ḥanīfah, and I shall cite authorities from recognised *rijāl* works. It was my intention to write brief notes on those forty of Abū Ḥanīfah's innumerable pupils who were associated with him in the preparation of his *fiqh* code. Unfortunately, however, I have been able to ascertain the names of only a few of them, namely, Abū Yūsuf, Zufar, Asad b. 'Umar, 'Āfiyah al-Azdī, Dāwūd al-Ṭā'ī, al-Qāsim b. Ma'n, 'Alī b. Mushir, Yaḥyā b. Zakariyyā, Ḥabbān and Mundal.[2] On these I write brief notes. Besides these there are some pupils worthy of mention who were acknowledged masters of Ḥadīth and *rijāl*. I begin with the latter.

Muḥaddithīn

Yaḥyā b. Sa'īd al-Qaṭṭān

He was the originator of *rijāl*. Al-Dhahabī says in the preface to his *Mīzān al-I'tidāl* that the first man to write on *rijāl* was Yaḥyā b. Sa'īd al-Qaṭṭān and that he was followed by his pupils Yaḥyā b. Ma'īn, 'Alī b. al-Madīnī, Aḥmad b. Ḥanbal, 'Amr b. 'Alī al-Fallās and Abū Khuthaymah, who in turn were followed by their pupils, such as al-Bukhārī and Muslim.

So high was his standing in Ḥadīth that while he lectured, Aḥmad b. Ḥanbal, 'Alī b. al-Madīnī and others stood respectfully in front of him, questioning him on points of Ḥadīth from the afternoon prayer, when he started his class, up to the evening prayer.[3] He had worked up so much skill in the verification and criticism of transmitters that imams of Ḥadīth often used to say that they would rule out any transmitter whom Yaḥyā rejected.[4] There is a famous statement of Aḥmad b. Ḥanbal to the effect that he had not with his own eyes seen the equal of Yaḥyā.[5]

Despite all this learning, he used to attend Abū Ḥanīfah's lectures and was proud of being a pupil of his. Although the system of *taqlīd* (conformity to a particular authority) had not yet crystallised, he followed Abū Ḥanīfah in most matters. He himself admitted that he had derived his views mostly from Abū Ḥanīfah's dicta.[6] Al-Dhahabī, speaking in the *Tadhkirah al-Ḥuffāẓ* of Wakī' b. al-Jarrāḥ, says, "Wakī' gave *fatwās* on the basis of Abū Ḥanīfah's sayings, and so also did Yaḥyā b. al-Qaṭṭān. He was born in 130 H and died in 198 H in Baṣrah."

'Abdullāh b. al-Mubārak

The traditionist al-Nawawī writes about him in the *Tahdhīb al-Asmā' wa al-Lughāt*, "The imam on whose leadership and greatness there is a general consensus, talk of whom invokes divine grace and love of whom promises salvation."

His standing in Ḥadīth can be gauged from the fact that *muḥaddithīn* used to call him "Commander of the Faithful in Ḥadīth." One day, a pupil of his having addressed him as *'Ālim al-Mashriq* (scholar of the east), the famous *muḥaddith* Sufyān al-Thawrī, who was present, exclaimed, "What do you mean by calling him *'Ālim al-Mashriq*? He is *'Ālim al-Sharq wa al-Gharb*[7] (scholar of both east and west)."

Aḥmad b. Ḥanbal asserted that none of 'Abdullāh b. al-Mubārak's contemporaries had been more sedulous than he in learning Ḥadīth. 'Abdullāh b. al-Mubārak himself claims to have learnt Ḥadīth from four thousand masters, of whom one thousand narrated traditions to him.[8] Thousands of traditions are recorded in the *Ṣaḥīḥs* of al-Bukhārī and Muslim on his authority, and there is no doubt that he is one of the great masters of Ḥadīth transmission. He wrote numerous works on Ḥadīth and *fiqh*, but unfortunately none of them is available today.

His learning and piety earned him a public esteem higher than that enjoyed even by royal personages and state dignitaries. On one occasion, when the caliph Hārūn al-Rashīd was on a visit to Ruqqah, 'Abdullāh b. al-Mubārak also arrived there. On hearing of his arrival, thousands of people rushed to the town, so that the whole landscape was covered with clouds of dust. A lady of Hārūn al-Rashīd's harem, who was watching the scene from a window, asked in surprise what was happening. She was informed that the "*'Ālim* of Khurāsān known as 'Abdullāh b. al-Mubārak" had come to the town. "This is real kingship," exclaimed the lady. Hārūn al-Rashīd's is no kingship; no one comes to him unless brought by soldiers and policemen."[9]

He is one of Abū Ḥanīfah's best-known pupils, who was specially attached to his master and who always acknowledged that he had acquired all that he possessed of knowledge through Abū Ḥanīfah and Sufyān al-Thawrī. There is a famous saying of his: "If Allah had not helped me through Abū Ḥanīfah and Sufyān, I should have been no better than an ordinary man."[10] There are several verses of his in praise of Abū Ḥanīfah which are often quoted. Al-Khaṭīb al-Baghdādī has quoted some of them in his *Ta'rīkh*. He was a native of Merv, born in 118 H and died in 181 H in Hīt.

Yaḥyā b. Zakariyyā b. Abī Zā'idah

He was a famous *muḥaddith*. Al-Dhahabī in his *Tadhkirah al-Ḥuffāẓ*, which comprises accounts of only those men who were known as *ḥuffāẓ al-ḥadīth* (those who knew *ḥadīths* by heart), includes him, placing him at the top of his class. ʿAlī b. al-Madīnī, one of al-Bukhārī's teachers, used to say, "In Yaḥyā, learning reached the highest point it reached in his time."[11] In the six *Ṣaḥīḥs*, many traditions are quoted on his authority. He was both a *muḥaddith* and a *faqīh*, being a finished scholar in both disciplines. Thus, al-Dhahabī, in the *Mīzān al-Iʿtidāl*, begins the note on him with the words "One of the great *fuqahā'* and acknowledged *muḥaddithīn*." He was one of Abū Ḥanīfah's favourite pupils and spent a long time together with him, so that al-Dhahabī in the *Tadhkirah al-Ḥuffāẓ* describes him as "*Ṣāḥib* Abī Ḥanīfah" (a close companion of Abū Ḥanīfah's). He was the leading figure among those who collaborated with Abū Ḥanīfah in the codification of his *fiqh*. According to al-Ṭaḥāwī, he was associated with this for thirty years. While this figure may not be accurate, there is no doubt that his collaboration lasted a long time and that the work of writing was specially entrusted to him.[12] *Mīzān al-Iʿtidāl* says that according to some people, Yaḥyā was the first author at Kūfah. This view may have been the result of misunderstanding of his position as the scribe of Abū Ḥanīfah's *fiqh*. He was a *qāḍī* at Madā'in and died there in 182 H at the age of sixty-three.

Wakīʿ b. al-Jarrāḥ

He is considered one of the pillars of Ḥadīth. Aḥmad b. Ḥanbal was proud of having been a pupil of his, so much so that whenever he quoted a tradition on his authority, he would begin by saying, "This tradition was transmitted to me by one whose equal you have not seen."[13] Yaḥyā b. Maʿīn, a leading master of *rijāl*, is reported to have said, "I have never met a man whom I could prefer to Wakīʿ b. al-Jarrāḥ."[14] Similar things have been said about him by most doctors of Ḥadīth. Al-Bukhārī and Muslim have included in their *Ṣaḥīḥs* many traditions narrated by him; and his narrations and views about *rijāl* are considered very authentic.

He was a special pupil of Abū Ḥanīfah's, from whom he heard traditions. He followed the Imam on most questions and gave *fatwās* according to his dicta. Al-Khaṭīb al-Baghdādī writes in his *Ta'rīkh*, "He gave *fatwās* according to Abū Ḥanīfah's statements and heard many things from him." Al-Dhahabī confirms this in the *Tadhkirah al-Ḥuffāẓ*. Wakīʿ died in 197 H.

Yazīd b. Hārūn

He is a famous imam of Ḥadīth who had many great imams of Ḥadīth among his pupils, such as Aḥmad b. Ḥanbal, ʿAlī b. al-Madīnī, Yaḥyā b. Maʿīn and Ibn Abī Shaybah. According to al-Nawawī, his pupils were innumerable. Yaḥyā b. Abī Ṭālib reports that on one occasion when he attended a lecture of his, there were approximately seventy thousand people present.[15] His name was proverbial for the large number of traditions he knew. He himself used to claim that their number was twenty thousand.[16] Al-Bukhārī's teacher, ʿAlī b. al-Madīnī, used to say that he knew of no one who knew more traditions by heart.

In Ḥadīth, he was a pupil of Abū Ḥanīfah's. Al-Dhahabī, in his *Tadhkirah al-Ḥuffāẓ*, includes him among those who heard traditions from the Imam. He was associated with the Imam for a long time and had ample opportunity of forming an opinion about his ways and habits. He is reported to have said, "I have associated with many people, but have not met one who was Abū Ḥanīfah's better."[17] He was born in 117 H and died in 206 H.

Ḥafṣ b. Ghiyāth

He was a very great *muḥaddith.* Al-Khaṭīb al-Baghdādī describes him as "*kathīr al-ḥadīth*" (one who knew a large number of traditions); al-Dhahabī includes him among the *ḥuffāẓ* of Ḥadīth; Aḥmad b. Ḥanbal, 'Alī b. al-Madīnī and others have quoted traditions on his authority. He was specially famous for narrating traditions from memory, without the aid of a book or record of any kind. The traditions narrated by him in this way number three or four thousand.[18] He was one of those specially dear pupils of Abū Ḥanīfah's to whom he used to say, "You are the comfort of my heart and the allayer of my sorrows." The *Mukhtaṣar Kitāb Ta'rīkh Baghdād* speaks of him as one of Abū Ḥanīfah's famous pupils.

He avoided worldly concerns for a long time, but was in the end compelled by circumstances to become involved in them. As luck would have it, Hārūn al-Rashīd, hearing of his fame, summoned him and offered him the post of a *qāḍī*, which he accepted because he was heavily in debt. Abū Yūsuf was at that time the *qāḍī al-quḍāh* (chief *qāḍī*), who administered the judicial department. As Hārūn al-Rashīd had appointed Ḥafṣ without consulting the *qāḍī al-quḍāh*, the latter minded this and instructed al-Ḥasan b. Ziyād to examine the judgements of Ḥafṣ critically whenever they came up to him on appeal. But after reading some of the judgements, he admitted that there was divine guidance behind them.[19]

Ḥafṣ was born in 117 H. He worked as *qāḍī* for thirteen years in Kūfah and for two in Baghdad. He died in 196 H.

Abū 'Āṣim al-Nabīl

His original name was al-Ḍaḥḥāk b. Mukhlad, and he is a famous *muḥaddith*, from whom many traditions have been quoted in the *Ṣaḥīḥs* of al-Bukhārī and Muslim. Al-Dhahabī says in the *Mīzān al-I'tidāl* that there is a general consensus about his reliability. He was very devout and pious. Al-Bukhārī quotes him as saying, "Since I learnt that backbiting is a sin I have not talked against anyone behind his back."

Nabīl, meaning "respectable," was his title. Accounts vary as to how he acquired it. One account is as follows. At one time, Shu'bah took a vow not to narrate traditions any more. As he was a very great *muḥaddith*, whose lectures benefited thousands of students, this caused much public concern. Abū 'Āṣim, on hearing of the vow, went to Shu'bah and said, "I free a slave of mine to compound your breaking your vow. Please break it and resume your *ḥadīth* classes." Surprised at Abū 'Āṣim's love of learning and courage, Shu'bah exclaimed, "*Anta nabīl.*" *Nabīl* from then on became his title.[20]

He was one of Abū Ḥanīfah's special students.[21] According to al-Khaṭīb al-Baghdādī, on somebody asking him once whether Sufyān al-Thawrī or Abū Ḥanīfah was more of a *faqīh*, he replied, "Comparison is possible only between things that resemble each other. Abū Ḥanīfah is the founder of *fiqh*, while Sufyān is only a *faqīh*."

He died in 212 H at the age of ninety.

'Abd al-Razzāq b. Hammām

Al-Dhahabī begins his notes on him with the words "One of the respected scholars." He is a highly renowned *muḥaddith*. The *Ṣaḥīḥs* of al-Bukhārī and Muslim are full of traditions quoted from him. On somebody asking Aḥmad b. Ḥanbal whether he had come across anybody greater than 'Abd al-Razzāq in narrating traditions, he is said to have replied in the negative. Many great imams of Ḥadīth, such as Sufyān b.

'Uyaynah, Yaḥyā b. Ma'īn, 'Alī b. al-Madīnī and Aḥmad b. Ḥanbal, were among his pupils. Students of Ḥadīth used to come from long distances to attend his lectures. Some people have said that after the Prophet (ṣ), there has been none else whom people came to see from such long distances.[22]

There is a voluminous book by him on Ḥadīth entitled *al-Jāmi'*, to which al-Bukhārī owes a debt and which al-Dhahabī, in his *Mīzān al-I'tidāl*, describes as a treasure house of learning.

He was a pupil of Abū Ḥanīfah's in Ḥadīth. It appears from a number of passages in *'Uqūd al-Jumān* that he was associated with the Imam for a long time. Consequently, many statements are quoted from him about the Imam's habits and manners. One of them is to the effect that he had not known anybody who was gentler in nature than Abū Ḥanīfah. He was born in 126 H and died in 211 H.

Dāwūd al-Ṭā'ī

He was a divinely gifted man. The sufis regard him as a perfect *murshid.* His high spiritual attainments are mentioned in the *Tadhkirah al-Awliyā'*. The *faqīhs*, especially Ḥanafī *faqīhs*, acknowledge his standing in *fiqh* and *ijtihād. The muḥaddithīn* have said that he was "incontrovertibly reliable."[23] He deserves all this honour. The famous *muḥaddith* Muḥārib b. Dithār used to say, "If Dāwūd had been one of the ancients, Allah would have spoken of him in the Qur'an."[24]

He started by learning *fiqh* and Ḥadīth and went on to achieve a high degree of proficiency in *kalām*, taking an active part in debates and polemics. One day, in the course of discussion with somebody, he threw a pebble at him. The man said, "Dāwūd, both your tongue and your hands have gone beyond your control." The remark struck home: Dāwūd gave up taking part in debates, but continued his studies. A year later, he threw all his books into a river and cut himself adrift from all worldly occupations. "I often used to go to Dāwūd," says Imam Muḥammad, "to consult him on legal questions. If my questions were of an important and practical nature, he would express his views on them, otherwise he would dismiss me by saying that he was preoccupied with other urgent things."

Dāwūd is a famous pupil of Abū Ḥanīfah's. Al-Khaṭīb al-Baghdādī, Ibn Khallikān, al-Dhahabī and other historians writing about him make particular mention of his being one of Abū Ḥanīfah's pupils. He collaborated with Abū Ḥanīfah in the codification of his *fiqh*, being an important member of the editorial board. He died in 160 H.

In addition to the above there are many famous *muḥaddithīn* who were pupils of Abū Ḥanīfah's, such as al-Faḍl b. Dakīn, Ḥamzah b. Ḥabīb al-Ziyyāt, Ibrāhīm b. Ṭahmān, Sa'īd b. Aws, 'Umar b. Maymūn and al-Faḍl b. Mūsā. But I have confined myself to those of his pupils who were specially close to him and were associated with him for long periods.

The *Fuqahā'* Who Participated in *Fiqh* Codification

Qāḍī Abū Yūsuf

Abū Yūsuf's greatness and high standing call for an independent memoir which could do justice to his accomplishments. But I must leave that to someone with more time at his disposal than I have at mine. All that is required of me in the context of the present book is to give a brief account of his life and scholarly attainments.

He traced his descent to the *Anṣār*, one of his ancestors, Sa'd b. Bajīr, having been a Companion of the Prophet's. His father was a poor man who earned his living as a labourer. He was born at Kūfah in 113 or 117 H. He was fond of learning from early childhood, but his father wished him to acquire some profession and add to the family's earnings. Nevertheless, whenever he could spare some time, he would spend it in the company of learned men. One day, his father forcibly took him away from Abū Ḥanīfah's class and admonished him thus: "My son, Allah has granted Abū Ḥanīfah freedom from worry so far as his livelihood is concerned. Why do you imitate him?" Abū Yūsuf consequently discontinued his education and started spending his time with his father. A few day later Abū Ḥanīfah inquired about him. On this being reported to him, Abū Yūsuf came to see the Imam and told him what had happened. The Imam quietly gave him a purse. When he opened it at home, he found that it contained a hundred dirhams. The Imam had also told him that after spending that money, he could ask for more. He went on helping Abū Yūsuf in this way until the latter had acquired complete mastery over all the current sciences and become an acknowledged authority.

Abū Yūsuf attended the lectures of many other doctors. He heard traditions from al-A'mash, Hishām b. 'Urwah, Sulaymān al-Taymī, Abū Isḥāq al-Shaybānī, Yaḥyā b. Sa'īd al-Anṣārī and others, learnt *maghāzī* (military history) and *siyar* (biography) from Muḥammad b. Isḥāq and acquired a knowledge of *fiqh* from Muḥammad b. Abī Laylā. Allah had endowed him with so much intelligence and such a good memory that he learnt all these disciplines simultaneously. 'Abd al-Barr, a well-known *muḥaddith*, writes that Abū Yūsuf used to visit different *muḥaddithīn* and at one sitting learn fifty to sixty traditions, all of which he would retain in his memory.

So long as Abū Ḥanīfah lived, Abū Yūsuf regularly attended his classes. After Abū Ḥanīfah's death, he thought of establishing connections with the caliphal court. The 'Abbāsid caliph al-Mahdī appointed him as a *qāḍī* in 166 H. Al-Mahdī's successor, al-Hādī, retained him in that post. Subsequently, Hārūn al-Rashīd, on learning of his attainments, appointed him as *qāḍī al-quḍāh* for the whole realm—a post which he was the first to hold in Islamic history and which after him was held by only one man, namely, Aḥmad b. Abī Dāwūd. The improvements he made in the judicial department belong, properly speaking, to a biography of his.

He died on the 5th of Rabī' al-Awwal 182, which was a Thursday. According to Muḥammad b. Samā'ah, his dying words were "O Allah! You know that I never deliberately gave a judgement which was against the facts. It was always my endeavour to judge in accordance with Your Book and the wont of Your Prophet (ṣ). Whenever confronted with a difficult problem, I sought Abū Ḥanīfah's guidance and, as far as I know, Abū Ḥanīfah understood Your commands well and never knowingly strayed from the path of truth."

Abū Yūsuf was a very wealthy man, and he put his wealth to good use. He bequeathed a large amount of money to the poor of Makkah, Madīnah, Kūfah and Baghdad.

He was a versatile scholar. Although famous mostly in *fiqh*, he was unrivalled in several other disciplines. The historian Ibn Khallikān quotes Hilāl b. Yaḥyā as having said, "Abū Yūsuf was a *ḥāfiẓ* of *tafsīr* (exegesis), *maghāzī* (military history) and *ayyām al-'Arab* (history of Arabia). *Fiqh* was one of his minor accomplishments." In Ḥadīth, he ranked so high as to be counted among the *ḥuffāẓ* of it, and al-Dhahabī has included an account of him in his *Tadhkirah al-Ḥuffāẓ*. Yaḥyā b. Ma'īn used to say, "There is no one among the *ahl al-ra'y* who cited more traditions than Abū Yūsuf did." Aḥmad b. Ḥanbal is reported to have said about him, "In Ḥadīth, he was just." Al-Muzanī, a famous disciple of al-Shāfi'ī, used to say, "Abū Yusuf[25] follows Ḥadīth more than anybody else." Al-Khaṭīb al-Baghdādī quotes this statement from Aḥmad b. Ḥanbal: "When I was first attracted to Ḥadīth, I went to Abū Yūsuf." Yaḥyā b. Ma'īn, Aḥmad b. Ḥanbal and many other imams of Ḥadīth have quoted traditions from Abū Yūsuf. There could be no better proof of his greatness."[26]

No one can deny his standing in *fiqh*. Abū Ḥanīfah himself acknowledged it. Returning once from a visit to Abū Yūsuf during the latter's sickness, he said to his companions, "If, Allah forbid, this man dies, the world will lose one of its great scholars." The other imams also acknowledged his quick intelligence and penetration. Al-A'mash, a famous *muḥaddith* of the time, having consulted Abū Yūsuf on a question, said on hearing his reply, "Have you any authority for this?" "Yes," replied Abū Yūsuf, and he reminded al-A'mash of a tradition which the latter had narrated to him on a certain occasion. "Ya'qūb," said al-A'mash, "I first heard this tradition when your parents had not yet married, but I have understood its meaning only today."[27]

Abū Yūsuf was the first to write a book on *fiqh*. There are many books by him on other disciplines too, which have been listed by Ibn al-Nadīm in *Kitāb al-Fihrist*, but I have seen only *Kitāb al-Kharāj* and will say something about it. The book is a collection of memoranda sent by Abū Yūsuf to Hārūn al-Rashīd on *kharāj* (tribute), *jizyah* (poll tax) and s on. It is mainly concerned with questions of *kharāj* and can, therefore, be described as the revenue law of the time. The classification of lands according to value and productivity, the different rates of revenue, variations in the status of the cultivators, kinds of product and similar matters have been dealt with so comprehensively, and rules have been framed on all of them so systematically, that one finds it a surprising document for its time. The style is free and easy. Along with rules and instructions, the irregularities prevailing in the administration have been mentioned, and the caliph's attention has been drawn to them boldly.

The most remarkable thing about Abū Yūsuf is that under a self-admiring autocrat like Hārūn al-Rashīd he performed his duties with courage and freedom seldom paralleled in the history of Asian kingdoms. Here, for example, is a bit of advice addressed to Hārūn al-Rashīd in *Kitāb al-Kharāj:* "Commander of the Faithful, if you had been holding court even once a month to dispense justice to your subjects, you would not have been bracketed with those rulers who veil themselves from their subjects. And if you had held court even once or twice altogether, the news would have spread far and wide, and wrongdoers would have desisted from wrongdoing. In fact, if the governors and administrators had got to know that you sat in court to dispense justice even once a year, wrongdoers would never have the audacity to do wrong."

Who else could have been bold enough to address Hārūn al-Rashīd in these words?

What is surprising is that even an independent-minded and high-souled man like Abū Yūsuf did not escape attacks by his enemies, who have called him a sycophant and time-server and have invented stories to prove this charge. Some undiscriminating historians have quoted these stories, which have misled superficial observers into believing the charge. Thus, some of the stories have been quoted in *Ta'rīkh al-Khulafā'*.

However, the passage I have quoted from *Kitāb al-Kharāj* furnishes positive proof of the unreliability of these stories. Leave alone uncritical historians, even some *muḥaddithīn* were so carried off by their animus that they did not care to verify the facts. Al-Bayhaqī, in his voluminous biography of al-Shāfiʿī, writes, "When Imam al-Shāfiʿī was produced under arrest in Hārūn al-Rashīd's court, Qāḍī Abū Yūsuf and Imam Muḥammad advised the caliph to have him put to death on the ground that, if he were not disposed of quickly, he would endanger the State. Alas! Al-Bayhaqī, for all his reputation as a *muḥaddith*, lost sight of the fact that Abū Yūsuf had died long before al-Shāfiʿī was arrested and produced before Hārūn al-Rashīd. Fortunately, some of his fellow-*muḥaddithīn* have proved the story to be false. Ibn Ḥajar, who was not followed by any *muḥaddith* greater than himself, wrote a book on al-Shāfiʿī[28] which has recently been published in Egypt. In that book, he writes, "This story is false, and the greater part of it is a fabrication, while the other part is derived from mixed narrations. What is obviously false in the story is the statement that Abū Yūsuf and Muḥammad b. al-Ḥasan induced Hārūn al-Rashīd to have Imam al-Shāfiʿī put to death."

There are a number of things of which Abū Yūsuf is said to have been the originator. Ibn Khallikān writes, "Qāḍī Abū Yūsuf was the first to propose a distinctive dress for the *'ulamā'*, which is still in vogue. Before that, they dressed like the common people."

Muḥammad b. al-Ḥasan al-Shaybānī

He is one of the twin pillars of Ḥanafī *fiqh*, the other being Abū Yūsuf. His family belonged to a village called Ḥarastā, in the close vicinity of Damascus, but his father had migrated to

Wāsiṭah, where he was born in 135 H. Early in his youth, he went to Kūfah and there started his education, attending the lectures of many eminent *fuqahā'* and *muḥaddithīn*. He heard traditions from Mis'ar b. Kidām, Sufyān al-Thawrī, Mālik b. Dīnār, al-Awzā'ī and others.

For about two years, he attended Abū Ḥanīfah's lectures, and after the latter's death, completed his education under Abū Yūsuf. Then he went to Madīnah, where he learnt Ḥadīth from Mālik. While still a youth, he became famous for his attainments. At twenty, he assumed the professorial chair, and students began to attend his classes. Hārūn al-Rashīd, having learnt of his attainments, appointed him as *qāḍī* and most of the time kept him near himself. Accompanying Hārūn al-Rashīd on a visit to Rayy in 189 H, Muḥammad died at a village called Ranbūyah in the neighbourhood of Rayy. By an unhappy coincidence, the famous grammarian al-Kasā'ī, who was in the royal party, also died at the same village. Hārūn al-Rashīd was greatly grieved by this double loss and said, "We have buried both *fiqh* and *Naḥw* today." Al-Yazīdī, a famous man of letters and courtier of Hārūn al-Rashīd, wrote a poignant elegy, one of whose verses said, "We asked ourselves who would solve our problems after your death."

Although Muḥammad spent the greater part of his life as a courtier, he never gave up thinking independently and speaking the truth. When, in 175 H, Yaḥyā al-'Alawī rebelled, Hārūn al-Rashīd was frightened out of his wits on seeing his strength in men and arms and signed an armistice with him. The armistice was countersigned by important divines, scholars and jurists. A few days after, Yaḥyā, having signed the armistice, returned to Baghdad, Hārūn al-Rashīd began to play with the idea of violating the armistice. All the *'ulamā'* from fear of the caliph gave a *fatwā* that in the circumstances it was permissible for him to do so. Muḥammad openly opposed the idea and adhered to his stand till the end.

Muḥammad's standing can be gauged from what the *mujtahid* imams said about him. Al-Shāfi'ī said, "Whenever Imam Muḥammad expounded a point of law, it seemed as if the revealing angel had descended on him." I have already quoted another saying of al-Shāfi'ī's: "I acquired from Imam Muḥammad a camel-load of learning." Asked where he had learnt all the subtle points of law he used to make, Aḥmad b. Ḥanbal replied, "From the books of Muḥammad b. al-Ḥasan."[29]

Although Muḥammad's school turned out many eminent scholars, al-Shāfi'ī stands in a class by himself among them. This statement will probably surprise people of superficial learning in our day. Even in earlier days, Ibn Taymiyyah denied that al-Shāfi'ī was a pupil of Muḥammad's. But the truth cannot be suppressed for ever. Hundreds of books of history and *rijāl* bear witness to the fact that al-Shāfi'ī acquired a lot from his association with Muḥammad, and, what is more, he himself acknowledged this. Ibn Ḥajar quotes him as having said, "Muḥammad b. al-Ḥasan was held in high esteem by the caliph. So I used to visit him. I told myself that he was of a high rank in *fiqh* too. Therefore, I made it a point to attend on him, and I used to take down his lectures."

Muḥammad for his part respected al-Shāfi'ī very much and treated him with more courtesy than he did other students of his. One day, while on his way to the caliph's court, he met al-Shāfi'ī, who was on his way to his house. He immediately dismounted and told his attendant to go and inform the caliph that he was unable to attend court at that time. Al-Shāfi'ī requested him to proceed to court, as he could see him some other time. Muḥammad, however, replied that it was not so necessary for him to go to court.[30] There were now and again debates between Muḥammad and al-Shāfiʿī which is why some people have denied the teacher–pupil relationship between them. The fact, however, is that in those days debate between teacher and pupil was not considered inappropriate—nor should it be in our day.

Although Muḥammad's fame rests mostly on his work in the field of *fiqh*, he has the rank of a *mujtahid* in exegesis, as well as Tradition and literature. Al-Shāfiʿī is reported to have said, "I have not come across a man more learned in the Qur'an than Imam Muḥammad."[31] There is no book of his on literature and Arabic linguistics, but the treatment, in *al-Jāmiʿ al-Kabīr*, of questions of *fiqh* based on grammatical points shows how high were his attainments in these disciplines. Thus, Ibn Khallikān and others make special mention of them.

In Ḥadīth, his book *al-Muwaṭṭa'* is famous. Besides, in his *Kitāb al-Ḥujaj*, which he wrote in refutation of Mālik, he has cited numerous traditions on different questions, pointing out that the traditions counter the claim of the Madīnah doctors that they follow Ḥadīth.

Muḥammad's writings are very large in number and they are the basis of Ḥanafī *fiqh* today. I give below a list of those of his works in which he has cited Abū Ḥanīfah's expositions and which are, therefore, considered the groundwork of Ḥanafī *fiqh*:

(1) *Al-Mabsūṭ*. This book was originally written by Abū Yūsuf. Muḥammad revised it, making the exposition clearer. This was his first work.

(2) *Al-Jāmiʿ al-Ṣaghīr*. This was written after *al-Mabsūṭ*. In it Muḥammad quotes all the dicta of Abū Ḥanīfah on the authority of Abū Yūsuf, dealing with 533 questions, on

170 of which different opinions have been expressed. The questions fall into three categories: (1) those mentioned only in this book, (2) those mentioned also in other books of Muḥammad, but not mentioned explicitly as Abū Ḥanīfah's rulings, which has been done in this book, and (3) those mentioned in other books of Muḥammad, but stated here in words which invest them with a new significance.

On this book many commentaries have been written, the names and brief particulars of which have been given in *Kashf al-Ẓunūn* and other works.

(3) *Al-Jāmi‘ al-Kabīr.* This was written after *al-Jāmi‘ al-Ṣaghīr.* It is a voluminous work in which the dicta of Abū Ḥanīfah have been quoted along with those of Abū Yūsuf and Zufar. On every question, the arguments have also been stated. Later Ḥanafī scholars formulated their principles of jurisprudence on the basis of the method of reasoning followed in this book. Many eminent jurists wrote commentaries on it, of which forty-two have been mentioned in *Kashf al-Ẓunūn.*

(4) *Al-Ziyādāt.* This is a supplement to *al-Jāmi‘ al-Kabīr*, as its name shows.

(5) *Kitāb al-Ḥujaj.* Muḥammad visited Madīnah after Abū Ḥanīfah's death, and for three years studied Mālik's *Muwaṭṭa'* under him. The Madīnans had their own school of *fiqh*, which differed on many questions from that of Abū Ḥanīfah. Muḥammad wrote the book on his return from Madīnah. In it he first states the dicta of Abū Ḥanīfah, then describes the views of the Madīnans and lastly proves, with the help of traditions and analogy, that Abū Ḥanīfah's *madhhab* is correct and that of others incorrect. Al-Rāzī mentions this book in the *Manāqib al-*

Shāfiʿī. It has been printed and is available everywhere. I have seen a manuscript of it too.

(6) *Al-Siyar al-Ṣaghīr wa al-Kabīr.* These are his last works. He first wrote *al-Siyar al-Ṣaghīr.* Al-Awzāʿī, seeing a manuscript of it, tauntingly remarked, "What do the Iraqis have to do with *siyar*?" Hearing of this remark, Muḥammad started writing *al-Siyar al-Kabīr.* When completed, it consisted of sixty parts. Muḥammad loaded it on a mule and had it carried to Hārūn al-Rashīd. The latter had already heard of it and so he sent the princes royal to study it with Muḥammad.

In addition to the above, there are some works by Muḥammad on *fiqh*, such as *al-Kayāniyyāt*, *al-Jurjāniyyāt*, *al-Raqqiyyāt* and *al-Hārūniyyāt.* But these books do not belong to *ẓāhir al-riwāyah* (exoteric narration in the terminology of the jurists). In fact, *Kitāb al-Ḥujaj*, mentioned earlier, does not either.

Zufar

Although he was a greater master of *fiqh* than Muḥammad b. al-Ḥasan, I have had to speak of him later than of the latter because no writing of his is extant and very little is known about him.

He was of Arab origin. In the beginning, he was interested exclusively in Ḥadīth and was therefore known as *ṣāḥib al-ḥadīth* (master of Ḥadīth), as al-Nawawī states in *Tahdhīb al-Lughāt.* Later he turned to *fiqh*, and was occupied with it till the end of his days.

Yaḥyā b. Maʿīn, an imam of Ḥadīth criticism, says, "Zufar, authentic and reliable."[32] Some people have tried to prove him a weak *muḥaddith*, but what they say is vague and not worthy of much notice.

He was particularly skilled in analogical reasoning. Abū Ḥanīfah used to call him the greatest of his companions in this respect. Wakī‘ b. al-Jarrāḥ, whom I have already dealt with, used to consult him. He also held the post of *qāḍī.* He was born in 110 H and died in 158 H.

Al-Qāsim b. Ma‘n

He was an eminent scholar, traditions from whom have been quoted in the six *Ṣaḥīḥs.* A finished scholar in Ḥadīth and *fiqh*, he was unrivalled in Arabic linguistics and literature. He frequently consulted Muḥammad b. al-Ḥasan. The caliph appointed him as a *qāḍī.* He accepted the post, but never drew any salary.

Abū Ḥanīfah held him specially dear. He was one of those people whom he used to call the comfort of his heart and the allayers of his sorrows. He in turn was sincerely attached to the Imam. One day somebody said to him, "You are an imam of both *fiqh* and Arabic linguistics. Which of these two is the vaster?" He replied, "By Allah, one piece of writing by Imam Abū Ḥanīfah is worth the whole of Arabic linguistics." He died in 175 H.

Asad b. ‘Amr

He was the first man to be appointed a member of Abū Ḥanīfah's editorial board. He was a scholar of high standing. Aḥmad b. Ḥanbal has quoted traditions from him, and Yaḥyā b. Ma‘īn calls him reliable.,

Hilāl al-Rāzī tells a story about him, from which the high esteem he enjoyed at court can be gauged. Hārūn al-Rashīd, says Hilāl, was on a visit to Makkah. After the *ṭawāf,* he went into the Ka‘bah and sat down. All the courtiers kept standing, except one who was made to sit next to the caliph. Hilāl was surprised at this and asked the people present who that man was. He was told that he was Asad b. 'Amr.[33]

He was a *qāḍī* in Baghdad. He died in 188 H.

'Alī b. Mushir

He learnt Ḥadīth from al-A'mash and Hishām b. 'Urwah. Al-Bukhārī and Muslim have quoted traditions from him. Aḥmad b. Ḥanbal acknowledged his scholarship. It was from him that Sufyān al-Thawrī obtained all his information about Abū Ḥanīfah's writings. He was the *qāḍī* of Mūṣil. He died in 189 H.[34]

'Āfiyah b. Yazīd

He is the one referred to in Abū Ḥanīfah's order "Do not record anything until 'Āfiyah comes." Al-Dhahabī writes about him, "He was among the best of judges."

Ḥabbān

He narrated a large number of traditions. Ibn Mājah quotes many traditions on his authority. Abū Ḥanīfah admired his memory. He died in 172 H.

Mindal

He was a brother of Ḥabbān. He narrated traditions from al-A'mash, Hishām b. 'Urwah, 'Abd al-Malik b. 'Umayr, 'Āṣim al-Aḥwal and Abū Ḥanīfah. He was extremely pious. He died in 163 H. Ḥabbān wrote a moving elegy on him, some verses from which have been quoted by al-Dhahabī in *Mīzān al-I'tidāl.* Here is a translation of two of the verses:

When I remember the loss of my brother,
I toss about in my bed.
What other brother could be like mine?
He was always ahead of me in good deeds.

Notes

1. Some superficial critics of our day will probably raise their eyebrows at this report and dismiss it as an invention of Ḥanafī writers. But they should know that the famous *muḥaddith* al-Nawawī has described it as authentic. See his *Tahdhīb al-Asmā' wa al-Lughāt*, notes on Imam Muḥammad.
2. The historian al-Khaṭīb has mentioned these people as Abū Ḥanīfah's pupils in his note on Abū Yūsuf.
3. *Fatḥ al-Mughīth* and *al-Jawāhir al-Muḍiyyah.*
4. Ibn Ḥajar, *Tahdhīb al-Tahdhīb*, notes on Yaḥyā b. al.Qaṭṭān.
5. Al-Dhahabī, *Mīzān al-I'tidāl.*
6. Ibn Ḥajar, *Tahdhīb al-Tahdhīb*, note on Abū Ḥanīfah.
7. Al-Nawawī, *Tahdhīb al-Asmā' wa al-Lughāt.*
8. *Khulāṣah Tahdhīb al-Kamāl*, note on 'Abdullāh b. al-Mubārak.
9. Ibn Khallikān, *Ta'rīkh*, note on 'Abdullāh b. al-Mubārak.
10. Ibn Ḥajar, *Tahdhīb al-Tahdhīb* note on Abū Ḥanīfah.
11. Al-Dhahabī, *Mizān al-I'tidāl*, note on Yaḥyā.
12. *Al-Jawāhir al-Muḍiyyah*, note on Yaḥyā.
13. Al-Nawawī, *Tahdhīb al-Asmā' wa al-Lughāt*, note on Wakī' b. al-Jarrāḥ.
14. Ibid.
15. Al-Nawawī, *Tahdhīb al-Asmā' wa al-Lughāt*, note on Yaīzd b. Hārūn.
16. Ibid.
17. Al-Mazzī, *Tahdhīb al-Kamāl*, note on Abū Ḥanīfah.
18. *Mizān al-I'tidāl*, note on Ḥafṣ.
19. *Al-Jawāhir al-Muḍiyyah*, note on Ḥafṣ.
20. Ibid., note on Abū 'Āṣim.
21. Ibid.
22. Al-Sam'ānī, *al-Ansāb*, and al-Yāfi'ī, *Ta'rīkh*, notes on 'Abd al-Razzāq b. Hammām.
23. Al-Dhahabī, *Mīzān al-I'tidāl.*

24. Ibn Khallikān, *Ta'rīkh.*
25. Al-Dhahabī has quoted these statements in *Tadhkirah al-Ḥuffāẓ.*
26. In books of *rijāl*, there are quoted criticisms of Abū Yūsuf, but these are, generally speaking, unreliable because they either are vague or seem to emanate from differences of judgement.
27. Ibn Khallikān, *Ta'rīkh*, note on Abū Yūsuf.
28. Entitled *Tawālī al-Ta'sīs bi Ma'ālī Ibn Idrīs* and published in 1301 H at the Mīriyyah Press.
29. All these sayings have been quoted by the traditionist al-Nawawī in *Tahdhīb al-Asmā' wa al-Lughāt.*
30. *Tawālī al-Ta'sīs*, p. 96.
31. *Al-Jawāhir al-Muḍiyyah*, note on Imam Muḥammad.
32. Al-Nawawī, *Tahdhīb al-Asmā' wa al-Lughāt.*
33. *Al-Jawāhir al-Muḍiyyah.*
34. I learnt these facts from *al-Jawāhir al-Muḍiyyah.*

Index

'Abbāsid(s), 42, 44, 45, 49, 51, 64, 103, 181, 253
'Abd al-'Alī Baḥr al-'Ulūm, 103
'Abd al-'Azīz al-Mājishūn, 124
'Abd al-'Azīz b. Abī Dāwūd, 109
'Abd al-'Azīz b. Rafī', 36
'Abd al-'Azīz b. Rawād, 86
'Abd al-Barr, Qāḍī, 119, 167, 252
'Abd al-Karīm al-Shahrastānī, 150
'Abd al-Karīm al-Waḍḍā', 134
'Abd al-Karīm b. Umayyah, 25, 36
'Abd al-Malik (caliph), 12
'Abd al-Malik b. Marwān (caliph), 6
'Abd al-Malik b. 'Umar, 36, 142, 263
'Abd al-Qādir al-Jīlānī, 118
'Abd al-Raḥmān b. Abī Laylā, 21
'Abd al-Razzāq b. Hammām, al-Ḥāfiẓ, 10, 127, 249, 250, 264
'Abdullāh al-Sahmī, 61
'Abdullāh b. 'Abbās, 26, 27, 91, 115, 121, 131-133, 146, 153, 173
'Abdullāh b. Abī Awfā, 8, 24
'Abdullāh b. Abī Ziyād, 37
'Abdullāh b. al-Ḥasan, 37
'Abdullāh b. al-Mubārak, 10, 29, 32, 50, 101, 127, 244, 245, 264
'Abdullāh b. al-Mu'tazz, 181
'Abdullāh b. al-Sā'ib, 26
'Abdullāh b. Dīnār, 37
'Abdullāh b. Mas'ūd, 18, 32, 62, 73, 74, 136, 141, 166, 168, 173-175
'Abdullāh b. Sarakhs, 24
'Abdullāh b. 'Umar, 22, 23, 26, 27, 36, 73, 74, 115, 121, 143, 153
Abū 'Abd al-Raḥmān al-Salạmī, 21
Abū 'Abdullāh Ḥunayn b. Muḥammad b. Khusrū al-Balkhī, 100
Abū Aḥmad 'Abdullāh b. 'Adī al-Jurjānī, 100
Abū al-'Abbās al-Saffāḥ (caliph), 44
Abū al-'Aṭūf, 37
Abū al-Baqā' Aḥmadī, 99
Abū al-Dardā', 26, 141
Abū al-Ḥasan al-Karkhī, 150
Abū al-Ḥasan Muḥammad b. al-Muẓaffar b. Mūsā b. 'Īsā, al-Ḥāfiẓ, 100

Abū al-Ḥuṣayn, 22
Abū al-Khaṭṭāb al-Jurjānī,, 63
Abū al-Maḥāsin, al-Ḥāfiẓ, 4, 9-11, 21, 41, 95, 129, 170, 178, 241
Abū al-Millah al-Ḥanīfah, 10
Abū al-Mu'ayyad Muḥammad b. Maḥmūd al-Khawārizmī, 99, 100
Abū al-Muḥāfiẓ al-Shāfi'ī, 35
Abū al-Qāsim 'Abdullāh b. Abī al-'Awwām al-Sa'dī, 100
Abū al-Qāsim Ṭalḥah b. Muḥammad b. Ja'far al-Shāhid, 100
Abū al-Sawwār, 37
Abū al-Ṭufayl 'Āmir b. Wāthilah, 6, 22
Abū al-Zubayr Muḥammad b. Muslim, 36
Abū 'Alī al-'Azzī, 177
Abū 'Āṣim al-Nabīl, 10, 31, 32, 39, 248, 249, 264
Abū Bakr Aḥmad b. Muḥammad b. Khālid al-Kulā'ī, 100
Abū Bakr al-Bayhaqī, 148
Abū Bakr al-Ṣiddīq, 115, 117, 121, 131, 137, 188, 215
Abū Bakr Muḥammad b. 'Abd al-Baqī Muḥammad al-Anṣārī, 100
Abū Dalāmah, 57
Abū Dāwūd, 122
Abū Dharr, 113
Abū Ḥafṣ, 35
Abū Ḥātim Ya'qūb, 23
Abū Hilāl al-'Askarī, 118, 196, 239
Abū Ḥujayyah, 37
Abū Hurayrah, 23, 26, 27, 121, 132, 140, 153
Abū Isḥāq al-Sabī'ī, 22, 23, 36, 126
Abū Isḥāq al-Shaybānī, 252
Abū Ja'far al-Manṣūr (caliph), 23, 44-49, 59, 57, 77, 91-93, 103
Abū Ja'far Mas'ūd, 51
Abū Khuthaymah, 243
Abū Laylā, Qāḍī, 78, 194
Abū Manṣūr al-Māturīdī, 15
Abū Mu'āwiyah al-Ḍarīr, 109
Abū Muḥammad 'Abdullāh b. Muḥammad b. Ya'qūb al-Ḥārithī al-Bukhārī, 100
Abū Mūsā al-Ash'arī, 143
Abū Muslim al-Khurāsānī, 45
Abū Muṭī', 4, 57, 104
Abū Na'īm al-Faḍl b. Dakīn, 10
Abū Nu'aym al-Aṣbahānī, al-Ḥāfiẓ, 100, 102
Abū Sa'd, 51
Abū Sa'īd Mawlā b. 'Abbās, 37
Abū Salamah, 132
Abū Sufyān al-Sa'dī, 36
Abū Ṭāhir al-Dabbās, 104
Abū Ṭālib al-Makkī, 118
Abū Thawr, 122
Abū 'Umar al-Nakha'ī, 20
Abū Wā'il Shaqīq b. Salamah, 21
Abū Yūsuf, Qāḍī, 10, 56, 57, 61, 82, 83, 100, 101, 108, 170, 177, 219, 239, 251-254, 256
Abū Zar'ah, 23, 122, 142, 154
Ādam b. Abī Ayās, 35
adhān, 86
'Adī b. Thābit al-Anṣārī, 22, 36
al-'Āfiyah al-Azadī, 177
'Āfiyah b. Yazīd, 178, 263
āḥād, 156
Aḥfaẓ al-Nās, 25

Ahl al-Bayt, 31, 42
ahl al-ḥadīth, 124, 125
ahl al-ra'y, 123-126, 253
ahl al-riwāyah, 124
Aḥmad b. Abī Dāwūd, 253
Aḥmad b. Ḥanbal, 22, 23, 25, 117, 119, 120, 122, 123, 125, 127, 183, 204, 209, 211, 214, 218, 222, 223, 226, 228, 233, 243, 244, 246-250, 254, 258, 262, 263
Aḥmad b. Ṣāliḥ al-Miṣrī, 164
Ahwaz, 41
'Ā'ishah, 22, 37, 115, 143, 144, 153, 166, 174, 189
'ajamī(s), 3, 107, 219
akhbār al-āḥād, 149, 150
akhbaranā wa ḥaddathanā, 139, 164
Akmal al-Dīn, 99
Alfiyyah al-Ḥadīth, 145
Algiers, 41
'Alī b Abī Ṭālib, 6, 13, 20, 27, 74, 87, 112, 121, 132, 133, 138, 190, 215
'Alī b. al-Aqmar, 36
'Alī b. al-Madīnī, 23, 154, 243, 246-248, 250
'Alī b. 'Āṣim, 81
'Alī b. Mushir, 177, 243, 263
'ālim, 47, 99, 244, 245
'Ālim al-Mashriq, 244
al-'Ālim wa al-Muta'allim, 99
'Allāmah al-Tābi'īn, 174
Alp Arslān al-Saljūqī, 50
'Alqamah b. Marthad, 22, 36, 126
Alzam, 41
'amal, 111, 112
al-A'mash, 24, 36, 38, 41, 126, 252, 254, 263. *See also* Sulaymān b. Mihrān
āmīn, 225
Amīr al-Mu'minīn, 25, 112; of Ḥadīth, 127
amīrs, 112
'Ammār b Yāsir, 165
'Amr b. 'Abdullāh, 24
'Amr b. 'Alī al-Fallās, 243
'Amr b. Dharr, 65
'Amr b. Dīnār, 32
'Amr b. Jubayr, 37
'Amr b. Murrah, 22, 36, 109
'Amr b. Qays al-Māṣir, 109
Anas b. Mālik, 6-9, 24
Anmūdhaj al-Qitāl, 175
al-Ansāb, 9, 11, 36, 264
Anṣār, 131, 216, 252
Anūshirwān, 196
al-'Aqā'id, 99
'Aqīl, 26
Arabia, 3, 5, 6, 12, 14, 19, 20, 22, 31, 117, 123, 181, 196, 209, 232, 253
'arḍ, 103
Aristotle, 71, 171
'aṣabāt, 235
Asad b. al-Furāt, 177
Asad b. 'Amr, 262, 263
Asad b. Khālid al-Tamīmī, 177
Asad b. 'Umar, 177, 243
Āṣaf b. Barkhiyā', 76
aṣḥāb al-ra'y, 150, 179
ashrafī, 204, 217
'Aṣim al-Aḥwal, 263
'Āṣim b. Abī al-Nujūd, 36
'Āṣim b. Sulaymān al-Aḥwal, 25, 36
aslāf, 27
asmā', 242
'aṣr, 70, 93
Astrābād, 41

al-Aswad b. Yazīd, 20
'Aṭā' b. Abī Muslim, 36
'Aṭā' b. Abī Rabāḥ, 26, 27, 36, 38, 39, 126
'Aṭā' b. al-Sā'ib, 22, 36
'Aṭā' b. Yasār, 4
āthār, 177
'Atiyyah b. Sa'īd, 36
'Awn b 'Abdullāh, 22, 23, 37
al-Awzā'ī, 8, 27-29, 36, 73, 101, 123-126, 179, 180, 183, 257, 261
āyah(s), 38, 68, 74, 76, 82, 95, 111, 143, 173, 187, 201, 225, 227, 236, 237
'Aynī, 9
ayyām al-'Arab, 253
Ayyūb (prophet), 38
'azīz, 156

badī', 181
Badr, Battle of, 20, 143, 184
baghāwah, 231
al-Baghawī, 127
Baghdad, 39, 41, 47, 49-51, 220, 248, 253, 257, 263
bāghin wa 'ādin, 231
Bahrain, 41
Banū Taymallāh, 4, 5
al-Bāqir, Imam, 29, 30, 36, 42, 126
Bashīr al-'Adawī, 132
Baṣrah, 8, 9, 15, 18-20, 22, 24, 25, 36, 37, 39, 41, 46, 50, 54, 117, 136, 174, 244
al-Bayhaqī, 137, 157, 179, 256
al-Bazzār, 140
Bentham, 207, 208, 239
Bukhārā, 41, 181
al-Bukhārī, 23, 25, 39, 79, 107-109, 114, 122, 123, 126, 127, 132, 134, 135, 140, 154, 158, 160, 162, 163, 168, 170, 222-225, 229, 243-247, 249, 250, 263; *Ṣaḥīḥ*, 108, 109, 114, 122, 132, 168, 222

Caspian Sea, 181
Chosroes, 4, 20
Circassians, 182
Companion(s), 7-10, 16, 18-20, 22-24, 26-28, 47, 58, 73, 102, 106, 107, 114-117, 120, 121, 124, 125, 130-133, 138, 140-146, 151, 153, 161, 165, 166, 169, 171-174, 184, 189, 190, 215, 216, 252
Constantinople, 181

al-Ḍaḥḥāk, 74, 75, 248
ḍa'īf, 156
Damascus, 41, 256
Dāmghān, 41
dār al-'ilm, 19
al-Dāraquṭnī, 23, 158
Dāwūd al-Ṭā'ī, 177, 193, 242, 243, 250, 251
Dāwūd b. Hind, 43
al-Daylamī, 102
al-Dhahabī, 9, 11, 20, 23, 32, 35, 36, 67, 88, 104, 109, 124, 128, 129, 131, 136, 141, 170, 243-251, 253, 263-265
dhawī al-arḥām, 224, 235
dhawī al-furūḍ, 235
dhimmī(s), 63,193, 206, 214-220, 232, 233
al-Dhuhalī, 107
dirāyah, 56, 126, 146-148
diyah, 80, 81, 217, 233, 234

ḍuʿafāʾ, 123

Egypt, 8, 13, 14, 41, 90, 182, 218, 256
Emessa, 41

al-Faḍl b. Dakīn, 10, 139, 251
al-Faḍl b. Mūsā, 251
Fakhr al-Islām al-Bazdawī, 103
fālūdah, 6
faqīh(s), 50, 65, 73, 79, 124, 166, 167, 172, 174, 186, 200, 246, 249
Faqīh al-ʿIrāq, 174
farḍ, 79, 166, 167, 172, 200; *kifāyah, 79*
Farghānah, 12
Fārisī, 3. *See also* Persian
Fatawa-i-Alamgiri, 219
Fatḥ al-Mughīth, 33, 35, 39, 145, 170, 264
Fāṭimah b. Qays, 166
fatwā(s), 8, 11, 24, 27, 69, 79, 175, 222, 224, 244, 247, 257
fiqh, 14-19, 21, 24, 25, 27, 28, 30, 31, 34, 40, 43, 69, 71, 72, 75, 76, 85, 87, 90, 93, 101, 106, 107, 120, 122, 125, 135, 136, 156, 160, 166, 167, 169, 171, 173-176, 179-182, 184-186, 189-193, 195-201, 203, 205, 207, 209, 214, 218, 221-223, 226, 239, 241-243, 245, 246, 249-254, 256-262; Madīnan, 28
al-Fiqh al-Akbar, 99, 103-105
al-Fuḍayl b. ʿIyāḍ, 69, 242
fuqahāʾ, 109, 118, 246, 251, 257

Georgia, 41
ghāʾiṭ, 228, 239
al-Ghazālī, 118, 154, 170

ḥabbah, 211
Ḥabbān, 263
ḥadd, 188
ḥaddathanā, 139, 140, 162
al-Hādī (caliph), 253
ḥadīth(s), 4, 7-10, 13, 14, 17-35, 56, 74, 77, 87, 99, 101, 102, 104, 107, 109, 113, 114, 119-121, 123, 124, 126-130, 134-137, 139-142, 144, 146-148, 152, 154, 155, 158-162, 164, 170, 173, 174, 177, 182, 184, 186, 188, 220, 222-226, 242-250, 253, 254, 257, 259, 261-263; *marfūʿ*, 135; *mutawātir*, 147; Nabawī, 33; school, 7
ḥāfiẓ, 95, 222, 253
Ḥafṣ b. ʿAbd al-Raḥmān, 60
Ḥafṣ b. Ghiyāth, 177, 242, 248
al-Ḥajjāj b. Yūsuf, 12, 13, 21, 50
al-Ḥakam b. ʿUtbah, 36
al-Ḥakam b. Ziyad, 37
Ḥakīm b. Jazlah, 51
al-Ḥakīm Isḥāq, 99
Hamadān, 37, 41
Ḥamīd al-Aʿraj, 37
Ḥammād b. Imam Abū Ḥanīfah, 100
Ḥammād b. Salamah, 101
Ḥammād b. Sulaymān, 109
Ḥammād b. Zayd, 134
ḥammām, 85, 175
Ḥamzah b. Ḥabīb al-Ziyyāt, 251
Ḥanafī(s), 9, 35, 49, 113, 136, 150, 151, 157, 158, 180-183, 185, 187, 192, 195-200, 203, 207, 214, 215, 218, 221-223, 228, 241, 250, 256, 259, 260,

264; *fiqh*, 49, 180-182, 195-197, 200, 203, 207, 214, 218, 221, 241, 256, 259; jurists, 35, 150, 180; *madhhab*, 181, 182, 218; *'ulamā'*, 151
Ḥanbalī, 181
ḥanīf, 10
Ḥanīf Mosque, 62
Haram al-Qurashī, 137
Ḥarastā, 256
al-Ḥārith b. 'Abd al-Raḥmān, 36
Hārūn al-Rashīd, 56, 57, 82, 183, 185, 215, 245, 248, 253-257, 261, 262
al-Hārūniyyāt, 261
ḥasan, 156, 160
al-Ḥasan al-Baṣrī, 4, 21, 24, 62, 76, 106, 140, 174
al-Ḥasan b. 'Ammārah, 50
al-Ḥasan b. Ziyād, 248
al-Ḥaṣfakī, 100, 102
Hāshimī(s), 184, 188
al-Hāshimiyyah, 46
Ḥashwiyyah, 15
Ḥasīn b. 'Abd al-Raḥmān, 37
Haytham b. Abī al-Haytham, 37
Herat, 41
al-Hidāyah, 9, 218
Ḥijāz, 13, 33, 174
Hilāl al-Rāzī, 262
Hilāl b. Yaḥyā, 253
Hishām b. 'Abd al-Malik (caliph), 42
Hishām b. 'Urwah, 23, 36, 126, 252, 263
ḥuffāẓ, 128, 129, 248, 253; *al-ḥadīth*, 246
Ḥujjah Allāh al-Bālighah, 95, 101, 153, 157, 208, 239
Ḥulwān, 41
al-Ḥusayn b. Ṣāliḥ, 89

ibādah, 178, 202
Ibāḍiyyah, 15
al-'Ibar fī Akhbār man 'Ghabar, 11, 104
Ibn 'Abbās, 133, 172
Ibn 'Abd al-Barr, Qāḍī, 58, 167
Ibn Abī Laylā, Qāḍī, 43, 79, 80
Ibn Abī Shaybah, 223, 247
Ibn 'Adī, 102
Ibn al-Athīr, 130, 196
Ibn al-Bazzāzī, 100
Ibn al-Hummām, 223
Ibn al-Jawzī, 147- 149, 160, 170
Ibn al-Nadīm, 254
Ibn al-Najjār, 102
Ibn al-Ṣalāḥ, 11, 137, 158, 159
Ibn al-Zubayr, 23, 26
Ibn 'Arūbah, 180
Ibn 'Asākir, 102
Ibn Ḥajar, 8, 9, 23, 25, 36, 118, 120, 146, 148, 149, 168, 169, 170, 226, 239, 256, 258, 264
Ibn Ḥazm, 161
Ibn Ḥibbān, 102
Ibn Hubayrah, 59, 66
Ibn Jazlah, 10, 11, 17, 239
Ibn Jurayj, 50, 180
Ibn Khaldūn, 81, 128, 136, 170, 185, 206
Ibn Khallikān, 9, 39, 52, 54, 70, 79, 95, 170, 182, 238, 239, 251, 253, 256, 259, 264, 265
Ibn Mahdī, 22
Ibn Mājah, 122, 143, 153, 263
Ibn Mu'īn, 23
Ibn Qutaybah, 43, 109, 124
Ibn Sa'd, 8, 22, 24
Ibn Sīrīn, 4, 41, 133, 174

Ibn Sufyān, 23
Ibn Taymiyyah, 31, 118, 258
Ibn ʿUliyyah, 35
Ibn ʿUmar. *See* ʿAbdullāh b. ʿUmar
Ibrāhīm (brother of Muḥammad al-Nafs al-Zakiyyah), 45, 46
Ibrāhīm (prophet), 111, 113, 167, 168, *millah of*, 10
Ibrāhīm al-Baṣrī, 67
Ibrāhīm al-Nakhaʿī, 33, 40, 63, 73, 136, 174, 175
Ibrāhīm al-Taymī, 109
Ibrāhīm b. al-Walīd, 42
Ibrāhīm b. Husām, 99
Ibrāhīm b. Maymūn, 45, 48
Ibrāhīm b. Muḥammad, 22, 36
Ibrāhīm b. Ṭahmān, 251
Ibrāhīm b. ʿUtbah, 62
ʿĪd, 130, 187
ʿiddah, 212
Idhā zulzilat, 68
iḥrām, 32
ijithād, 120
ijmāʿ qaṭʿī, 147
ijtihād, 188, 192, 207, 222, 250
ikhtilāf, 25
ʿIkrimah Mawlā b. ʿAbbās, 37, 164
ʿillah khafiyyah, 154
al-ʿilm al-ʿaqlī wa al-naqlī, 153
al-Imām al-Aʿẓam, 6, 170
īmān, 77, 112
India, 54, 181, 182
Iran, 4, 51, 188, 196
Iraq, 12, 13, 22, 25, 29, 33, 42, 43, 72, 123, 132, 174, 185, 196
irjāʾ, 109
ʿĪsā (prophet), 111
ʿĪsā b. al-Malik al-ʿĀdil, 182
ʿĪsā b. Ibān, 150
ʿĪsā b. Mūsā, 59, 64
Isfahan, 41
Isḥāq b. Rāhwayh, 122
ʿishṣāʾ prayer, 55, 68, 70, 226
ism al-aʿẓam, 76
Ismāʿīl (Abu Ḥanīfah's grandson), 3, 5
Ismāʿīl b. ʿAbd al-Malik, 36
isnād, 127
ʿIyāḍ, Qāḍī, 148

Jābir al-Juʿfī, 164
Jābir b. ʿAbdullāh, 26
Jaʿfar al-Ṣādiq, 30, 31, 150
Jahm b. Ṣafwān, 106, 117
Jahmiyyah, 15, 106, 117, 169
jahr bismillāh, 224
Jalāl al-Dīn al-Suyūṭī, 149, 169
al-Jāmiʿ al-Kabīr, 127, 259, 260
al-Jāmiʿ al-Ṣaghīr, 104, 225, 239, 259, 260
al-Jāmiʿ al-Ṣaḥīḥ, 225
jarḥ, 163, 164, 221, 222
Jarīr b. ʿAbd al-Ḥamīd, 101
al-Jawāhir al-Muḍiyyah, 51, 178, 264, 265
jawhar, 103
jawr, 107
Jawwāb al-Taymī, 37
Jawzaqānī, 102
Jerusalem, 181, 182
Jew, 94, 95
Jewess, 143
jizyah, 187, 188, 216-218, 254
jubbahs, 57
al-Junayd al-Baghdādī, 193
Jundub b. ʿAbdullāh, 22
al-Jurjāniyyāt, 261
Juzʾ al-Qirāʾah, 224, 225

Ka'bah, 216, 217, 262
Kabul, 4, 5, 12, 181
kāfir(s), 27, 77, 91, 92
kalām, 14-17, 39, 92, 106, 117, 118, 167, 190, 198, 199, 250
al-Kāmil, 102
Kashf al-Ẓunūn, 260
Kashghar, 181
Kathīr al-Aṣamm, 37
kathīr al-ḥadīth, 248
al-Kayāniyyāt, 261
al-khabar al-wāḥid, 157
Khālid b. 'Alqamah al-Widā'ī, 37
Khālid b. al-Walīd, 174
Khalīfah, 48
Kharāfah, 187
kharāj, 254
Khārijah b. 'Abdullāh, 37
Khārijah b. Muṣ'ab, 81, 109
Khārijah b. Zayd b. Thābit, 128
Khārijī, 74
Khārijites, 91, 92, 106, 109, 117
al-Khaṭīb al-Baghdādī, 9, 39, 115, 222, 241, 245, 247-249, 251, 254
Khawārij, 15, 16
Khawārizm, 12, 41
Khayzurān, 50
Khuḍayb, 32
khul', 210, 213
Khurāsān, 36, 43, 245
khuṭbah, 225
Kirmān, 41
Kitāb al-Ansāb, 9, 11
Kitāb al-Āthār, 37, 138
Kitāb al-Awā'il, 118, 196
Kitāb al-Ḍu'afā', 102
Kitāb al-Fihrist, 254
Kitāb al-Ḥudūd, 203
Kitāb al-Ḥujaj, 73, 138, 198, 259-261
Kitāb al-'Ilal, 133
Kitāb al-Intiqā' fī Faḍā'il al-Thalāthah al-A'immah al-Fuqahā', 119
Kitāb al-Jināyāt, 203
Kitāb al-Kharāj, 239, 254-256
Kitāb al-Madkhal, 163
Kitāb al-Rahn, 178
Kitāb al-Ṣiyānah, 179
Kitāb al-Siyar, 179
Kitāb al-Uṣūl, 103
Kūfah, 6-8, 14, 15, 18-24, 29, 36, 37, 39-43, 45-47, 50, 55, 59, 65, 74, 75, 77-79, 88, 89, 94, 126, 129, 131, 136, 164, 173, 174, 184, 196, 246, 248, 252, 253, 257
Kūfans, 46, 226
kufr, 91, 92
kunyah, 3, 10

al-Layth b. Sa'd, 8, 90, 224
Levant, 12, 14

Ma'ānī al-Āthār, 151, 198
al-Ma'ārif, 109, 124
al-Mabsūṭ, 259
Madā'in, 20, 41, 246
madhhab(s), 181-183, 199, 203, 206, 218, 224, 238, 260
Madīnah, 8, 20-22, 25, 28, 29, 34, 36, 37, 39, 41, 44, 126, 150, 173, 181, 184, 216, 217, 253, 257, 259, 260
Madīnans, 260
madrasah, 51
maghāzī, 22, 252, 253
Maghrib, 185
maghrib prayer, 38, 70

Magians, 116
al-Mahdī (caliph), 253
Maḥmūd al-Ghaznawī, 182
mahr, 89, 90
Makḥūl al-Shāmī, 28, 126
Makkah, 19-21, 25-28, 31, 32, 36, 37, 39, 41, 43, 47, 50, 72, 90, 126, 181, 184, 216, 217, 253, 262
Makkī b. Ibrāhīm, 10
Mālik b. Abī ʿĀmir (imam Mālik's grandfather), 184
Mālik b. Anas, 8, 23, 28, 32, 35, 67, 79, 119-121, 123, 125, 135, 137, 138, 140, 142, 145, 182, 183, 185, 204, 217, 224, 233, 235
Mālik b. Dīnār, 257
Mālikī, 182
Ma'mūn al-Rashīd, 54, 117
Maʿn, 37
Manāqib al-Shāfiʿī, 73, 101, 110, 119, 150, 157, 169, 170, 179, 215, 224, 260
Manṣūr b. al-Maʿmar, 22
Manṣūr b. al-Muʿtamir, 36, 126
Manṣūr b. Zādhān, 36
Maʿqil b. Yasār, 236
maqṭūʿ, 162
al-Mārdīnī, 223
marfūʿ, 56, 161; *ḥadīth*, 161
Maʿrūf al-Karkhī, 193
Marwān al-Ḥimār, 42
masā'il, 179, 182
masfūḥ, 231
Mashhad Abū Ḥanīfah, 51
mashhūr, 156, 157, 166, 167
Masīsah, 41
masnūn, 166, 172
Masrūq b. al-Ajdaʿ, 20
al-Māwardī, 100
Mawlā Aḥmad b. Muḥammad al-Maghnīsāwī, 99
Mawlā Ilyās b. Ibrāhīm al-Sīnūbī, 99
mawlās, 4
Maymūn b. Siyāh, 37
al-Milal wa al-Niḥal, 104
Mindal, 263
Minorca and Majorca, islands of, 12
mīrāth, 178
Misʿar b. Kidām, 41, 68, 89, 109, 257
Mīzān al-Iʿtidāl, 109, 124, 163, 243, 246, 249, 250, 263, 264
muʿallal, 154, 155
muʿāmalāt, 178
muʿanʿan, 161, 162
Muʿāwiyah, 87, 89, 115
muʿawwadhatayn, 168
al-Muʿizz b. Bādīs, 181
mudraj, 154
muḥaddith(s), 21-25, 27, 32, 35, 41, 60, 75, 76, 109, 119, 120, 124, 129, 136, 140, 147, 149, 154, 155, 159, 160, 163, 198, 224, 244-246, 248-250, 252, 254, 256, 261, 264
muḥaddithīn, 9, 102, 104, 106-109, 113, 114, 119, 120, 122, 128, 129, 136-139, 148, 154, 158, 160, 165-168, 179, 223, 243, 244, 246, 250-252, 256, 257
Muhājirs, 216
Muḥammad al-Anṣārī, 81, 100
Muḥammad al-Munkadir, 36
Muḥammad al-Nafs al-Zakiyyah, 44, 45

Muḥammad b. 'Abd al-Raḥmān, 78
Muḥammad b. Abī Laylā, 252
Muḥammad b. al-Faḍl, 32
Muḥammad b. al-Ḥasan, 49, 149, 157, 192, 198, 256, 258, 261, 262
Muḥammad b. al-Sā'ib al-Kalbī, 37
Muḥammad b. Bashshār al-Miṣrī, 164
Muḥammad b. Ibrāhīm, 44
Muḥammad b. Isḥāq, 252
Muḥammad b. Mālik, 37
Muḥammad b. Muslim al-Zuhrī, 37, 126
Muḥammad b. Samā'ah, 253
Muḥammad b. Sīrīn, 21, 142
Muḥārib b. Dithār, 22, 23, 36, 126, 250
Muḥyī al-Dīn b. 'Arabī, 118
Muḥyī al-Dīn Muḥammad b. Bahā' al-Dīn, 99
mujtahid(s), 40, 119, 120, 123, 125, 127, 128, 138, 142, 153, 155, 160, 172, 173, 180, 181, 183, 186, 192, 193, 198, 200, 201, 203, 205, 207, 208, 214, 221, 222, 224, 226, 228, 230, 232, 235, 237, 238, 242, 258, 259
mujtahidīn, 165
Mukhtaṣar Kitāb Ta'rīkh Baghdād, 10, 36, 239, 248
Mullā 'Alī al-Qārī, 99, 100, 145, 170
mu'min(s), 76, 77, 109-113
munkar, 154
Muqaddamah, 11, 137
muqtadī(s), 225, 229
al-Muqtadir Billāh (caliph), 51
Murji'ah, 15, 108
Murji'ite, 109, 111
murshid, 250
Mūsā (prophet), 111, 112
Mūsā b. Abī 'Ā'ishah, 22, 37
Mūsā b. Kathīr, 40
Musallam al-Thubūt, 150
mushaddid fī al-riwāyah, 136, 137
Mūṣil, 41, 263
Muslim (imam), 79, 122, 126, 140, 158, 160, 163, 223, 243, 245, 249; *Ṣaḥīḥ*, 131, 159, 163, 165, 170
musnad(s), 99-102
mustaḥabb, 166, 171, 172, 200, 211
mutawātir, 147, 156, 157, 166-168
Mu'tazilah, 15, 110, 117, 138, 166, 169, 199
Mu'tazilite, 107
Muṭṭalibī, 184
muttaṣil, 56, 159, 161, 162, 165, 177
muwālāh, 226, 227
al-Muwaṭṭa', 36, 120, 137, 138, 224, 259, 260
al-Muzanī, 254

nabīl, 249
al-Naḍar b. Yaḥyā, 125
Nāfi' b. 'Umar, 36, 126
nafls, 68
Nāmah-i-Dānishwarān, 42, 46
al-Nasafī, 99
al-Nasā'ī, 23, 122
Naṣībīn, 41
Nāṣir al-Dīn Qājār, 51

Naṣr b. Muḥammad, 57
naṣṣ, 191, 220
al-Nawawī, 8, 9, 23, 127, 158, 163, 244, 247, 261, 264, 265
Nawrūz, 6
Nazār, 20
Nihāwand, 41
Nihistār, 41
Nisā, 41
Nīshāpūr, 41
niyyah, 200, 226, 227
Niẓāmiyyah *madrasah*, 51
Nūḥ (prophet), 111, 114
al-Nu'mān b. Bashīr, 23
al-Nu'mān b. Thābit, 3, 5, 29
Nūr al-Dīn Zangī, 182, 238
nuṣūṣ, 220

Pathan, 182
Persia, 4, 5, 14, 196
Persian(s), 3-6, 15, 131, 196, 197, 201, 219, 229, 239. *See also* Fārisī
pīrs, 58

Qābūs b. Abī Ẓabyān, 37
qaḍā', 27
qadar, 27
Qadariyyah, 15, 116, 169
qāḍī(s), 9, 22, 23, 43, 47, 50, 53, 54, 77-79, 83, 84, 123, 175, 182, 183, 210, 238, 246, 248, 253, 257, 262, 263; *al-quḍāh*, 248, 253
qadr, 106, 107
Qalā'id 'Uqūd al-'Iqyān, 11, 175, 179
al-Qāsim b. Ma'n, 177, 242, 243, 262
al-Qāsim b. Muḥammad, 142
al-Qāsim b. Qaṭlūbaghā, 223
al-Qasṭalānī, 114, 122
Qatādah al-Baṣrī, 75
Qatādah b. Di'āmah, 21
Qays b. Ḥāzim, 21
Qays b. Muslim, 36
qiblah, 112, 116, 117
qidam, 108
qirā'ah, 17, 108, 200, 201
qiyās, 150, 152, 153
al-qiyās al-jalī, 150
Qūmas, 41
qunūt al-fajr, 224
Qurayshī, 184
Qurrah, 13
al-Qurṭubī, 145
Qurẓah, 132

Rabī' b. Khuthaym, 21
al-Rabī'ah, 37
Rabī'ah al-Ra'y, 123, 124
Rāfi', 26
Rāfiḍah, 15
al-Rāfi'ī, 127
Rajā' b. Ḥayah, 142
rak'ahs, 26, 130, 226
Ramaḍān, 45, 151
Raqqah, 41
al-Raqqiyyāt, 261
rāwī, 104
Rayy, 37, 41, 257
al-Rāzī, 73, 110, 122, 150, 151, 179, 183, 215, 224, 227, 230
rijāl, 39, 242, 243, 246, 247, 258, 265
riwāyah, 20, 22, 33, 109, 127, 134, 261
Roman, 131, 195-197, 207
rukn, 171
rukū', 73, 200

Sa'd b. Abī Waqqāṣ, 20, 226
Sa'd b. Bajīr, 252
al-Saffāḥ (caliph), 45
Ṣafwān, 27
Ṣaḥā'if, 104
Ṣāḥib Abī Ḥanīfah, 246
Ṣāḥib al-Fiqh al-Akbar, 104
ṣāḥib al-ḥadīth, 261
ṣaḥīḥ(s), 56, 119, 121, 122, 124, 126, 129, 153, 154, 156, 159, 160, 245-247, 249, 262
Sahl. b. Sa'd, 6
Sa'īd b. al-Marzubān, 37
Sa'īd b. al-Musayyib, 24, 25
Sa'īd b. Aws, 251
Sa'īd b. Jubayr, 27
Sa'īd b. Masrūq, 36
al-Sakhāwī, 9, 35, 135, 140, 144, 160
ṣalāh, 171, 178, 225
Ṣalāḥ al-Dīn, 182
Salamah b. Kuhayl, 22, 36
Sālim al-Afṭas, 37
Sālim b. 'Abdullāh, 28, 73
Sālim b. Abī al-Ja'd, 142
al-Ṣalt b. Bahrām, 37
Samāk b. Ḥarb, 22, 23
al-Sam'ānī, 9, 36
Samarqand, 12, 41
Ṣana'an, 41
sanad, 22, 28
Sarakhs, 24, 41
Sayf b. Jābir, 8, 9
Ṣaymarī, Qāḍī, 5
sayyids, 44
Seljukians, 181
al-Sha'bī, 6, 14, 22, 27, 33, 34, 38, 72, 174
Shaddād b. 'Abd al-Raḥmān, 37
al-Shāfi'ī (imam), 25, 79, 87, 110, 119-122, 129, 137, 141, 145, 157, 161, 168, 169, 183, 184, 190, 192, 193, 201, 204, 206, 208, 210-212, 214, 217, 218, 223, 224, 226-228, 230, 231, 233, 235, 236, 254, 256, 258, 259
Shāfi'ī(s), 73, 113, 181, 182, 198, 199, 222
Shāh 'Abd al-'Azīz, 42
Shāh Waliullāh, 101, 102, 153, 154, 157, 170, 171, 186, 187, 208, 239
al-Shām, 22
Shams al-A'immah al-Kurdarī, 179
Sharḥ al-Maqāṣid, 104
Sharḥ al-Mawāqif, 104
Sharī'ah, 28, 59, 74, 83, 128, 155, 185, 186, 189, 190, 197-201, 203, 231
Sharīk, Qāḍī, 94, 108
al-Shawkānī, Qāḍī, 189
Shaybān b. 'Abd al-Raḥmān, 37
shaykhs, 126
Shī'ahs, 30
al-Shiblī, 193
Shī'ism, 42
Shi'ite, 94
Shu'bah, 24, 25, 33, 35
Shurayḥ b. al-Ḥārth, 21
Shurayḥ b. Hānī, 21
shuyūkh, 120
Simāk b. Ḥarb, 36
Sind, 12, 181, 185
Sistān, 41
siyar, 252, 261
al-Siyar al-Kabīr, 261
al-Siyar al-Ṣaghīr, 261
Spain, 12, 41, 182, 185

Sufyān al-Thawrī, 22-25, 33, 63, 67, 80, 88-90, 101, 124, 125, 127, 164, 178, 223, 244, 245, 249, 257, 263
Sufyān b. ʿUyaynah, 21-23, 249
Ṣughrjyyah, 15
sujūd, 200
Sulaymān al-Shaybānī, 37
Sulaymān b. ʿAbd al-Malik, 13
Sulaymān b. Mihrān, 24. *See also* al-Aʿmash
Sulaymān b. Yasār, ʿAbd al-Raḥmān b. Hurmuz al-Aʿraj, 126
sunnah, 161, 200
Sunnīs, 30
sūrah(s), 148, 168, 225
Syria, 8, 14, 22, 28, 36, 72, 76, 99, 112, 123, 174, 183, 195

Ṭabaqāt al-Ḥuffāẓ, 36, 131, 170, 221
al-Ṭabarī, 119
Ṭabaristān, 41
Tābiʿ al-Tābiʿīn, 58
Tābiʿī(s), 7, 8, 22-24, 26-28, 37, 58
Tābiʿīn, 18, 19, 141
Tabūk, 188
Tadhkirah al-Awliyā', 250
Tadhkirah al-Ḥuffāẓ, 11, 21, 32, 35, 39, 141, 244-247, 253, 265
tadhkirahs, 55
taʿdīl, 163, 164, 221, 222
tafsīr, 253
al-Tafsīr al-Kabīr, 167, 227, 230, 236
tahajjud, 70
ṭahārah, 178
al-Ṭaḥāwī, 145, 151, 177, 198, 222, 223, 246
Tahdhīb al-Asmā' wa al-Lughāt, 11, 221, 244, 264, 265
Tahdhīb al-Kamāl, 36, 37, 39, 221, 264
Tahdhīb al-Tahdhīb, 11, 21, 25, 36, 170, 221, 239, 264
Taḥṣīl al-Sabīl ilā Maʿrifah al-Thiqāt wa āl-Majāhīl, 35
takbīr, 26, 200, 201, 229
takbīrah al-taḥrīmah, 229
Ṭalīq b. Ḥabīb, 109
taqlīd, 244
Ta'rīkh al-Kabīr, 122, 170
Ta'rīkh al-Khulafā', 255
Ta'rīkh Baghdād, 10, 11, 17, 95, 239
tartīb, 226, 227
tashbīh, 107
tasmiyah, 227
Tawālī al-Ta'sīs, 120, 169, 265
tawātur, 67, 159, 168, 169, 191
tawrīth dhawī al-arḥām, 224
Ṭāwūs b. Kaysān, 37
tayammum, 38, 165, 227, 228
Thaqīf, 36
al-Thawrī, 8
Tīmūr, 182
Tirmidh, 41
al-Tirmidhī (imam), 120, 122, 133, 153; *Ṣaḥīḥ*, 223
Torah, 4
Tuḥfah, 42
ṭuruq, 21

ʿUbaydah b. ʿUmar, 20
ʿUbaydullāh b. ʿUmar, 37
ʿudwān, 231
al-ʿUjaylī, 23

'ulamā', 58, 76, 79, 81, 82, 86, 88, 100, 170, 256, 257
'ulūm, 171
'Umar al-Fārūq, 69, 121. *See also* 'Umar b. al-Khaṭṭāb
'Umar b. 'Abd al-'Azīz, 12, 13, 34
'Umar b. al-Khaṭṭāb, 20, 26, 94, 112, 131, 137, 165, 166, 173, 187-189, 219, 226. *See also* 'Umar al-Fārūq
'Umar b. Dīnār, 27, 36, 126
'Umar b. Ḥasan al-Ushnānī, al-Ḥāfiẓ, 100
'Umar b. Maymūn, 251
'Umar Hubayrah, 43
Umayyad(s), 13, 44, 107, 190; caliphs, 13, 44; princes, 13
Umm Zar', 187
Ummah, 116
'Uqbah b. 'Amr, 27
'Uqūd al-Jumān, 10, 11, 16, 17, 24, 35, 37, 39, 48, 70, 95, 101, 129, 150, 170, 238, 250
Usāmah b. Zayd, 26
uṣūl, 142, 190
'Uthmān al-Battī, 110, 114
'Uthmān b. 'Abdullāh b. Ḥawshab, 37
'Uthmān b. 'Affān, 94, 121, 132, 138, 216
al-'Uyūn wa al-Ḥadā'iq, 72

waḥy ghayr matlū, 156
waḥy matlū, 155
wājib, 166, 167, 171, 172, 200
Wakī' b. al-Jarrāḥ, 127, 222, 239, 241, 244, 246, 247, 262, 264
al-Walīd b. Yazīd (caliph), 42
Wāṣil b. 'Aṭā', 106, 117, 190, 239
Wāsiṭ, 41
Wāsiṭah, 257
waẓīfah, 86
wuḍū', 38, 55, 149, 171, 228

Yaḥyā al-'Alawī, 257
Yaḥyā al-Maṣmūdī, 182, 239
Yaḥyā b. 'Umar b. Salamah, 37
Yaḥyā b. Abī Ṭālib, 247
Yaḥyā b. Abī Zā'idah, 127, 177
Yaḥyā b. al-Qaṭṭān, 244
Yaḥyā b. Ma'īn, 25, 129, 243, 246, 247, 250, 253, 254, 261, 262
Yaḥyā b. Sa'īd, 36, 77, 127, 222, 243, 252
Yaḥyā b. Salām, 33
Yaḥyā b. Zā'idah, 242
Yaḥyā b. Zakariyyā, 109, 127, 243, 245
Yamāmah, 41
Yazīd al-Nāqiṣ, 42, 43
Yazīd b. Hārūn, 127, 247
Yazīd b. Kumayt, 63, 68
Yemen, 19, 20, 37, 41, 76, 173

Ẓāhirites, 155
Zā'idah b. Qudāmah, 139
zakāh, 130, 199, 201, 202
Zanādiqah, 134
Zayd b. 'Alī, 42
Zayd b. Arqam, 23, 26
al-Zayla'ī, 223
Zayn al-Dīn al-'Irāqī, 9, 134
ẓihār, 38
zindīq, 63
Zirr b. Hubaysh, 20
Ziyād b. 'Ilāqah, 36
ẓuhr, 70
al-Zuhrī, 13, 22, 27, 33, 34, 73, 135
zunnār(s), 218, 219
Zurqah, 66

www.ingramcontent.com/pod-product-compliance
Lightning Source LLC
Chambersburg PA
CBHW031827090426
42741CB00005B/162
* 9 7 8 9 8 3 9 5 4 1 9 9 1 *